"This book is not a defense for anything or anybody, but a poignant testimony to pain and perplexity being finally swallowed by love, forgiveness, fidelity, hope, and an increase of intimacy and family solidarity. The supreme impression left is of the unbounded goodness of God."

J. I. PACKER

"You'll be hard-pressed to find a more vulnerable account of a marriage that's faced a dark night of the soul than this one. Gayle Haggard's courageous 'risk of love' reveals a healing path that few would have ever predicted. Her authenticity is disarming. Her faith is inspiring. And her story will take you deeper into God's healing grace. You won't be able to put this book down."

DRS. LES & LESLIE PARROTT
Founders of RealRelationships.com
Authors of Saving Your Marriage Before It Starts

Excerpts from letters the Haggards received after granting a series of interviews about the HBO documentary The Trials of Ted Haggard.

"Words cannot express how much you all have touched my heart this evening [seeing you on *Larry King Live*]. My husband (of only five years) and I are separated due to far less severe circumstances. I am calling him as I write this."

CHERYL

"Your choice to allow the journey to redemption to be public has helped more souls than you'll ever know."

KELLY

"God has blessed you with a love that I cannot grasp. Do you have a book that can explain how you got to this level of love? I just do not understand."

GLORIA

"To see a woman stick with her man after so much misery is truly a modern-day miracle."

ANONYMOUS

"Ted, even now I thank God for your wife, who has stuck by you when she had a biblical reason to leave you."

JASON

"Your story, however sad it was (and still is), brings a powerful message. It's a message of hope, love, compassion, and support. Exactly what religion should be."

VINCENT

"Ted, you have no idea how profoundly your wife's attitude toward you has touched me."

EMMANUEL

"Gayle, you are an amazing woman, and my wife and I hurt for you because of what happened; but we have also found hope through your belief and action."

ANONYMOUS

WHY I STAYED

The Choices I Made in My Darkest Hour

GAYLE
HAGGARD

with Angela Hunt

Tyndale House Publishers, Inc., Carol Stream, Illinois

Visit Tyndale's exciting Web site at www.tyndale.com.

TYNDALE and Tyndale's quill logo are registered trademarks of Tyndale House Publishers, Inc.

Why I Stayed: The Choices I Made in My Darkest Hour

Copyright © 2010 by Gayle Haggard. All rights reserved.

Front cover photo of Ted and Gayle Haggard copyright © by Reuters/Phil McCarten. All rights reserved.

Front cover and author photo of Gayle Haggard by Stephen Vosloo, copyright © 2009 by Tyndale House Publishers, Inc. All rights reserved.

Inside flap photograph taken by Nora Feller.

Author photo of Angela Hunt by Jeff Callenberg, copyright © by Angela Hunt. All rights reserved.

Designed by Jessie McGrath

Edited by Dave Lindstedt and Susan Taylor

Back cover quote from ABC News: http://abcnews.go.com/GMA/story?id=2626067&page=1.

Back cover quote from *Rocky Mountain News*: http://www.rockymountainnews.com/drmn/local/article/0,1299,DRMN_15_5112770,00.html.

Back cover quote from MSNBC: http://www.msnbc.msn.com/id/15536263/.

Library of Congress Cataloging-in-Publication Data

Haggard, Gayle.
  Why I stayed : the choices I made in my darkest hour / Gayle Haggard with Angela Hunt.
    p. cm.
  Includes bibliographical references (p.   ).
  ISBN 978-1-4143-3585-8 (hc)
  1. Sexual misconduct by clergy. 2. Haggard, Gayle. 3. Haggard, Ted. I. Hunt, Angela Elwell, date. II. Title.
BV4392.5.H35 2010
261.8'35766092—dc22
[B]   2009042431

Printed in the United States of America

16   15   14   13   12   11   10
7   6   5   4   3   2   1

Most important of all,
continue to show deep love for each other,
for love covers a multitude of sins.

1 PETER 4:8

For Ted . . .

and the rest of us as well.

Author's Note

WHY I STAYED is *my* story. In these pages, I share my observations of the events leading up to the fateful day when my world came crashing down and of the choices I made, along with my husband and many others, in the three years that followed.

In recounting this story, I have searched my heart, my memory, my journal, and my records. Conversations are told from my perspective and are recorded as clearly as I can remember them. I've done my best to present events accurately, but others may recall things differently.

Of course, much of what follows has already been made public. But because I want readers to think about the ideas I am presenting rather than about individual personalities, I have avoided using names where doing so might cause someone hurt or embarrassment. My hope is that through this story of my darkest hour, we all can achieve grace.

—Gayle Haggard

Contents

Special Thanks

. . . to the men and women at Tyndale House Publishers who believed that my story needed to be told.

. . . to Angela Hunt, whose keen insight, biblical understanding, and courageous heart compelled her to come alongside and help me put my story on the page.

. . . and to our dear friends who chose to stand by us and lighten our load when they could have heaped more burdens on us as we walked through our greatest heartache, shame, and despair.

To all these friends, I am forever grateful.

FROM MY JOURNAL ENTRY FOR WEDNESDAY, NOVEMBER 1, 2006:

Today we found out that a man in Denver is accusing Ted of sin . . .

FROM MY JOURNAL ENTRY FOR THURSDAY, NOVEMBER 2, 2006:

Today our world changed. Ted confessed the truth to me . . .

Whom have I in heaven but you?
I desire you more than
    anything on earth.
My health may fail, and my
    spirit may grow weak,
but God remains the
    strength of my heart;
he is mine forever.

PSALM 73:25-26

1

THIRTY YEARS AGO, Ted Haggard stepped into my life because he lost an argument.

We were attending Oral Roberts University—Ted was a senior; I was a junior—and along with several other students, we had been chosen as spiritual-life directors in the dorms. As custom dictated, each women's dorm had been paired with a corresponding men's dorm. The campus chaplain expected the spiritual-life directors from each pair of dorms to share responsibilities and plan activities together. Though Ted and his friend Paul Osteen had lived in the same dorm for the past three years, if both men wanted to be spiritual-life directors, one of them would have to move and take the dorm paired with mine. In other words, the loser got me.

I preferred to work with Paul because I knew of him. He was a really nice guy, good looking and well liked; but I kept asking my friends, "Who is this Ted Haggard?" Actually, I was surprised he and I hadn't met before, because loads of my friends knew him.

Still, as I watched the two men argue over who would move, I couldn't help thinking, *Please, God, don't let Ted Haggard be the one who gets the dorm paired with mine.* But I had a feeling things weren't going to go my way.

To my dismay, Ted lost. He had to move to my partner dorm, and he had to work with me.

I wasn't attracted to Ted right away. For one thing, I was engaged to my high school sweetheart at the time. He had recently asked me to marry him, so I certainly wasn't looking for a boyfriend.

After getting to know Ted a bit, I found that he was not only friendly and outgoing but was also a veritable whirlwind of activity. In addition to going to school full-time, he was serving as the interim pastor of a church in Tulsa. In fact, he was so busy that I found it difficult to pin him down and get him to work with me on spiritual-life activities for our dorms.

One of the first activities we planned was a combined men's and women's retreat. When I arrived at the evening meal on the first night, I discovered that the organizers had arranged for guy-girl seating around the tables. I spotted Ted seated across the room and walked over to ask him about a joint presentation our chaplains would be giving later that night. What I didn't know was that Ted had just joked to the other guys at his table that he was going to marry the girl who sat next to him.

As I slid into the chair beside him, he yelled, "No! You can't sit there!"

While the other guys snickered, I shook my head. "Don't worry. I don't plan to stay."

At that moment, the other guys burst out laughing. "Don't leave, Gayle," they said. "Stay put. We all want you to stay."

"Well," I said, shrugging, "I do need to talk to Ted for a few minutes." Then, sensing that I had somehow missed a punch line, I raised an eyebrow and looked around the table quizzically. "What's going on here, anyway?"

One of the guys explained the joke while Ted grimaced. I smiled, telling myself that Ted Haggard was the last person on earth I would want to marry.

After covering for him a time or two, I didn't think I was going to like working with Ted, but his genuine friendliness and quick smile began to grow on me. He made me laugh, and I began to see why so many people liked him. When I was feeling burdened and taking our responsibilities too seriously, a quick conversation with him could lighten my load. When he absolutely had to miss a meeting or delegate a responsibility, I found I looked forward to helping him out.

Then I heard him speak in front of a group. As I listened to him teach the Bible with more thoughtfulness, pragmatism, and relaxed humor than I was accustomed to, I thought, *I could learn to respect this guy.* I liked the way his mind worked, and I admired his direct and down-to-earth approach with people.

I began to see Ted Haggard in a new light. I tried to keep myself from developing a crush on him, because I was committed to someone else, but I did begin to think he was the sort of man I'd like to spend more time with.

These new thoughts left me feeling confused and disconcerted and caused me to question my engagement to my high school sweetheart. My parents and friends thought I was crazy. Everyone expected me to marry the great guy I had dated for so long. In fact, those expectations were part of the reason I had accepted his proposal, even though I'd felt unsure about it at the time.

When my fiancé came to visit me at school, Ted greeted him cordially, but privately he joked that my high school sweetheart was "way too serious" for me. I didn't think so—in fact, I *liked* serious—but Ted's teasing made me further reconsider whether or not I was ready to enter into a lifetime commitment with the guy.

On occasion, I caught myself admiring Ted's profile as I sat catercornered and a few rows behind him in a psychology class we shared that fall. And after a while, I found myself standing at my dorm room window one day, watching Ted walk to class as I quietly sang Karen Carpenter's "Love, look at the two of us, strangers in many ways. . . ."

But I was engaged, and Ted was dating a good friend of mine. I considered him off-limits—until my friend confessed that although she liked Ted, she didn't see the relationship going anywhere in the long term. Then Ted confidentially told me the same thing: He liked my friend, but he didn't see a future in their relationship.

I found myself wondering if my future didn't lie with a man like Ted Haggard.

Ted and I began to meet each other for meals and to walk to class together—as friends, nothing more. Other students would greet us and ask, "Now, when are you two getting married?" and we'd laugh at the question.

One day, the campus chaplain called Ted into his office and asked him about his relationship with me. He said that his wife had had a dream that Ted and I were getting married, and then he told Ted, "You'd better not hurt Gayle. She's one of my favorites."

Ted was stunned, because at that point we weren't even dating.

As the months passed, I realized that I couldn't marry my high school sweetheart—not when I felt the way I did about Ted. I didn't want to hurt my fiancé, but I finally realized that if he wasn't right for me, then I wasn't right for him, either. And the more I learned about Ted Haggard, the more convinced I became that *he was* right for me—or that I at least needed to find someone *like* him. I determined that I wanted to be with someone who had all the same qualities, someone I could admire and respect the way I did Ted, and someone who made me feel as if there were fireworks going off every time I was with him.

Once I had broken things off with my fiancé, word trickled out that I was once again "available." When a friend heard the news, he told Ted that he was on his way to call me and ask me out. Ted bolted to his room and phoned me first, so when the other guy called, he got a busy signal.

Ted, on the other hand, got a solid *yes* to his invitation.

By the time Ted and I went on our first date, we had both developed a sense that we were right for each other. I remember our eyes meeting as we sat in the car in front of a friend's house. In that moment, I felt that somehow, in God's divine plan, he had brought us together.

Two years earlier, when I was a freshman pondering whether I should continue dating my high school boyfriend or date the guys at ORU, I had asked God to simplify the process and show me who I would marry. (The idea seems silly now, but I was serious at the time.) That afternoon, I fell asleep with that prayer on my lips and awoke with an image in my mind: a young man, standing some distance down a road marked by telephone poles. The young man remained far away, so I couldn't see him clearly. But I could see that he had blond, blown-back hair and a ruggedly handsome complexion and that he wore blue jeans and a reddish plaid shirt. Because he hadn't moved toward me, I intuited that our first meeting would take place at some point "farther down the road."

I never told anyone about that fleeting vision. I tucked the picture away in my heart, a little wary of believing it was a message from God. I chose instead to maintain a "we'll see" attitude. But my high school sweetheart—who had dark hair and dark eyes—was definitely not the man I'd seen in my dream.

After our first date, Ted and I ate most of our meals together. In the evenings after classes, we took long walks around campus and talked about everything. One night, Ted got so giddy that he ran onto the grass outside my dorm and started turning somersaults while he yelled, "I am just so excited about *us*!" I laughed, watching him, and knew that life with Ted would always contain a dash of fun, drama, and the unexpected.

That year, my birthday fell on a Saturday, and to celebrate, Ted asked me to pack a picnic lunch. We planned to spend the day on a sandy beach bordering a nearby river. We spread our picnic in a deserted area and didn't see another soul until we decided to walk along the water's edge. We were talking, not really looking around, when we noticed a shirtless, barefoot man with long, brown hair. He seemed to have appeared out of nowhere, and without a word of explanation, he began to walk with us and eventually joined our conversation. The man spooked me a little, but Ted seemed so comfortable with the situation that I simply followed his cues.

When we decided to sit on a pile of logs beside the river, the stranger sat with us. At one point, conversation died, and we fell into a comfortable silence. I was hoping the guy would take the hint and leave, but at that point our beachcomber friend turned to Ted and said, "Do what you've come to do." Then he stood.

I didn't know what the man meant, but apparently Ted did, because surprise flickered across his face. Ted glanced at me, and when we looked back, the man was gone. He must have slipped away when we weren't looking, but though we shaded our eyes and scanned the beach, we saw no sign of him.

"That was strange," Ted said, turning back to me.

"No kidding," I agreed. "I felt strange the entire time he was with us."

Who was he? We had no idea.

Once the sun sank toward the horizon, Ted and I built a campfire on the beach. As we warmed ourselves beside the flames, Ted shared what he felt God was calling him to do with his life. He told me what he believed God had shown him about his future. When he finished, he swallowed hard and looked at me, and then he asked if I would want to share that life with him.

My heart had been pounding as I listened, but now it skipped a beat. My love for him and excitement over what he was planning grew with every word out of his mouth. I knew what he was asking, and my answer came easily to my lips: "I'd love to!"

"And would you marry me?"

My answer was a confident *yes*.

As I looked at Ted in the firelight, I saw a young man with blond, blown-back hair and a ruggedly handsome complexion. He was wearing blue jeans and a red-and-gold plaid shirt.

Then we kissed for the first time.

LORD, you alone are my inheritance,
*   my cup of blessing.*
You guard all that is mine.
The land you have given me
*   is a pleasant land.*
What a wonderful inheritance!
I will bless the LORD who guides me;
Even at night my heart instructs me.
I know the LORD is always with me.
I will not be shaken, for he
*   is right beside me.*

PSALM 16:5-8

2

I GREW UP in a military family, so we moved every few years. My dad, who was an officer in the Air Force, served at the Pentagon and retired as a full-bird colonel just before his promotion to general. Because Dad was a strong leader, my siblings—two sisters and a brother—and I grew up feeling sheltered and safe.

From the time I was a little girl, my dad has held my deep respect. Though he was strict, I always felt secure in his love for me. I shared his sense of humor and always enjoyed making him laugh. My mother was—and still is—totally devoted to my father and our family. Fun and easy to love, she is the glue that held everything together through the many moves we made as a military family.

My parents seemed to glide through life gracefully, and I don't remember a single disruption in their relationship. To this day, they are still dancing with each other and wowing us at weddings and other celebrations.

My paternal grandmother was a devoted Christian who spent many years praying for all of us. When I was three or four, my dad was stationed in Colorado Springs, and I attended Vacation Bible School at a church near our home. That's where I remember hearing about Jesus for the first time. The teachers taught me that Jesus had been born to a girl named Mary and that he was going to come again someday. Later that night, as I lay in bed, I quietly asked God if he'd let me be the next Mary. That's the first prayer I remember praying.

As I grew up, my family and I lived in North Carolina, Maine, Florida, California, Colorado, and Virginia, just outside Washington, D.C., which is where I attended high school. When I was fourteen, we lived at Edwards Air Force Base in California, and I attended a youth meeting at the base chapel. At that meeting, for the first time, I fully understood what it meant to follow Jesus—it meant that I accepted that God is who the Bible says he is and that he sent Jesus, his Son, to redeem me from the eternal consequences I deserved for my sins. It meant that I would choose God's ways over my own. It meant that Jesus would be closer to me than a brother and that God would become a very real Father to me.

I prayed and dedicated my life to Jesus Christ that evening. I also asked God to use me in some significant way.

Around the time I decided to become a Christian, my parents made the same decision. Within a few months, my entire family was regularly attending church and learning how to apply Jesus' teachings to our everyday lives.

I developed a love for the Bible during my teen years. A wise old man in our church told me that if I read a chapter from the book of Proverbs each day of the month, I would grow in wisdom. That appealed to me, so during high school I read one of the thirty-one chapters of Proverbs every day. I read other books of the Bible, too, and would often embark on "read the Bible in a year" plans, with plenty of false starts. But my goal was to know God and to understand what Christianity was all about, so I kept reading and praying.

I wasn't a completely compliant child, but because I was serious about serving God, I never went through a time of overt rebellion, even in adolescence. My desire to fulfill God's purpose for me was part of the reason I chose to attend a Christian university. It was also part of the reason I believed that God brought Ted and me together.

Not long after Ted proposed to me, he graduated from ORU with a degree in biblical literature. He spent most of the following summer working in Ghana, West Africa, with a West-German missionary whose organization had its U.S. office at Bethany Baptist Church in Baton Rouge, Louisiana. In the late 1960s, this heroic missionary had smuggled Bibles to believers behind the Iron Curtain and had jumped out of low-flying planes to bring food to the starving people in Biafra. During the fall of Saigon in 1975, he and his wife rescued orphans who would have been killed by the encroaching Vietcong, guiding the children through a treacherous war zone until they reached one of the last military cargo planes to leave the capital city. Ted and I were excited about working with this man and his missions organization.

While Ted was in Ghana, I spent the summer waitressing at a local restaurant and daydreaming about our upcoming wedding.

Because Ted wasn't scheduled to return from Africa until the week before our big event, I knew I'd have to handle most of the preparations myself. Just before he boarded the plane for Africa, he called me to say good-bye and to tell me that he'd sent me a brochure about a trip that would be a great honeymoon idea. He wanted me to look it over and, if I agreed, to make the necessary arrangements.

I looked forward to receiving the brochure and was excited to see what Ted had in mind—but I was a little shocked when I opened the envelope. Apparently, his idea of a great honeymoon was a weeklong *group* camping and backpacking trip. I wasn't as concerned about the river rafting and hot-air ballooning as I was about doing those things with a group . . . and sleeping in tents at night.

How in the world could he think such a trip would be *romantic*?

Ted later told me that he had anticipated adventure-filled days and romantic nights in our own private tent. But because he was on one side of the globe and I was on the other, I had to rely on my imagination. I could just see us as "the newlyweds" having to put up with the group's constant surveillance. I had hoped for something a little more private.

I was beginning to realize that I—a fairly private woman—had agreed to marry a very public man.

Since Ted had given me the freedom to make the honeymoon arrangements and I thought he *couldn't* be all that serious about the outdoor adventure trip, I booked a suite for us at an old Victorian hotel in Durango, a town nestled in the beautiful mountains of Colorado. When Ted finally arrived home, he couldn't believe I preferred a clean, beautiful room and lots of private time to white-water rafting and canvas tents.

That's when another truth began to dawn on me: We weren't as alike as I'd thought. I should have suspected that life with Ted would push me out of my comfort zone.

In August 1978, we married at The Church in the Wildwood in Green Mountain Falls, about fifteen miles outside of Colorado

Springs, where my parents had retired. At the conclusion of our mostly private Victorian honeymoon (with a few outdoor adventures thrown in), we piled our belongings into our car and headed south to Baton Rouge, Louisiana, where Ted planned to help develop a U.S. office for the ministry World Missions For Jesus and I planned to finish my college career at Louisiana State University.

Soon after we arrived in Baton Rouge, I decided to put my degree on hold in order to join Ted in working for the missionary organization, whose U.S. office had consisted of little more than a mailing address until we arrived. With our meager earnings, we purchased our first home, and we moved the operations for World Missions For Jesus into a large room on the back of our house. I also took a position as a teacher's assistant for middle schoolers at a Christian school. For two years, Ted and I ran the American office for the missionary organization, and then for another four years we served Bethany Baptist Church as youth pastors.

Those early years of our marriage were more trying for me than for Ted. We both loved the church and the work we felt God had called us to do, but Ted really seemed to thrive on it. He was always doing something with the church and our youth group, whereas the private side of my nature led me to long for more personal time alone with him. Sometimes, when Ted recognized my longing, he'd go to extraordinary lengths to make sure we had time together.

Once we started working for the church, we were allowed to live in a guesthouse on church property, and we were then responsible for hosting church visitors from out of town. Sometimes we were so overwhelmed with having a house full of guests that we would slip into our bedroom and crawl out the window in order to enjoy some time for just the two of us.

In those early days, as I watched Ted pull out of the driveway to rescue yet another teenager from some foolish antic, or listened to him spend hours on the phone counseling a young person locked in depression, I felt he was the most compassionate person I knew. He was always willing to give of himself in order to help someone else. Sometimes I thought he forgot about me in the process, but I honestly admired the way he unselfishly cared for other people.

While we were in Baton Rouge, our first two children, Christy and Marcus, were born, so my days were filled with caring for my little ones. I wanted to continue to be active in the ministry, but my priorities naturally shifted.

In 1984, we went to visit my parents in Colorado Springs. I spent time with my mom and dad while Ted took a pup tent and a gallon of water and went camping on the back side of Pikes Peak. While praying and fasting, Ted felt God speak to him and entrust him with several visions—one of a large church in the city, one of a high-tech world prayer center, one of a prayer and fasting center, and another of a stadium filled with twenty thousand men.

Not long after we arrived back in Baton Rouge, Ted and I went for an evening walk around the Bethany Baptist Church property. Crickets chirred as we walked hand in hand past the playground and the street where the church owned several parsonages. Lights twinkled from the windows of the velvet night, and towering pecan trees whispered in the gentle breeze.

At the quiet conclusion of what had otherwise been an uneventful day, Ted told me that he felt God wanted us to move to Colorado Springs and start a church. I halted in midstep. Move to Colorado? Our focus had been on overseas missions! I had been thinking that our next assignment would be in Calcutta or Mexico City, and I could barely speak over my surprise. What would our missionary friends think when they heard we'd now been called to beautiful, *American*, Colorado Springs?

I stared at Ted for a long moment and then felt him squeeze my hand. "Gayle?"

"I'm okay," I said, shaking my head. "It's not that I'm opposed to going home or anything. I'm just . . . surprised."

I trusted Ted's discernment, but most of all, I trusted God's guidance in our lives.

I wasn't surprised that Ted sensed God's direction for our future. The Bible is full of examples of God's speaking to people. And the New Testament clearly states that his sheep hear his voice (for example, John 10; Revelation 3). But I was caught off guard by what seemed to be a significant change of focus.

I believe—I *know*—that God speaks to people in many ways. He speaks to us through the magnificence of creation, which bears witness to his awesome power and skillful design. He speaks to us through the Bible, which relates the history of God's activity with humankind and explains the work of salvation. Sometimes he speaks to us through our spiritual leaders and authorities, especially when we are children or are immature in the faith. And sometimes he speaks to us in a still, quiet voice we hear within our hearts. Because I believed that Ted had heard a message from God, I said good-bye to our friends in Baton Rouge (albeit sadly) and rallied our small family for the adventure of a move.

At first, Roy Stockstill, our pastor in Baton Rouge, didn't want to let us go. He had become like a father to us in our early days of ministry. We loved him, and we felt his deep love and concern for us. He flew to Colorado Springs to check out the situation, and on his return he told us that he agreed God was leading us to that city. So we packed up Christy and Marcus and our few belongings, and we moved to Colorado.

When we first arrived in Colorado Springs, in 1984, it was not the "Evangelical Mecca" that some say it is today. Back then, fewer than 10 percent of its residents attended church on an average weekend; by 2006, that number would reach 25 percent. Not long after we started New Life Church, a wave of Christian ministries moved to the area. By the late 1980s, Colorado Springs had become home to hundreds of Christian organizations.

On January 6, 1985, after walking through neighborhoods to distribute door hangers, purchasing three-minute radio spots in which Ted taught small portions of Scripture, and spreading the word any way we knew how, Ted and I, along with Christy and Marcus, held the first meeting of what would become New Life Church. About thirty people gathered in the basement of our home on that first Sunday, and Ted and I were delighted to see how God had blessed our hard work. New Life would be an independent body, only loosely affiliated with Bethany Baptist, our parent church in Baton Rouge. They had offered to send us five hundred dollars a month to support our start-up efforts, but not long after our first Sunday, we asked them not to send any more checks, because we didn't want to be dependent on their financial help. Ted has always been trusting when it comes to finances. With confident faith he believes God will provide.

Our fledgling church expanded at an amazing rate. We soon outgrew our basement, so we moved our meeting to a hotel, and then to a storefront. From its inauspicious beginning in January 1985, New Life Church grew by double-digit percentages every year for twenty-two years, never once suffering any major traumas, splits, controversies, or scandals.

During the early months of the church start-up, Danny Ost, another paternal figure in Ted's life, came to visit us. He and Ted had often traveled together on missions trips, and I'm sure Danny was partly responsible for planting a deep love for missions in Ted's heart. They drove around the Colorado Springs area and looked for sites where our church might someday relocate. As they rounded a curve on Highway 83, about a mile east of Interstate 25, Danny said, "Pull the car over. This is your site." He pointed to a large, grassy field where nothing but antelope lived. "I can see you building a great church here—a church they can see from the Air Force Academy chapel across the way. Dignitaries will come to the Air Force Academy, and they will look across the valley and see your building. When they ask about it, they'll learn that God has built a great church in Colorado Springs."

Ted came home and told me about the field, but to my knowledge, he never told anyone else. Danny Ost passed away within a few months of that meeting, but five years later, when New Life desperately needed a permanent meeting place, a real-estate agent took Ted to that same grassy field north of town. "This acreage is available," he said, "and the price is so low you really should consider it." That field became the permanent home of New Life Church.

Ted and I loved serving the Lord by serving the people of New Life. The church grew to a congregation of fourteen thousand, and some of our innovative ministries became nationally known. Because Ted felt a special love and concern for young people, our ministry emphasized programs for youth. Each week we had more than one thousand college-age students attending meetings, and another thousand in high school and middle school groups. New Life's Desperation Conferences drew young people from across the nation, and the Desperation Band became world renowned. Our worship leader and members of his team also wrote songs that are sung by Christians all over the world.

Knowing that some people feel lost and disconnected in a large church, Ted began a program called "free market small groups"—a way for people to choose a common interest and meet during the week to discuss that interest in the light of Christian living. To present the value of small groups to a larger audience, Ted wrote a book called *Dog Training, Fly Fishing, & Sharing Christ in the 21st Century.* At one point, New Life had more than 1,300 small groups meeting each week.

When the Lord blessed us with Jonathan, our third child, our eyes were opened to the world of people with special needs. Because Jonathan suffered learning delays and was speech disabled, we realized the importance of reaching out to individuals with special needs. Every Sunday, New Life volunteers drove vans and buses all over the city to pick up special-needs children and adults and bring them to our church for worship. Under the leadership of our good friend Beth Kraiss, this ministry quickly became a hallmark of New Life.

Missions continued to be a huge emphasis in our lives. New Life supported hundreds of missionaries and missions organizations with an annual budget of multiple millions of dollars. The high-tech World Prayer Center, which Ted had envisioned years before, became a reality. Via the Internet, people from all over the world could post their requests and have them prayed for in real time by volunteers who felt called to the ministry of prayer. New Life Church also built Praise Mountain, a retreat center for prayer and fasting, which the church later sold to a couple who managed the operation.

Because we believe Christianity affects every area of a person's life, our church developed practical programs to support people who needed help with diverse issues—marriage and family, physical fitness, job training, child care, and education. Ted preached about our responsibilities as Christians and American citizens to participate in civil government.

In May 2005, an article in *Harper's Magazine* said, "No pastor in America holds more sway over the political direction of evangelicalism than does Pastor Ted, and no church more than New Life."[1] Some pastors might have been flattered by such an observation, but Ted didn't feel like an evangelical kingpin. He knew that a key ingredient of our church's success was the simple act of empowering people in the church to serve others.

While Ted worked hard at New Life, I worked hard at raising our family. In time, we had other babies, adding Alex and then Elliott to our lineup of Christy, Marcus, and Jonathan. I focused on our children, particularly when they were young and needed more of my time.

Some of those early years were difficult and exhausting, especially because Jonathan had special needs. In light of Ted's busy schedule, I often felt that I parented alone. I developed compassion for single parents and appreciated how difficult it could be for them to manage the demands of children, work, and family. I knew how bone tired and weary I was at the end of the day.

Often, after an exhausting day of cleaning, laundry, and keeping up with my kids—especially Jonathan—I would fall asleep right in the middle of a bedtime story and start to mumble. My kids would laugh and say, "Mom, you're doing it again!" I would kiss them good night and retreat to my bedroom, grateful that my husband would soon be home.

As our lives grew busier and the church grew larger, I learned to embrace each day. I looked forward to waking up and starting my day with reading the Bible and prayer—those were my moments of quiet reflection and bliss.

I felt grateful to have been called to my role as Ted's wife and the mother of our wonderful children . . . but I wasn't completely happy. I carried a hidden heartache, and though I cried out to the Lord about my pain, I couldn't talk about it openly without feeling selfish.

I wanted more of my husband.

Please don't misunderstand—I don't think Ted ever slighted me intentionally. He frequently told me that he loved me, and he was present for our children as often as he could be. But the trouble was, that wasn't often enough. Other people usually consumed his attention.

I had listened to enough women talk about their marriages to know that Ted and I shared something special. Friends often commented about how our eyes lit up whenever the other person entered the room. A friend whose family had vacationed with us told me that her daughter remarked that Ted and I "must really love each other" because of the way we looked at each other.

Yet there were plenty of times when I felt Ted wasn't with me in the moment—when his attention was diverted to something else and his emotional energy was spent on others, leaving little time and energy for the kids and me. I felt I was important to Ted, just not important enough. I would restrain my comments again and again, biting my tongue until my disappointments churned in a raging flood. Then, when I tried to talk to Ted about my frustration—usually waiting until the dam holding my pent-up emotions had burst—I would tearfully unload, nearly drowning him in a tide of reproach.

He would be shocked, as if I'd blindsided him, and I could tell he considered my outburst another burden on his shoulders, another concern added to his already-full plate. Afterward, I would feel embarrassed at how petty and possessive I sounded. What did I expect him to do, give up his life's work? I loved his work and felt called to it with him. I hated appearing so emotionally needy. I didn't want to be clingy; I wanted to be strong. And so, gathering up my determination, I would resolve to deal with my feelings privately.

Prayer became my lifeline.

I told myself I was expecting too much of Ted as long as he had so many other commitments. His devotion to his work and other people was admirable, even necessary. I knew that part of his drive to take care of so many people stemmed from his belief that his investment in New Life was an investment in our family's security.

Yet even though I knew he loved me sincerely, I longed for a deeper connection. Sometimes, even in the midst of our busy family, he seemed distant and preoccupied, and I sensed that he kept part of himself walled off from the rest of the world, including me. I wanted to understand what lay behind that wall. I wanted to know Ted on deeper levels. My inability to reach that private place left me feeling isolated . . . and frustrated.

Still, I knew Ted loved me. Sometimes I'd wake in the morning and find him staring at me. He'd say, "You are so beautiful," or "I am so blessed to have you. I love you so much." And my heart would melt.

One of our enduring morning rituals was to reach out and take the other's hand upon waking and lie beside each other as we talked about our lives and how grateful we were for God's blessings.

When Ted was home with the children, he tried to be available to them. He loved long, vibrant discussions at the dinner table. One of his greatest delights was to lie in his favorite recliner with an open book on his chest and listen to our children talk and laugh in the next room. I think those were his "all is well with the world" moments, and he treasured them. As our children grew older, he especially enjoyed taking one or more of them with him when he traveled so they could see the world and share his experiences.

Because Ted is bright, pragmatic, and extremely entertaining, he was regularly invited to speak at various national and international events, which frequently required him to travel far from home. When he was in Colorado Springs, he made himself available to meet with people in his church office. After services, he would usually stay after the people were dismissed in order to meet with anyone who wanted to speak with him. His door was always open to his staff, and he spent a great deal of time in meetings with his staff, elders, and trustees—men and women with whom he shared the privilege of caring for a large, vibrant church. He had an inner circle of senior staff members, and these men enjoyed investing their lives in ministry together. They were often on the phone with Ted or in our home discussing some exciting idea or new venture. Many times our families vacationed together, or they would join us for barbecues in the backyard.

Sometimes I found myself in the unique position of being jealous—not of another woman but of my husband's best friends. I would watch them gather around Ted in his office, after meetings and services, and in our backyard. They'd laugh and talk endlessly. Sometimes they drew together in a conspiratorial knot. They knew Ted so well—at times, I thought they knew my husband better than I did. They certainly spent more time in conversation with him. They shared more daylight hours with him. They shared confidences about things that were happening in the church, and I felt left out when I heard them discussing situations I knew nothing about. I wanted to know everything about my husband, to enjoy life with him, to share experiences so we could grow together.

I would think back to the day Ted proposed; I'd remember how he'd shared his dreams with me. I yearned to feel that closeness again and to be reminded of his conviction that we'd be a team for the rest of our lives. Yet if I had asked him who he saw as his "team members," I really believed that he'd list the names of his executive staff.

In my mind, I had gone from being a ministry partner to being simply the woman at home—Ted's wife and the mother of his children.

I told myself that I couldn't expect to be completely up-to-date on the ministry because I had to think about our children. I tried to put my dissatisfaction behind me, to tell myself that no human relationship could ever meet my every emotional need—which is true—and I found tremendous fulfillment in my relationship with God and in caring for our household.

But God designed the marriage relationship for intimacy, and though Ted and I had always enjoyed physical intimacy, I yearned for greater emotional intimacy with him. I wanted to be my husband's confidante and his best friend. I wanted to be the person he called first with good news, the person he ran to for comfort or to share a fleeting thought.

But as New Life grew and the demands on Ted increased, I realized that my desire for closeness wasn't going to be fulfilled anytime soon. I had married a popular and successful man; now I was paying the price. Because so many other people wanted to be close to Ted, the children and I would simply have to surrender some of our claims on him.

Somewhere along the way, I decided to be happy with my many blessings: a role in a thriving, exciting ministry; five beloved children; and a loving husband. After all, I knew my marriage was still better than most.

❖

When our third child, Jonathan, was born, I experienced an uneventful pregnancy, but the delivery was more difficult than anything I'd endured before. I noticed a look of concern on the nurses' faces when they first handled Jonathan, but I couldn't see any obvious birth defects. I thought he was fine, but the doctor noted that Jonathan had very low muscle tone.

"There's a chance we're going to find other problems," the doctor told me, but I barely heard him because I was so thrilled with my new son. So what if his muscles were a little weak? He'd grow stronger. I wasn't going to worry.

Because I wanted to do what I thought was best for my baby, I breast-fed Jonathan. At his three-month well-baby checkup, I watched as the doctor weighed Jonathan, frowned, and wrote the words *failure to thrive* on his pad.

"Don't!" I cried, alarm sending a surge of adrenaline through my bloodstream. I knew what "failure to thrive" meant; I'd seen videos of thin, forlorn babies who withered away because they weren't cuddled or loved in their first few months of life. "I love my baby!"

The doctor shook his head. "I know you love him. I'm writing this because he's not growing. He should have put on more weight."

Alarmed, we allowed Jonathan to undergo a barrage of medical tests. We visited heart doctors, metabolic doctors—all kinds of doctors. But from the time of that three-month checkup until Jonathan was a year old, he never weighed more than twelve pounds.

I think he was starving. Because I knew that breast milk is good for babies, I nursed him regularly, but Jonathan gagged and spit up almost constantly. Finally, a doctor friend stopped by the house, examined Jonathan, and said, "Either you start giving him high-fat formula or we're going to have to put him in the hospital."

We started giving Jonathan high-fat formula right away, and he soon began to gain weight.

Throughout that first year, we worried primarily about his physical health, but once he began to grow, we noticed that he wasn't achieving normal developmental milestones. Though he was a sweet-natured baby, he was experiencing developmental delays. But it wasn't until he was two that we realized he couldn't communicate the way he wanted to. While other children his age babbled, Jonathan remained silent.

We began speech therapy. We learned sign language and tried a communication device, but Jonathan preferred to gesture and speak the few words he could force out. When we couldn't understand him, he grew frustrated and threw tantrums, but at that point, he was still small enough for me to manage.

By this time, we had come to understand that Jonathan had a condition similar to autism. Though he was bright, active, and relational, he didn't process things in the same way his brother and sister did. We understood him, we loved him, and we were convinced God had a wonderful plan for his life, but parenting Jonathan brought challenges we couldn't have anticipated.

We decided that we were not going to let Jonathan's condition define our family; instead, we wanted to let the family define Jonathan. I had seen many other families center their lives around caring for their special-needs child, but I didn't think that would be fair to our other children. Jonathan is unique, but so are our other kids. Jonathan has special challenges, but so do his brothers and sister. We all do.

Our family is a vocal family. We love to tell stories, and our dinner table is always filled with conversation. Ted and I encourage discussion and laughter, but though Jonathan tried to listen patiently to his brothers' and sister's stories, he became agitated when he couldn't participate. It seemed we couldn't get through a meal without having him throw his food or slam his hand on the table in frustration. As much as we tried to make him a part of things, his limitations discouraged him and made him sad.

I remember the night when we were able to really accept Jonathan as Jonathan. He had gone to bed, and Ted and I were getting ready for bed ourselves. We heard Jonathan begin to cry, which he rarely did except when throwing a fit. Yet on this night, there was something different in the sound, something deep and wounded and heartbreaking. We could tell he was despondent.

Ted went into Jonathan's room while I stood outside the door. I heard Ted say, "Jonathan, Mommy and I have made a big mistake. We keep praying for God to heal you, but we're not going to try to fix you anymore. You are fine just the way you are. We love you just the way you are."

I strained to hear as silence filled Jonathan's room.

"Something else," Ted added. "I've never told you something you should know. Everybody is retarded. I'm retarded, Mommy's retarded—everybody is. None of us is perfect."

After a brief silence, I heard Jonathan giggle.

When Jonathan was seven or eight, we moved to a house in the Black Forest area of Colorado Springs, where we were literally surrounded by trees. We loved it, but our happiness quickly turned to panic when Jonathan began to wander away from home. We would search for him, our entire family fanning out as we ran to neighbors' houses and searched the woods. We frequently found Jonathan walking through the trees or strolling down a neighboring dirt road.

After outgrowing that phase, he replaced it with a fascination for the 911 emergency number. At school, he learned about calling 911 in an emergency, but he couldn't understand that the number was to be used *only* in an emergency. Jonathan soon became well-known to the 911 operators. Police officers and rescue vehicles visited our home, sometimes in the middle of the night, because Jonathan had dialed 911.

We tried to explain to the emergency personnel that punishment didn't work with Jonathan but that he did respond to positive reinforcement. So the emergency dispatchers worked with us to institute a reward system. If Jonathan went an entire week without calling 911, the following Monday he could call the emergency operator. If he went an entire month without calling 911, we would take him to visit the dispatch facility. The first time he visited, you'd have thought he was a celebrity—and no movie star on the red carpet ever looked happier than our son did on that visit.

When Jonathan reached middle school, he learned words and hand gestures from his classmates—things I'd have preferred he not learn at all. Many times I would be driving down the road in our minivan and catch a startled look from another driver. Without being told, I knew that behind me Jonathan was displaying his newfound knowledge through the car window. I learned to just smile and wave. What else could I do? Cry? I had discovered that laughter and looking on the "bright side" would lift my spirits and enable me to face less than optimal circumstances. Often, I was faced with situations that boiled down to a choice between laughter and tears. I found that laughter, whenever possible, is definitely the better option.

My years with Jonathan taught me how to walk through embarrassing situations with my chin up and a smile on my face. From the time I was a child, I had prayed that God would help me stop being so easily embarrassed. Now virtually nothing fazes me.

As Jonathan approached adolescence, I realized that caring for him and four other children was exhausting me physically and mentally. The bigger Jonathan grew, the more damage he could inflict when he threw things or acted out in anger. I decided that we needed a little peace—not a permanent break, but a temporary reprieve. I hoped to find a school nearby that Jonathan could attend during the week and then come home on weekends.

Until then, I had never dreamed I'd even consider such a thing; but I'd become desperate for a little relief, and I was concerned for our other children.

I made an appointment at Children's Hospital in Denver to discuss Jonathan's situation with a psychologist. When we arrived, Ted and I sat in guest chairs, but Jonathan didn't take the chair that was offered him. Instead, my long-legged thirteen-year-old curled up in my lap and buried his face in my shoulder.

After briefly describing what we were going through at home, I caught the psychologist's eye and tried to wordlessly relate my feelings of desperation. I had hoped that Jonathan would wait outside, but he clung to me as though he sensed my intention. I didn't want him to hear that I wanted to send him away, even for brief periods. I wasn't sure he'd understand the concept of a boarding school.

With a breaking heart, I looked at the doctor and tried to communicate my frustration and exhaustion. Tears spilled onto my cheeks as my overgrown boy tightened his grip as if he would never let me go.

The doctor studied us for a moment, and then she looked me squarely in the eye. "No one," she said, "is going to love him like you do."

I blinked as those words sank into my heart. They settled and expanded as I began to understand. In that moment, I felt a renewed determination to love Jonathan better. I knew I could stretch a little more. God would give me the strength and flexibility I needed for the task he'd given me.

I dashed the wetness from my eyes and gave the doctor a smile. "You're right." Ted and I stood and took Jonathan home.

Jonathan attended a public middle school in Colorado Springs, and he had always loved his classes; but when the time came for him to move to high school, he told me he didn't want to go to the school in our neighborhood. He was adamant in his refusal.

Though I didn't understand his reasons, I remembered that years earlier I had jotted down information about a special private school in Kentucky. I'd been at the orthodontist with one of the other kids, and I'd seen an article in an issue of *Southern Living* magazine. I'd written the school's name on a green envelope.

After rummaging through a drawer in my nightstand, I found the envelope and called the Stewart Home School for more information. The institution had been founded in 1883 by a Dr. Stewart, who observed the lack of positive schools for special-needs people. Since then, five generations of Dr. Stewarts have overseen that residential program. Everything sounded perfect for fifteen-year-old Jonathan, so Ted, Jonathan, and I flew to Kentucky to check out the school.

At that time, Jonathan had traded his fixation on 911 calls for a fascination with water hydrants. He was desperate to see someone open a hydrant, but Colorado was suffering a severe drought, so no one was likely to let the water flow for Jonathan's sake. On the flight to Kentucky, Jonathan kept asking if the school had fire hydrants. "I don't know," I told him. "I think it's a big farm."

But the first thing we noticed as we drove onto the school property were several large, green fire hydrants. We got out of the car, and Jonathan started jumping and running around in his excitement. When the school director stepped out to meet us, Jonathan took her hand and led her over to a fire hydrant. Lifting a brow, she said, "Do you like fire hydrants, Jonathan?"

He beamed at her. "Yes!"

She smiled. "Well, now. We use them to water the grounds, and we're looking for a man to open them for us. Maybe you could be that man."

Jonathan nearly exploded with excitement . . . and I cried. God had answered our prayers, and I knew we had found the right place.

You keep track of all my sorrows.
You have collected all my
    tears in your bottle.
You have recorded each
    one in your book.

PSALM 56:8

3

WHEN I TURNED forty, I felt as though I had come to a milestone in my life. The youngest of my children had reached school age, and New Life Church was thriving under Ted's pastoral leadership. Until that point, I had always thought of myself as Ted's partner in ministry, but I tended to be more of a behind-the-scenes person than one involved in a public leadership role. I felt united with Ted in his call to pastor, but my focus was on raising our children, taking care of our home, which always seemed in need of some kind of maintenance work, and making life as pleasant as possible for my family.

Though I still yearned for greater intimacy with my husband, I loved New Life and our shared roles of serving the people of our church family. I've met leaders who unconsciously limit their influence because they tend to micromanage their staff, but Ted never wanted to control every aspect of the ministry. He constantly encouraged others to fulfill their God-given ministries, and he gave them free rein to be innovative, relevant, and effective in helping people.

We all enjoyed that kind of liberty. In the creative and relaxed atmosphere of a life-giving church, I watched hundreds of people rise to leadership positions and use their gifts without limitation or hesitation. When we hired a youth pastor, Ted allowed him to follow his dreams and do everything in his heart to reach young people.

Many different ministries sprang up. One of our programs, 24/7, was a sort of spiritual boot camp for young men and women. Under the leaders of this disciplined program, hundreds of students trained to be physically, mentally, and spiritually fit so they could minister anywhere in the world.

Because of Ted's openhanded leadership style, I never felt pressure to be something I wasn't. As I walked down the halls of our church on Sunday mornings, I didn't worry that I had to fit a particular image of what a pastor's wife should be. People seemed genuinely happy to see me, and I was happy to see them. I felt they loved me and prayed for my family. I loved them and prayed for their loved ones as well. We belonged to each other. We were a family.

One morning, just before my fortieth birthday, I was lying on the floor of our bedroom, praying and seeking the Lord's direction in my life. In the quiet of the moment, I felt God speak to my soul: *Do you want the hearts of women?*

"I'm not sure I understand what you mean," I answered, in all honesty, "but if that's what you want to give me, I will step into that role."

To care for the hearts of women . . . a daunting task when I thought about all the women who attended New Life. I got up from the floor and moved through my regular routines, but over the next few days I noticed doors opening to new opportunities for ministry with women. Prior to this, I had been an advisor for the women's ministry, which was a behind-the-scenes, volunteer position. But after my morning prayer experience, I felt the time had come for me to step into a public leadership role.

With Ted's approval, and the support of the women in the church, I became the first full-time director of women's ministries at New Life, which was a paid staff position. I began to work with small groups and then watched as the number of women-only groups grew from ten to more than 150. On Sunday mornings, I taught one women's class, and on Sunday evenings I taught the college-age women. My focus was on teaching women how to live in relationship to God and to others. I also endeavored to teach women to value the beauty and strength they bring to their relationships in their homes, workplaces, communities, and the church. I taught them not only to value their own femininity but also to value one another. Several women told me that they hadn't liked other women when they entered my class but they'd left with a new appreciation for their feminine gender.

I enjoyed my role as director of the women's ministry and felt I was fulfilling what God had empowered me to do. I was pleasantly surprised at how much enjoyment and satisfaction I derived from teaching and working with the women. They became friends and confidantes, more like sisters than casual acquaintances. I especially enjoyed teaching the younger women. On several occasions during the summer, I invited all the young pastors' wives to our house. We ate lunch around the pool and then crowded into our living room to just laugh, talk, and share stories. Once, I had a party for all the women who worked on the custodial staff. They were shocked when I jumped into the pool and challenged them to a game of volleyball. I think they were even more shocked when I played like a real competitor!

Being with all these women brought me joy and helped fill

the deep well in my heart. Sometimes I'd look over the crowd of lovely, shining faces and say, "If only we had more time, we could all be best friends." I may have sounded like Pollyanna, but the sentiment was sincere. I was surrounded by women I loved, and I frequently referred to our group as a "community of friends."

Throughout my time in the women's ministry, where so many were infused with the love of God and a love for one another, I rarely saw any evidence of backbiting, gossip, or criticism. The other leaders worked with me to create a supportive environment in which we followed the biblical admonitions in working out our difficulties. We weren't without flaws, but we were healthy and growing in the right direction in our relationships with God and with one another. I never minded a bit of contention because I saw it as evidence of growth and life. Our goal was not to avoid conflict but to work through it. I felt our women's ministry was alive and thriving, and I loved it.

In the fall of 2006, I launched a weekly women's meeting called Women Belong to address the issue of loneliness, which has become an epidemic in our society. I had certainly experienced it in my own life. I wanted to make sure that each woman knew she belonged to the Lord and that we belonged to one another. I would often say, "You need never feel alone, because you belong here." Soon I had enlisted other women who were willing to teach and lead, and I loved seeing these women flourish. Like Ted, who has always believed in empowering others, I was thrilled to see others exercise their gifts.

My motto in ministry came from a Bible passage, Romans 12:3-8:

Because of the privilege and authority God has given me, I give each of you this warning: Don't think you are better than you

*really are. Be honest in your evaluation of yourselves, measuring
yourselves by the faith God has given us. Just as our bodies have
many parts and each part has a special function, so it is with
Christ's body. We are many parts of one body, and we all belong
to each other. In his grace, God has given us different gifts for
doing certain things well. So if God has given you the ability to
prophesy, speak out with as much faith as God has given you. If
your gift is serving others, serve them well. If you are a teacher,
teach well. If your gift is to encourage others, be encouraging.
If it is giving, give generously. If God has given you leadership
ability, take the responsibility seriously. And if you have a gift for
showing kindness to others, do it gladly.*

I believed that if each woman did her own part, none of us would
be overburdened, and we could all enjoy doing our work together.
I rejoiced when a woman told me she wanted to pursue a particular ministry, because that meant she had discovered her gift and
an avenue for service.

Over the years, I frequently opened our home to meet with the
wives of other staff members. I loved getting to know them and
encouraging them in their marriages and ministries. Ted and I
also threw open our doors to meet with many of our church leaders, and during the summers we hosted executive staff meetings
and staff-family barbecues in our backyard. We loved the people
we worked with, and we enjoyed spending time with them. We
expected to be involved in these friendships for life. Ted always
saw his leadership position as a gift, but what he valued most was
being part of this New Life team.

The Bible often describes the church as a family, and that was certainly our experience at New Life. I realize that not everyone has positive associations with the word *church*. Some people think of church as an institution or a bastion of ritual, or as a legalistic, guilt-inducing organization. I am saddened when I hear those sorts of comments, because they don't represent what Jesus had in mind when he established the church. The church is simply a group of people who believe in Jesus Christ. If they are living and growing in God's grace, they are wonderful to be around—relational, warm, and kind. You could never find a more supportive or loving group of people. The Bible says we are "no longer strangers and foreigners" but "citizens along with all of God's holy people. [We] are members of God's family" (Ephesians 2:19).

To my way of thinking, New Life Church was the epitome of what a church should be: a vibrant group of dedicated but imperfect people who loved Jesus and were willing to love one another. For Ted and me, they were indeed family.

For me, being among the leadership staff of New Life often felt like a bit of heaven on earth. That's why I wasn't surprised when Ted's influence began to extend far beyond Colorado Springs. As our church family continued to grow, people came from all over the world to observe how our staff interacted, and many expressed amazement at how much we enjoyed working with each other.

In addition to serving as senior pastor of New Life Church, Ted added several other responsibilities to his workload, including leadership of worldprayerteam.org and the Association of Life-Giving Churches. He also joined the National Association of Evangelicals (NAE), an organization composed of forty-five thousand churches from most of the major evangelical denominations. (If you're not familiar with the term *evangelical*, it refers to someone who believes that Jesus is the Son of God, the Bible is the Word of God, and that a person must be spiritually reborn to enter heaven.) Ted liked the NAE's bipartisan nature and its involvement with global issues beyond hot-button American political causes.

In the fall of 2003, Ted was elected president of the NAE, a position that frequently required him to act as a media spokesperson for the evangelical point of view. As president of the NAE, he participated in regular phone calls from the White House—though not, as some have reported, directly from President George W. Bush. Instead, Ted was part of a weekly conference call with Timothy Goeglein, a White House liaison who briefed several evangelical leaders on a regular basis.

I loved the NAE role for Ted because of the way he thinks. He's well-read, he's thoughtful, and he often looks at things more broadly than some others in the evangelical community. Ted's comments and perspectives were like a breath of fresh air. I think his open-mindedness is what got him elected to the position of president, because he certainly never campaigned for the job. He wasn't even present at the executive committee meeting where he was selected.

During Ted's time as president of the NAE, the organization grew from twenty-three million to thirty million members, but Ted began to feel the strain of running four major ministries. He enjoyed his work with New Life, the NAE, the Association of Life-Giving Churches, and worldprayerteam.org, but their combined demands were starting to overwhelm him.

In the summer of 2006, as Ted's four-year term as president of the NAE was drawing to a close, he repeatedly told me that he was becoming exhausted by all the travel. He felt he'd done the best he could do in the position, and he thought he ought to resign.

He wanted to stay home more to focus on me, our family, and pastoring New Life Church. Ted asked his assistant not to accept any more speaking engagements for him, and we made plans to refurbish a room in our barn so he could have a quiet place to write. The kids and I were thrilled at the prospect of having him home more often.

Yet while Ted was trying to lighten his workload, members of his staff encouraged him to keep going. They believed in him and wanted to help him achieve even more. Although well-intentioned, some of their efforts led to embarrassing situations that left Ted ill-prepared for difficult interviews. I remember him coming home after an interview with a well-known atheist. He had been so turned off by what he saw as the man's arrogance that he had allowed himself to become upset and had over-reacted. After hearing the story, I thought, *Ted is definitely not on his game. He's getting way too emotional. Something is wrong; he isn't himself.*

One opportunity he'd been asked to accept led to a humiliating scene in the 2006 documentary film *Jesus Camp*. In a jocular moment with the crew, Ted looked straight into the camera, pointed his finger, and smirked. "I think I know what you did last night," he said, hamming it up. "And if you send me a thousand dollars, I *won't* tell your wife." Then he grinned and told the cameraman, "And if you use that, I'll sue you."

Ted was only joking around with the camera crew, but he violated one of his own rules: *Don't film anything if you're not serious about it.* The crew recorded every word, and that unfortunate video clip has been distributed all over the Internet.

I could see that Ted was losing his edge and growing weary. In the previous few weeks, I had seen signs of stress in him—sudden outbursts of temper that weren't at all like him. I told him I was becoming concerned. On several occasions, he even made off-color remarks.

A couple of times, I pulled him aside and said, "You're scaring me, Ted. What is wrong with you?"

"Nothing." He would draw a deep breath and shrug away my concern. "I'm tired, that's all."

When he finally settled on resigning from the NAE, he felt a great sense of relief. He knew he desperately needed to simplify his life.

Ted went to the NAE board meeting in October 2006 with a resignation letter in hand. Even though I felt he was the best person for the job, I supported his decision because I knew he somehow needed this for his own health and well-being.

One of our senior staff members, however, flew out to the meeting site to encourage Ted *not* to resign. He convinced Ted that he would personally relieve some of the pressure by taking on more of Ted's responsibilities. He was determined that Ted should remain president of the NAE, and Ted reluctantly agreed to accommodate him.

When Ted went to the executive committee meeting the following day, he offered his resignation, but without much resolve. When the board refused to accept it, he didn't argue. He kept the position, and he came home feeling depressed and pressured.

Ted had called me from his hotel room the night before to tell me about the change of plans. My heart sank when I heard the news. I said, "No, Ted. Remember how settled you were about resigning. Don't let anyone talk you out of it."

"Well," he answered, "I think these guys have come up with a plan to help me."

I felt a heaviness sweep over me. I sensed darkness approaching like a cloud of impending grief. That night I slept fitfully. I kept waking with a trembling prayer on my lips: "Help us, God." And I couldn't explain why.

The next morning, as I read my Bible and prayed, my emotions were again stirred. I could still feel the heaviness from the night before, and I wept as I prayed. Later, as I worked on a lesson for our weekly Women Belong meeting, I felt impressed to share a story I had prepared at an earlier point in my life: the story of the Shunamite woman.

Our women were studying a series on the church, and I had planned to teach on the church as the family of God. But just before I stood to deliver that lesson, I once again felt the Spirit of God whisper, *The Shunamite woman.*

I had taught that story, found in 2 Kings 4, many times before. It is part of the history of the prophet Elisha. Most of the teaching I've heard on that passage focuses on Elisha's raising a dead boy to life, but the Shunamite woman herself has always held my attention.

I opened our meeting by reading the Scripture passage, 2 Kings 4:8-37. Then I lowered my Bible and looked out at the women in the room. "The Shunamite was a woman of means, and she used her resources to serve the man of God. She asked her husband's permission, and her husband, who knew he could trust her heart, appears to have given his blessing to proceed with her plan. So she built and furnished a room for the man of God, and whenever he came by, he stayed there. Like her husband, the prophet knew he could trust her with his reputation. She was a godly woman. A trustworthy woman. A woman worthy of respect.

"The prophet wanted to show his gratitude for her kindness,

and he asked what he could do for her. Her response? 'I am fine. You don't need to do anything for me.'

"But the prophet called his servant aside for more information, and the servant pointed out that the woman had no child. When Elisha told the Shunamite woman that she would have a son by that same time the following year, the woman responded, 'No, my lord. Don't go there. Don't touch that place in my heart.'"

I knew that I was about to broach a sensitive topic, so I stepped away from the podium as I continued. "In those days, in that culture, infertility was a disgraceful condition. We don't know whether this woman had had miscarriages or was barren, but she had closed her heart to the hope of ever having a child and had moved on to do the things she knew she could do with what she had. She used her gift of hospitality to serve others.

"Nonetheless, Elisha persisted in his prophecy, and twelve months later, the woman had a son, just as the prophet had foretold. But while the boy was still young, he developed a sudden headache one day and died."

Some of the women in our group had suffered from infertility; others had buried children or husbands or had experienced other forms of loss. This story was bound to strike a sensitive nerve in the hearts of women who had suffered pain over situations they couldn't change, and now I turned my focus to a different part of the room.

"Can you imagine what was running through this woman's mind?" I asked. "Hadn't she told the man of God that she was fine and not to open the sealed door of her heart? Hadn't she told him, 'Don't do anything; it is well with me'? She had resolutely moved on. But Elisha had opened the door anyway, and now what the woman feared most had become a reality.

"She had finally received what she thought she never would

have: a precious son. She had rejoiced at his birth, but now that promised child had just died in her arms. The woman's greatest joy had become her greatest loss. The representative of God had insisted on granting her prayers. So now she faced a choice: Did she surrender to grief and despair? Did she rage against God or his servant? Or did she dare to hope?

"She lifted her beloved son tenderly and carried him upstairs to the prophet's chamber. After laying him on the bed, she went out to visit her husband. She told him that she wanted to go see the man of God, and when he asked why, she assured him that all would be well.

"Why did she tell her husband everything would be all right? She was saying, 'As far as things are between you and me, it is well. You cannot answer the cry of my heart right now.' She didn't even tell her husband that their son had died. Why not? Surely he would have grieved the loss of the boy with her. But she couldn't, not yet. I think she would have lost it. She was restraining her emotions, holding them in a delicate balance—and we all know how it feels when one concession, one admission, will tip the emotional balance, spill the flood of our tears, and send us spiraling into despair. So instead of offering explanations, the Shunamite woman remained silent and went to find the man of God.

"Elisha saw her coming in the distance and immediately sent his servant to check on her. She told Elisha's servant the same thing she had told her husband: 'It is well.' Then she pressed on, seeking the One who could help. And when she reached Elisha, she fell to the ground and clutched his feet.

"In that moment, she had reached her destination. She had reached the One who could help. When she found the representative of God, she was finally able to pour out the burden of her heart. She wrapped her arms around Elisha's legs and cried, 'Didn't

I tell you not to take me there? This is the place of my greatest pain.'

"Elisha was deeply moved. Likewise, the heart of God is deeply moved when we seek him. When we look to him for comfort. When we say, 'No one else can help me. Only you, God. Only you.'

"There are times when other people can help us, but sometimes only a direct connection with God will suffice. In those moments, only God can provide what we need, because only he understands the deep inner workings of our hearts.

"There are moments in our lives when we have to communicate our utter dependence to the Father. That's what faith is. It's not just praying a prayer and believing you will have what you have prayed for with every ounce of strength in your 'believer.' It's depending on God and trusting him with the answers for your life.

"When Elisha returned to the Shunamite's house, the dead child was lying on the prophet's bed. Elisha went in alone, shut the door behind him, and prayed. Then he lay down on the child's body, placing his mouth on the child's mouth, his eyes on the child's eyes, his hands on the child's hands. And as he stretched over him, the child's body grew warm. Elisha got up, walked back and forth across the room, and then stretched himself over the child again. This time the boy sneezed seven times and opened his eyes!

"Then Elisha returned the boy to his mother."

That October morning, I looked out at the dear faces of the women at New Life Church and choked back tears of my own. When I had told the story of the Shunamite woman on previous occasions, I usually thought of my struggles with Jonathan, our special child. But that morning, a sense of unease stirred in my heart, as if God were preparing me for something I couldn't yet identify.

"I want us to think about our deepest fears," I told the women in the auditorium. "Even if they're closed-off areas of our hearts from which we've moved on. We would commend the Shunamite woman for not dwelling on her frustrated desires, and I think she did the right thing. But you know what? Our Father loves us. He will not let those sealed-off areas go untouched. He will go to those areas of our hearts and heal them.

"Your deep need may not involve raising a dead child, and it may not involve physical healing. Your lowest point may lie in some aspect of your marriage, your finances, or one of your children. But God is going to go there with you. He's going to touch you at your most vulnerable point, and he's going to heal you.

"We can do many things for each other; we can bring each other joy and comfort; but when God opens that wounded place in our hearts, he is faithful to heal. So if you are carrying a fear, or if you're facing your darkest hour, cling to him. Run to him, and hold on tight. Don't let go."

The room remained hushed as I finished teaching, and then I heard sniffling and muffled sobs. I invited women who wanted to pray to come to the front, where others would pray with them. Many came forward, and I was deeply moved by their response.

As the meeting ended, I dashed wetness from my eyes and watched the women of New Life make their ways toward the exits. Many of them stopped to talk; others embraced.

I didn't know it then, but I would teach at Women Belong only one more time; and on that last day, I would teach about how the church is the family of God. Like human families, we have good days and bad days, but none of us ever needs to feel alone, because we will always belong to the family.

As I looked out over the room, I pondered why the Lord had led me to spend that morning talking about the Shunamite woman.

I honestly thought I was delivering that lesson for someone else in the room. I had no idea that someone was me.

If you fail under pressure,
your strength is too small.

PROVERBS 24:10

4

FOR THREE WEEKS after I spoke on the Shunamite woman, I suffered through restless nights. I would jolt awake from a deep sleep, sit straight up in bed, and peer into the darkness. Then I'd pray, "Lord, help us. Something is wrong." This conviction plagued me through the nights, but during the day, I put the thought out of my mind and went about my routine.

During much of that time, Ted was traveling with Ron Luce, founder and president of Teen Mania, to raise awareness of that ministry among pastors. Ted took two of our sons, Marcus and Elliott, on the last of those trips, and they returned home on Wednesday morning, the first of November.

I met Ted at the church, just in time for our executive staff meeting. We sat side by side in a classroom, catching up as we ate a quick lunch. Around us, forty people were eating at tables that had been pushed together in a rectangular configuration. As usual, the atmosphere was buoyant with laughter and jocular conversation.

When Ted's cell phone buzzed, he glanced at the message on the screen, and his countenance changed. He handed me his phone so I could read the text he'd received from a pastor friend. A homosexual "escort" in Denver had leveled an accusation against a nationally known evangelical pastor from Colorado Springs. The escort hadn't yet identified the man he was accusing; he said he would do that on a Denver radio station the following morning.

I knew that Ted would be considered the most nationally known evangelical pastor in the Springs.

My stomach tightened, and my appetite vanished, replaced by a feeling of dread.

As I pushed my plate away, Ted abruptly brought the meeting to a close. As people moved toward the doorways, Ted pulled a few key staff members to the side and showed them the text message. One of them looked Ted in the eye and asked what he knew about the charge. Ted replied that he knew nothing, and he assured us there was no truth in the man's allegation.

Though I was apprehensive, I wasn't immediately alarmed. People who achieve national prominence are often targets of misinformation, so I braced myself for a possible encounter with someone who only wanted attention for a political agenda. "Do you know this guy?" I asked Ted. "Do you know anything about this?"

"I don't know him," Ted reassured me. "But I'll arrange a meeting with our church attorney and a couple of the staff guys so we can figure out the best way to answer this."

We were in the midst of a volatile political season in Colorado, with two amendments affecting gay rights at the forefront of the upcoming election. None of us would have been surprised if someone took a jab at Ted. People frequently assumed he represented the "Religious Right," though Ted strongly disliked that title and didn't agree with the tone or substance of many of the Religious Right's views.

Because Ted had spoken against same-sex marriage from the pulpit, I assumed the accusation was designed to embarrass him. What the accuser didn't realize, apparently, was that Ted has always believed that we need to show compassion to everyone. The doors of our church were open to everyone, and our purpose was to encourage people—*all* people—to grow in their relationships with God.

That evening, we arranged a meeting with the church's attorney to discuss how we should protect ourselves and the church from the still-unspecified accusation. Before we left our home for the meeting, I caught Ted in the upstairs hallway and pulled him into one of the bedrooms. I had been uneasy all afternoon, and as the day progressed, a knot of fear had grown in my chest. I didn't want to doubt my husband, but a sharp jab of suspicion drove me to ask him if any part of the accusation was true.

"Ted, is there anything to this?" I searched his eyes as we sat across from each other on our son's bed. "Do you know this man? Don't let me be surprised."

"I don't know this man," he answered.

I pushed my doubts aside and chose to believe him. As I exhaled, I caught a glimpse of my face in the mirror. The line between my brows had disappeared; I could relax again.

That night, we talked to the church's attorney. At one point, Ted left the room, and the lawyer quietly asked if I believed my husband.

"Absolutely," I told him, my voice firm. "I believe him."

We called our head elder and told him of the accusation. We asked him to call the overseers, the next step mandated by our church bylaws in the event that an accusation was brought against the senior pastor. I took a deep breath, reassured that everything was progressing as it should.

Years before, while setting up our church constitution and bylaws, Ted had established an overseers committee, whose sole purpose was to provide accountability for the senior pastor. If Ted's qualification for leadership ever came into question, the five-member board of overseers (we had four active members at the time), all of whom were senior pastors of other churches, would be responsible for investigating the accusations leveled against Ted and, based on their findings, determining whether he should remain as pastor of New Life. The bylaws stated that the overseer board had no authority within New Life unless the overseers were contacted by the elders to fulfill this specific function. Their sole responsibility was to ask Ted to give an account of his actions and evaluate his response to determine whether he should be disciplined or fired.[1] Ted had set up this system to protect the hearts of the people in the congregation from having to investigate and pass judgment on their senior pastor.

Later that night, when we pulled into our driveway, we found a news team assembled on the front lawn. As we drove past, I averted my eyes, unable to believe that anyone could make such a scandalous charge against my husband.

Ted parked the car in the garage and pulled the key from the ignition. "I'll go talk to them."

While he went out to tell the reporter that he didn't know any homosexual escorts in Denver, I went inside to check on our children. Ted told the reporter that the accusations were not true, and I told our kids that this was someone's desperate bid for attention and that all the fuss would soon blow over.

When Ted came inside, we went to bed and talked late into the night about the implications of this charge coming right before the election.

Politics, I told myself as I finally drifted off to sleep. *That's all it is.*

❖

On Thursday morning, we turned on the radio and listened to the show on which the accuser, a masseur in Denver, stated that he and Ted had been involved in a three-year homosexual affair and that Ted had obtained drugs from him. Even though I had braced for a blow, I was still shocked to hear the man say my husband's name. I was so convinced of Ted's innocence that I actually laughed as I listened to the allegations of drug use.

"There you have it," I said, relaxing when the show was over. "Anyone who knows you has to realize the absurdity of this man's accusations." Anyone who knew Ted knew he didn't drink alcohol or smoke anything.

I knew the man had to be lying. A three-year affair with a homosexual escort? Out of the question.

I believed Ted had been honest with me, and our physical relationship certainly didn't indicate that homosexuality was even a possibility. Our sexual relationship had always been strong and satisfying, and I didn't believe for one instant that Ted had been regularly visiting a gay escort.

As far as the charge of illegal drug use was concerned, I knew Ted had never had anything to do with marijuana or any other kind of illegal drug, even in high school or college. In my mind, that charge was even more ludicrous than the idea that Ted had visited a gay escort.

The phone rang. My good friend Julia was on the line, and she was laughing. "Can you believe it? I can't believe he expects anyone to take him seriously."

"I know," I answered. "I laughed too when I heard it."

"I can't believe anybody would go so far as to accuse Ted of those kinds of offenses. *Ted*, of all people!"

When I hung up, Ted suggested that I get ready to go with him to see our church's attorney a second time. Though the charges were clearly false, I assumed we needed to further discuss how to protect ourselves and the church from the fallout of the accusations. While I got dressed, Ted went outside to call the attorney.

We drove to the lawyer's office mostly in silence, realizing the gravity of the situation. My earlier laughter had turned to anger toward the man who was taking advantage of Ted's position to try to damage my husband, my family, our church, and Christians everywhere. *How dare he!* Though angry, I expected the trouble to fade quickly because the man *had* to be lying. Everyone who knew Ted would come rushing to his defense.

When we arrived at the law firm, I stopped in the restroom while Ted proceeded to the lawyer's private office. When I returned, the lawyer met me in the hallway. He looked at me gravely and said, "Go on into my office; Ted has something he wants to tell you."

My heart skipped a beat when I heard the serious tone in his voice. When the door closed behind me, I felt the life begin to drain from my body.

I sat down across from Ted at the attorney's conference table, and as I looked at him, I saw that his expression had changed. This was not the confident man who had entered the building with me only a few moments before. This man's face had contorted with anguish.

I sat stunned in my chair as Ted looked at me with the saddest eyes I have ever seen on his face.

"It's true, Gayle—not all of it, but part of it, enough of it. The man exaggerated things, but some of it is true."

Tears rolled down his cheeks while life continued to seep out of my body. I felt myself trembling, tears flooded my eyes, and my throat tightened until I could barely get words out.

"Who *are* you?" I sobbed from the depths of my soul. "Didn't I tell you not to let me be surprised? You lied to me! How could you?"

Ted sat silently.

"What about our children? What about the church? Who are you, and how could you have done this?"

Ted looked at me through red, swollen eyes. "I am sorry. I am so sorry, Gayle. I never wanted to hurt you. I love you. I thought I could fix this before you ever found out. I never wanted you to know. I was afraid you wouldn't love me if you knew. I didn't want to break your heart. I didn't want to lose you."

Tears poured down my face, and I tried vainly to stifle my sobs. My mind spun in bewilderment. I knew the implications. I understood the potential loss. My heart was breaking beneath the weight of my husband's confession. I could hardly breathe.

A knock interrupted the heavy silence. The lawyer opened the door and tilted his head toward the hallway. "The other men are waiting."

I swallowed hard as we stood, and Ted clasped my hand. I didn't resist. I didn't feel much of anything as we left the office and stumbled toward a conference room down the hall. I might have been walking with a stranger . . . but I wasn't. The hand in mine felt familiar; I knew it as well as I knew my own.

I knew who we'd find waiting for us in the conference room: four of our closest friends at the church, senior associates with whom we'd shared years of joy and service. Ordinarily, I'd have been smiling when I greeted them, but in that hour I needed their strength, their comfort and support.

We stepped into a room so filled with tension that moving through it took real effort. The men glanced at Ted; then they looked at me, and I knew the tears on my face told them all they needed to know. After Ted and I were seated at the table across from them, Ted looked at his dear friends and associates and confessed, confirming what he'd told me in the other room.

Their responses varied as the shock hit them. One man wept while another, fighting back tears, tried to comfort him. One apologized to Ted for not having been a good enough friend. Another's face clouded in anger.

I watched without speaking, mentally recording each man's reaction even as my own emotions roiled in shock.

I didn't realize it at the moment, but in that conference room I witnessed a microcosm of the various reactions we would face as news of Ted's guilt broke. Our friends would be devastated. Church members would be hurt and confused. Some would blame themselves for not having been the friends they should have been. Others would become angry. Many would be ashamed.

Ted and I wept as the flood of our impending loss threatened to drown us.

Then Ted asked one of the men in the room to call a group of local media and city officials to ask them to cancel a public meeting they had arranged for that afternoon. They had planned to gather on the courthouse steps and proclaim their support for Ted.

Finally, he asked about the group of overseers he had named for the purpose of disciplining or firing him if his actions ever warranted it. They had been called the night before, but Ted wanted to be sure they were on their way to Colorado Springs. Three lived within driving distance, but one had to catch a flight. We learned they were all scheduled to arrive at the attorney's office later that afternoon.

Ted and I both knew that our next step had to be telling our children.

Somehow, I got up from the chair and managed to tell our friends good-bye. Somehow, we walked out of the building and into the covered parking garage where our car waited. Somehow, we called our children and arranged to meet them at the house.

Christy, Marcus, and Alex got off work or left school and met us at home. Elliott was already there because he was homeschooling at the time. Sarah, Marcus's wife, couldn't get there until later. Jonathan was at school in Kentucky—which was a relief, because the emotions of that day would have only confused and upset him.

Our children were used to hearing their father's name in the news, but for this rumor to be true—I knew they'd be shocked to the core. We drove home, and Ted and I were both red-eyed and crying when we walked into the kitchen. Our kids looked at us, wide-eyed, and Marcus asked, "So . . . what's going on here?"

We gathered in the living room. Ted sat in his recliner by the fireplace. Too emotional to sit, I stood nearby as Ted apologized to our children. He confessed to using drugs, and he confessed to having had contact with the escort in Denver. He apologized for his sin, and he apologized for the shame his sin was going to heap on them.

I looked around the circle as my heart went out to my children. Next to Ted, they were the most precious people in the world to me. I didn't want them to have to go through this. I didn't want them to endure the embarrassment and the shame. I didn't want them to suffer ridicule from their peers. They didn't deserve it. For years they had done nothing but love us and put up with having to share their dad with so many others.

Marcus and Christy wore expressions of shock. Alex, our internal processor, looked pained and thoughtful. Thirteen-year-old Elliott's face had darkened in anger and disbelief. I could tell he was quickly assessing the damage.

After a few moments of stunned silence, their response was . . . remarkable.

Christy and Marcus, our two older children, admitted that in one way the news made them feel better about themselves. "We've always seen you and Mom as being perfect," Christy explained, looking from Ted to me. "I thought something was wrong with me because I'm not. To know that you have struggles too—that's a relief."

The Haggards have always been good at comic relief, and though her point was well-taken, Christy must have sensed that this would be a good time to make us all laugh.

After absorbing the news, the kids looked to me for direction.

"I don't know what's going to happen," I told them, my voice trembling. "I know we'll have to work some things out, and it won't be easy. But Dad and I love each other, and we love you all. We will get through this."

In those critical moments, I felt my family pull together in a solid show of support. I felt agreement from each of our kids, and it cheered my heart. We were in this as a team; we would face this crisis as a *family*.

Two years later, I would hear Marcus tell Oprah Winfrey about that day: "It was shocking, almost otherworldly. But there was an immediate relief—mixed with anger and frustration."

I don't remember many other details from that day, but I do remember making another trip with Ted to the attorney's office to meet with the overseers. We didn't meet at the church—and I couldn't help sensing that our presence there would be viewed as inappropriate.

When we arrived for the meeting, the four pastors and the

attorney—all of whom we considered friends—were seated at the table in the conference room. They rose from their chairs as we entered the now-familiar room, and as they gathered around Ted, he crumpled into their arms.

"Help me, brothers," he sobbed. "I'm in trouble."

After a moment of murmured consolations, Ted straightened, wiped his eyes, and said, "Your job is done. There is no need for an investigation. I know I need to resign. I just need you to help me."

He confessed that he had sinned, and that he had lied about it when asked.

"I lied to the news media," he explained, "because I didn't want *this* to happen, but now I'm beginning to see that this is the hand of God in my life."

The attorney took notes while Ted admitted buying drugs from his accuser and participating in sexual immorality. As he poured out his confession, fresh tears streamed down my face. But even through my pain, I began to sense God's mercy. As hurtful as the facts were, I knew I'd rather wrestle with the truth than live a lie. Confession and coming to terms with the truth, I believe, are the beginning of real healing.

The overseers prayed for us. When they had finished, the lawyer, who had been a good friend and the church's attorney for many years, told us that because he represented New Life, we would need to hire our own attorney.

Ted and I looked at each other in surprise. "I don't need an attorney," Ted said. "I'm not setting myself against the church in any way. Obviously, I can't continue to pastor, but I'm not the shepherd; Jesus is. I've only been an undershepherd, so let me be part of the body like everyone else. Let me serve among the people and heal. Let me mow the lawns or something. I'll do anything to serve the body."

We waited while the overseers looked at the lawyer for direction.

"You need your own lawyer," the attorney repeated. "I have a friend in Denver I can call for you."

While we listened, shell-shocked, the attorney called a Denver law office and arranged an appointment for us for the next morning.

We didn't talk much on the drive home from the lawyer's office.

Before we arrived, our children called and said, "Don't come home. The front of the house is crammed with reporters and camera crews. We've had to tack blankets over the windows to keep them from shining lights into the house."

As we neared the drive, we saw that the kids were right. Hordes of reporters clustered at the entrance to our driveway, so we didn't pull in. Instead, we kept going until we reached the home of our friends Adam and Julie Taylor. They quickly ushered us in and provided a safe haven from the media.

Not long after we arrived, our kids came by, one by one. A news van pursued our boys, who considered outrunning the media an adventure. Christy, however, was not amused. She was deeply concerned and protective of us.

As we waited for the news vans to leave, we moved to the Taylors' basement. From there, I called my parents and my sisters to give them the awful news. After absorbing the shock, they promised to pray for us. I promised to keep in touch about further developments.

When we finally went home, around midnight, the reporters had gone. After I cleared the kitchen counters and locked the doors, I stood in the middle of the house and realized I was exhausted and needed to go upstairs to bed—to the bed I shared with Ted.

I climbed the stairs to our room with mixed emotions. Our bedroom had been our private place, the room devoted to marital intimacy, but now it felt like an empty mockery.

How could I sleep with the man who'd been unfaithful to me? Ted had taken something that was mine alone—the right to physically enjoy his body—and shared it with a so-called escort. A *male* escort.

I quickly closed the lid on those thoughts; I wasn't ready to consider all the implications. Instead, I slipped into the bathroom to brush my teeth. As I ran the water over my toothbrush, I couldn't avoid my reflection in the mirror. My face looked worn, my eyes empty. All traces of my mascara were long gone, wept away in a flood of tears.

I bent over the sink and rinsed my mouth, then froze as a rogue thought slammed into my mind. *What if this man in Denver has AIDS? What if Ted has picked up some other sexually transmitted disease and infected me?* How could I face our family doctor and explain that I needed to be tested for AIDS, syphilis, gonorrhea, and whatever other venereal diseases were making the rounds?

The thought made me sick to my stomach.

Ted had already climbed into bed by the time I came out of the bathroom. I slid between the sheets and let my head fall to the pillow.

And then I felt Ted reach for me.

My heart broke in that instant. I knew the importance of physical touch in a marriage. I knew its power to bring comfort, healing, and validation. And I knew the damage rejection could cause. Broken people need to be touched, and by reaching out, Ted was pleading for my help. I wanted to help him; I didn't want to reject him—but what was I supposed to do with the anger, revulsion, and pain that were warring in my heart?

I had coached other women through this. Now it was my turn. I would have to press through my feelings and not lose this important opportunity, because it might not come again.

And so that night I began my journey of choosing . . . choosing to love. I chose to press through my feelings of anger. I pressed through my feelings of revulsion and took the hand I had held so many times, the hand that had brought me such comfort in the past. And in that moment, I realized how much I still loved my husband.

I turned and slid into his arms, but a fresh wave of sorrow overwhelmed me. I sobbed so loudly that I was sure the children could hear me. Waves of anger and sadness swept through me, and within seconds I felt Ted's shuddering sobs as well. I didn't stop to comfort him; I let my tears flow. I needed to cry, because I was terrified. I didn't know what Ted's confession meant, and I didn't know what I was going to discover about him now that he'd opened the door to the sealed-off place in his life. I didn't know what the impact of any of this was going to be on our future or our children. I was afraid of losing everything we loved at the church. I knew Ted had lost his position, but what would that look like? How would we relate to the people of New Life now?

And what effect would Ted's sin have on the body of Christ at large? So many Christian brothers and sisters were scattered throughout the world; how many would be mocked and scorned because of Ted's sin?

As the storm raged all around us, Ted and I clung to what little we had. We drew nearer, each of us sobbing out our sorrow while we held each other tight. Somehow, I felt closer than ever to Ted;

and even in my pain, I found comfort in the strength of his arms around me.

I don't know how long we clung to each other and wept. Eventually, wrapped in a heavy blanket of grief and exhaustion, Ted rolled over and went to sleep, but I remained awake. Finally I could sort through my thoughts without worrying about what others might read on my face.

Though I was shocked, heartbroken, and afraid, I felt as though I had spent my entire life training for that moment. I thought about my faith in God and my belief in the Bible. I considered my convictions about marriage and family, friendship, and the body of Christ—concepts I had taught to the women of our church. I remembered how I had learned to stretch in order to love Jonathan more.

I realized that everything I believed was being tested. Now I had to determine whether I had the strength to pass the test. Everything I valued was at stake—my marriage, my children, my church, and my understanding of God.

In those quiet moments, I decided to rise to the challenge. I was going to demonstrate my love by fighting for the dignity and honor of everyone and everything I held dear.

I had no idea how the battle would take shape; I had no idea how the opposition would present itself; but that night I settled the question within my own mind: My faith and the people I loved were worth fighting for. So fight I would, no matter how difficult the battle.

LORD, *don't hold back your*
  tender mercies from me.
Let your unfailing love and
  faithfulness always protect me.
For troubles surround me—
too many to count!
My sins pile up so high
I can't see my way out.
They outnumber the hairs on my head.
I have lost all courage.
Please, LORD, *rescue me!*
Come quickly, LORD, *and help me. . . .*
May all who search for you
be filled with joy and gladness in you.
May those who love your salvation
repeatedly shout, "The LORD *is great!"*
As for me, since I am poor and needy,
let the Lord keep me in his thoughts.
You are my helper and my savior.
O my God, do not delay.

PSALM 40:11-13, 16-17

5

I AWOKE EARLY the next morning, keenly aware that my world had shifted on its axis but uncertain of how much of it had changed. Because I have always taught that consistency contributes to sanity, I did what I always do: I slipped out of bed, put on my robe, and went downstairs to the kitchen to make a pot of coffee. After pouring myself a cup, I settled into my favorite overstuffed chair in our cozy den and read from my Bible and prayed. I don't remember what I read that morning, but the act of reading felt important. Afterward, I prayed more fervently than ever, "God, help us and show us what to do. Show me how to do this."

My emotions had settled somewhat overnight, and I was beginning to process the news about Ted more rationally. As I went into the kitchen for coffee, I remembered a Chinese proverb: "A journey of a thousand miles begins with a single step." I knew that Ted and I were embarking on a difficult journey, and I also knew what my first step had to be: forgiving Ted.

All Christians know that forgiveness is the proper response when we have been wounded or offended in some way. Forgiveness, the way God intended it, meant that I would no longer hold Ted's sins against him. I would cancel the penalty and surrender my desire to punish him. If I forgave Ted, I would restore him to the place he held before the offense.

I knew I wouldn't be able to forgive Ted in a single step—forgiveness would take some time. But I didn't know where to begin. I really wanted to forgive him, but first I wanted to know what he was thinking. Was he really sorry? And if so, was he sorry he'd hurt me or just sorry he got caught? Was he willing to change? Was he willing to *repent*? In religious vernacular, *repentance* means "to turn from sin and commit to doing what is right." Was Ted ready, willing, and able to do that? The day before, he had repeatedly answered yes to all those questions, but I had to be sure of him before I could be sure of my own response.

Ted made the call that morning to the head trustee at New Life to resign his position as senior pastor. He also resigned as president of the NAE. Later that morning, Ted and I prayed together before leaving. We prayed for each of our children by name, and we prayed for the church. Our hearts were heavy, and our voices were thick and afflicted with sorrow. Then we prepared for the drive to Denver to meet with the lawyer the church had hired for us.

Christy, Alex, and Elliott wanted to go with us to offer their support. As we were heading to the garage, the phone rang, and we received word that Ted's accuser had once again been a guest on a Denver radio show. He had taken a lie detector test live on the air—and the results had indicated some level of deception.

The media had been buzzing with reports that the masseur had a recorded voicemail message that could be identified as Ted's voice. The man on the voicemail had called himself "Art," and everyone who knew Ted well knew that his middle name was Arthur. The moment I heard the voicemail, I recognized Ted's voice and heard him ask where he could get "more stuff."

Despite the damning evidence of the voicemail, Ted seemed thrilled with the result of his accuser's polygraph. I think he felt it validated his assertion that many of the charges were not true. Even so, I knew he was in a vulnerable state. The media were lined up outside the house; we were still numb with shock, and we'd just heard that Ted's accuser had failed a lie-detector test. Maybe that news tempted Ted to believe he could still deny the drug charge, even though he'd already confessed to part of it. Yes, he told me and the kids, he had bought drugs from the man in Denver, and he had used them. But there had been no "three-year affair," as the masseur claimed.

The five of us got into the truck and backed out of the garage. My stomach tightened as we neared the gate at the end of the driveway. A reporter and her camera crew waited by a news van; I could see a mike and cameras.

I reached out to touch Ted's arm. "Don't say anything," I urged him. "Tell them you can't speak right now."

We pulled through the gate, and Ted stopped the truck. He has always been good about cooperating with the media, and he'd always been on good terms with most of our local reporters. A microphone shot toward me as I rolled down the window, confident that Ted would shake his head and say, "Sorry, but I can't make a statement right now."

"Can you step out of the vehicle and talk to us a minute?" a female reporter asked. I had seen her before and knew she worked for 9News out of Denver. An attractive woman with kind eyes, she had interviewed Ted on our front lawn that first night. She looked at me now with a sad expression, wordlessly apologizing for the question she was about to ask.

"Well, we can't get into much; we're a little late for an appointment," Ted said, "but—"

My heart lurched at the word *but*.

"—as we talked the other night, we're so grateful that he failed the polygraph test this morning. My accuser did."

As Ted continued to talk, the reporter and cameraman moved in closer. "The man who's making the accusations did fail *part* of the polygraph," the reporter clarified. "He showed deception about having any kind of a relationship. He did not fail or did not directly address the aspect of any use of illegal drugs."

Ted nodded. "Yeah, and all that's—"

"That's another question that's out there."

"All that's got to be processed through," Ted continued, "and I'm sure they're gonna do that."

I shifted my gaze from the woman to Ted, but he didn't see my warning glance. He remained focused on the reporter.

"I have to ask you," she said. "Have you used meth?"

I knew he had. Christy and Alex and Elliott knew he had; he had confessed to all of us. I closed my eyes as I heard him say, "No, I have not."

"Okay. And the voice expert that is in Denver . . . has now matched eighteen of the words left on the voicemail message—"

"Yeah, I did call him," Ted said, his voice firm. "I did call him."

"What did you call him about?"

"I called him to buy some meth, but I threw it away."

"And who were you buying the meth for?"

"No one. I was buying it for me, but I never used it."

I suppressed a sigh. What were the children thinking? To my

knowledge, before this moment they had never heard a lie from their father. I turned away, afraid the reporter would read my thoughts in my eyes.

The woman kept questioning. "Have you ever used meth before?"

"No, I have not. And I did not ever use it with him."

"And did you ever have sex with him?"

"No, I did not."

"At what point did you decide to throw away the meth?"

"Right after. I never kept it very long because it's wrong. I was tempted, I bought it, but I never used it."

"And how did you know that he would sell it to you?"

"He told me about it. I went there for a massage."

The reporter concluded her questioning, and I rolled up the window as Ted pulled the truck onto the road. As we approached the traffic light nearest our house, his confident expression melted, and his forehead dropped to the steering wheel. When he spoke again, his voice came out in tatters: "What have I just done?"

"You just lied," I answered, my tone flat. "And everybody's going to know it."

No one said much on the drive to Denver. I felt so empty and disheartened. What could I say? How could I explain this to our kids? On Thursday, Ted had confessed his drug use in private, but today he'd denied his confession in public. I didn't know what was going on in his head, but I knew he was miserable. He drove silently with a pained expression on his face.

The attorney in Denver, Leonard Chesler, proved to be a good friend to us. He was a grandfatherly sort, and his desire to protect us seemed genuine and sincere. He cleared his calendar, allowing us to spend the entire day with him. He advised us not to say anything to the media—and I wished we'd heard that wise counsel an hour earlier. He explained that the church would be paying him. We explained that we did not know why the church had hired him—because we didn't see our relationship with the church as adversarial. We told him we planned to submit to the overseers, to the church, and to its leaders.

"What's the role of these overseers?" Leonard asked.

Ted replied that the overseers were to discipline or fire the senior pastor if he was found guilty of engaging in sexual immorality, embezzling funds, or teaching heresy. "At that point," Ted continued, "their function is finished. But I've asked these men, as my brothers, to help me recover and heal."

"And what about the church?"

"The church has an excellent staff," Ted answered. "Wonderful elders and a capable board of trustees. New Life is a strong body. They'll do fine."

I knew Ted was thinking of our senior associate, who would step in as interim pastor. We had total confidence in his ability to lead the church. In addition to the senior associate, Ted and I had earlier identified at least six other associates with the potential to become senior pastor. No matter what happened, these men were capable of working well together, so the church would be in good hands.

Nonetheless, Leonard emphasized that he would work to protect us.

When we realized that the meeting was going to take more time than we'd planned, we decided to let Christy and the boys drive the truck home. A friend would bring it back to us later in the day. In the early afternoon, we said good-bye to the kids and continued our discussions with our lawyer.

When Leonard wanted to speak with Ted alone, I stepped into the foyer. While I waited, I received a call from one of the overseers, who was obviously upset about something. "What just happened?" he demanded. "Ted granted another interview."

"Yes," I answered, not emotionally prepared to explain my husband's muddled reasoning. "And he lied. He knows he lied, and we've discussed it."

Frustrated and weary, I raked my hand through my hair and stared out the window. I was upset with Ted, too, but I was torn between protecting my husband and cooperating with the overseer as he fired questions at me. Ted seemed so vulnerable, and he already felt guilty. I knew enough about psychology to know that he was traumatized. He wasn't thinking clearly; he was still being self-protective. He had been lying to himself and others for months, maybe years. I understood that denial kicks in when a person cannot emotionally handle the truth.

And now, in the public arena, Ted had to face himself, his loved ones, and everyone he cared about. I could understand why he lied that day. He didn't want to face himself or anyone else. Not like this. He wanted it all to go away.

I wished he'd chosen a different course, but I understood that he had tried to hide his sin because he was so deeply ashamed of it. So many people depended on him, and he was sure I'd leave him and no one would understand or love him if they knew the truth. When he acted on his temptations, he was so ashamed afterward that he'd try to hide his sin from others, receive forgiveness from God, and move on.

But I also knew that he was only digging himself in deeper. I could hear anger in the overseer's voice and knew he must have felt that Ted had betrayed him.

I don't remember the rest of our conversation. I only remember disconnecting the call and thinking that I'd be grateful when the day finally came to an end. I sent Ted a quick text saying, "I'm totally miserable out here." So he and Leonard invited me back into the inner office.

As Ted and I prepared to drive home, Marcus called and said that the area outside our driveway had again filled with dozens of reporters and film crews. Media people were chasing our children as they pulled in and out of the gate. To deter prying cameras, the kids had again draped blankets over the sheer curtains at the windows.

"Don't come home tonight," Marcus warned. "You'll be ambushed."

Without any luggage, Ted and I checked into a hotel in Denver. On Saturday morning, we were supposed to attend a meeting with the overseers and both attorneys, so we wanted to be well rested. Or as well rested as we could be.

Again we held each other as we went to sleep; again we sobbed out our sorrow and our fears. When we were spent, we nestled together like spoons.

As I closed my eyes to sleep, I couldn't help thinking that what I wanted most was for Ted to confess *everything*, without lying or holding anything back. Only then could he begin to heal among the people he'd loved and led for twenty-two years.

The next morning, we drove to the church's attorney's office. On the drive, I could tell that Ted was beginning to think clearly again. He said, "I know this is hard on you, but I am feeling relieved to finally be able to talk about this. I believe Jesus is answering my prayers and finishing the work he began in me."

I knew what he meant in referring to Philippians 1:6: "I am certain that God, who began the good work within you, will continue his work until it is finally finished on the day when Christ Jesus returns." As Christians, we don't magically become perfect people the moment we decide to follow Christ. Instead, we begin a lifelong journey of growing and maturing in our relationship with God and in the way we relate to others. God begins to purify us, teach us, and discipline us so that we are changed over the course of our lives. Ted believed that God was using even these events to continue this work in Ted's life.

I wondered if people would understand that principle and grant him grace—favor and forgiveness—while he went through this process.

I thought most people at New Life would love Ted enough to let him be human, because in twenty-two years of pastoring, he had never presented himself as the model of perfection. While teaching the Scriptures, he would often say, "This is for me; I need this." I think his self-effacement was one of the qualities that drew people to him and to the church.

One of the themes of Ted's ministry was "living in the tree of life," meaning that we should give each other grace to keep growing and not judge or limit each other in that process. Ted always said you could either live in the "tree of life" or in the "tree of the knowledge of good and evil." "Living in the tree of the knowledge of good and evil" means that we judge and scrutinize one another according to some measure of perfection. It's the tree that God warned Adam and Eve not to eat from, or they would surely die. Being a Christian is not about seeing how holy or perfect we can be for the sake of appearance. It's about living in relationship with Jesus and his body, the church. It's about receiving life from God and giving it to others, experiencing the transformation that only Jesus can bring in the process.

I felt certain that our New Life family would extend grace to Ted. I knew the situation would be difficult for everyone and that Ted would have to face people who felt he had betrayed them. He'd have to answer to their anger. But that is a necessary part of the relational healing process outlined in the Bible in Matthew 5:23-24. I was convinced that the people of New Life Church were strong enough to handle Ted's very human journey.

God had brought Ted to a place where he could face his sins honestly and confess them. He needed the church to extend forgiveness and grace now that he had publicly acknowledged his sins. This would be the path to healing and restoration. I knew this process would take a while, but I welcomed the idea of spending some time alone with my husband and family.

My thoughts turned toward the immediate future. I could take a sabbatical from leading the women's ministry. Ted could get the rest he desperately needed. We could heal together and with our children. And then we could return and continue to heal with the church. I could draw strength from my friends at the church; our children could receive love and support from the youth ministries; and Ted could serve in whatever jobs were available. I knew he would do anything the church asked.

What a testimony to our city this would be! What a testimony to our world of the church's power to forgive and heal.

When we arrived at the attorney's office, the overseers were present, as was our lawyer, Leonard Chesler. During the meeting, the overseers presented us with their plan. We were frazzled and emotionally exhausted from our lack of sleep and the events of the preceding days, and we wept as one of the overseers explained that they felt we needed to leave the church—not for a set period of time for the purpose of healing, but *permanently*.

We couldn't even grasp what he was saying. We couldn't imagine being permanently separated from New Life. For the first time, I heard that I would have to relinquish my role as director of women's ministries. That news felt like a blow to the stomach. God had called me to that position, and I had found such joy in it.

We felt so weak. We nodded and cried and tried to cooperate.

The overseers told us that our salaries would continue for three months, until they could determine a severance package. One of them looked at Ted and said, "I know you are a dad, and as a dad, concern for Jonathan must be at the forefront of your thinking. I'm going to set up a fund to help pay the bill so you can keep Jonathan at his school."

We wept again, struck by his thoughtfulness and the incredible loss we faced. Ted pleaded, "Let me clean the bathrooms; let me do this right. I have watched other churches successfully transfer leadership, so I know I can do this. I don't have to lead, but I need to be part of the body. New Life is our family."

The overseers shook their heads. "Too risky," one of them said. "You're such a strong leader, the people might not be able to let go of you."

I believed the overseers were mistaken. New Life was unique, and so was Ted's role in it. The church had never hired him to preach. The church had grown from a small group that had met in our basement, so we didn't fit the mold of other church communities that regularly hire and fire pastoral staff. We functioned as a community of family and friends. We were functionally and relationally members of a church body. Because Ted had never taught, or demonstrated, a clergy-laity divide, I thought that over time he could assume a different role in the church. I know some people will think I was being naïve, but I believed we could navigate the process biblically if given the chance. I deeply believed that we needed the body's help in order to heal.

Ted was willing to serve the church in whatever capacity he could. He knew how to point people toward new leadership and how to model submission. He knew he would have to walk through his repentance with humility.

I knew that most New Life members were mature enough in their faith to understand that no one is perfect and that everyone fails. Sin is part of our human experience and only confirms our need for a Savior.

I know that some pastors view the people in their congregations as sheep, in the sense that they are immature in their faith and cannot think for themselves. But Ted and I had never seen the people of New Life that way. Our congregation was composed of mature and maturing Christians—men, women, and young people who would be intelligent in their response if given the chance. We felt honored to be among these people and often said how grateful we were that God had placed us among this body of believers. They knew that only Jesus never sinned.

Of course, watching Ted step down from his former role would be difficult for some; but with good leadership everyone could learn from the process. Forgiveness and healing are part of the function of a healthy church, and both clearly communicate the biblical message that no one is without sin. The goal would be for a healthy church to restore Ted to spiritual health again, just as it would for any other member of the body of Christ.

I wanted the overseers to give New Life an opportunity to do what I believed their hearts would lead them to do. But the overseers felt a different approach would be in order.

They then informed us that they had chosen three men to be responsible for our restoration process. We wanted to be restored by the people in our church—the people who knew us best. But the overseers felt that because of all the national publicity, Ted's process would require national leaders. We wondered how such busy men would find the time to walk us through such an intimate process.

For several reasons, I didn't have a great deal of confidence in the overseers' plan. First, the men they'd chosen were incredibly busy leaders. Ted knew and respected all three, but I didn't see how they could have regular interaction with him while they were actively involved with their own full-time ministries. Second, they lived in three separate states, so logistically I didn't see how we could all meet on any kind of regular basis. And finally, even though we respected these leaders, none was familiar with the unique culture of New Life Church.

The plan made little sense to Ted and me, but we were too frazzled to question it. At that point, I wasn't sure what "restoration" entailed or what we were being restored *to*.

After my emotions settled, I realized that I did have some expectations about what would happen next. Because Ted had confessed his sin and had chosen to repent, I expected the restorers to give him time to personally heal while they offered their love and support. I expected that we would go through marital counseling to heal our wounds and uncover blind spots that had helped create our problems. I expected that we would receive tools we could use to make our marriage stronger and better.

I thought our children would be brought into the restoration process to help them heal their own wounds and strengthen our family relationships. I believed that after a few months, we would begin to reenter the life of the church, giving Ted time to heal with those who felt he had let them down. While Ted walked out his repentance in a supportive environment provided by people who cared about him, I anticipated feeling the love and support of the church around me as well. And I expected that my children would also experience the love and care of the congregation.

I was confident that the people of New Life would set a biblical example and would demonstrate how the church was a safe place in which people could work out their personal struggles with sin.

I believed that even those people who were angry or hurt could walk through a process of reconciliation and healing in keeping with Christian teachings. Perhaps that sounds like a lot to expect, but New Life had always been an exceptional church.

"There remains one other matter," another overseer said. "How do we announce this development to the church?"

I held my breath as everyone looked at Ted. He knew he had failed the Lord, his family, and the people of New Life. He was deeply ashamed of his personal incongruity and the hurt he had caused. He wanted to stand before the church, to confess and ask for forgiveness, but he knew the auditorium would probably be filled with cameras, and he did not want to create another emotional media moment.

So instead, Ted suggested that we write letters to the church. The chief overseer could read them to the congregation on Sunday morning.

The overseers agreed that this was a good idea.

We thanked them for their hard work and went home. After eating a light lunch, Ted and I retired to separate corners to write the most significant letters of our lives. I went to my desk in our bedroom while Ted settled into his favorite chair by the fireplace in our den.

Tears streamed down my face as I wrote my letter in one draft. I knew exactly what I wanted to say, though it broke my heart to say it.

Later that afternoon, I met with my three closest friends for the first time since the crisis. These women had partnered with me in life and ministry. When I was writing *A Life Embraced*, my book for pastors' wives, these three friends often met and prayed with me. They had played key roles in helping me build the women's ministry, and they were my closest confidantes. We had spent hours laughing, praying, and planning together. I loved these women and felt safe with them.

On that Saturday, they listened as I wept and tried to explain what had happened and what the outcome was going to be. I knew they were experiencing the same shock I'd felt. Ted was their pastor; New Life, their church. I was going through the last experience on earth they would have predicted for me.

They tried to comfort me, but no one really knew what to say. I wanted to smile and assure them that I was still the same person but was just going through a really tough situation.

Finally, I looked at one of the women who had assisted me in teaching the women's classes and asked if she would oversee the women's ministry. "I don't know how long you'll have to do it, and I don't know what things are going to look like in the next few weeks—"

"I'll do it," she said. "Don't worry about a thing." My other friends offered to help her.

And then we said our good-byes, none of us knowing what the future held. But I felt confident about the stability of those friendships.

After I arrived home, another associate pastor from New Life came by the house with his wife. They sat on our sofa while he apologized for not having been a better friend to Ted. "I saw signs that you were in trouble," he told Ted, "but I didn't know what to do about it."

Ted thanked his friend but pointed out that the fault was his alone. Then we said good-bye.

We went to bed that night wondering what would happen the next morning when our letters were read in church. I knew it would be a sad day for many people. Most were still in shock at the news and stunned by the media whirlwind that had swept down to surround their pastor and the church. Many still refused to believe the story. Tomorrow, some would be angry; others would be heartbroken.

But as I considered what possible good could come out of all this, I envisioned people weeping as our letters were read aloud. I could see individuals standing, one at a time, all over the congregation as the realization hit home: "Yes, Pastor Ted sinned, but I am a sinner too." "Me, too. I am a sinner as well."

I knew the media would be present—probably scores of reporters. And what a testimony the world would see as members of the church realized that their pastor shared their sinful condition. Like every man and woman in those pews, Ted was an imperfect human being who could never claim righteousness or holiness except through Jesus. What a powerful opportunity to present the gospel.

I couldn't imagine a more validating testimony. And if this was what God had in mind when he allowed this situation to happen, perhaps I could begin to make sense of it.

Suddenly, Jesus was standing there
among them! "Peace be with you,"
he said. As he spoke, he showed them
the wounds in his hands and his side.
They were filled with joy when they
saw the Lord! Again he said, "Peace
be with you. As the Father has sent
me, so I am sending you." Then he
breathed on them and said, "Receive
the Holy Spirit. If you forgive anyone's
sins, they are forgiven. If you do not
forgive them, they are not forgiven."

JOHN 20:19-23

6

Dear Women of New Life Church:
I am so sorry for the circumstances that have led me to write this letter to you today. I know your hearts are broken; mine is as well. Yet my hope rests steadfastly in the Lord who is forever faithful.

What I want you to know is that I love my husband, Ted Haggard, with all my heart. I am committed to him until death "do us part." We started this journey together, and with the grace of God, we will finish together.

If I were standing before you today, I would not change one iota of what I have been teaching the women of our church. For those of you who have been concerned that my marriage was so perfect I could not possibly relate to the women who are facing great difficulties, know that this will never again be the case. My test has begun; watch me. I will try to prove myself faithful.

I love you all so much, especially you young women—you were my delight.

To all the church family of New Life Church—Ted and I are so proud of you. You are all we hoped you would be. In our minds, there is no greater church.

As you try to make sense of these past few days, know that Ted believes with all his heart and soul everything he has ever taught you, those things you are putting into practice. He is now the visible and public evidence that every man, woman, and child needs a Savior.

We are grateful for your prayers for our family.

I hold you forever in my heart.

Gayle Haggard

My dear New Life Church family, I am so sorry. I am sorry for the disappointment, the betrayal, and the hurt. I am sorry for the horrible example I have set for you.

I have an overwhelming, all-consuming sadness in my heart for the pain that you and I and my family have experienced over the past few days. I am so sorry for the circumstances that have caused shame and embarrassment to all of you. I asked that this note be read to you this morning so I could clarify my heart's condition to you.

The last four days have been so difficult for me, my family, and all of you, and I have further confused the situation with some of the things I've said during interviews with reporters who would catch me coming or going from my home.

But I alone am responsible for the confusion caused by my inconsistent statements. The fact is, I am guilty of sexual immorality, and I take responsibility for the entire problem. I am a deceiver and a liar. There is a part of my life that is so repulsive and dark that I've been warring against it all of my adult life. For extended periods of time, I would enjoy victory and rejoice in freedom. Then, from time to time, the dirt that I thought was gone would resurface, and I would find myself thinking thoughts and experiencing desires that were contrary to everything I believe and teach.

Through the years, I've sought assistance in a variety of ways, with none of them proving to be effective in me. Then, because of pride, I began deceiving those I love the most because I didn't want to hurt or disappoint them.

The public person I was wasn't a lie; it was just incomplete. When I stopped communicating about my problems, the darkness increased and finally dominated me. As a result, I did things that were contrary to everything I believe.

The accusations that have been leveled against me are not all true, but enough of them are true that I have been appropriately and lovingly removed from ministry. Our church's overseers have required me to submit to the oversight of [three mature Christian leaders]. Those men will perform a thorough analysis of my mental, spiritual, emotional, and physical life. They will guide me through a program with the goal of healing and restoration for my life, my marriage, and my family.

I created this entire situation. The things that I did opened the door for additional allegations. But I am

responsible; I alone need to be disciplined and corrected.
An example must be set.

It is important that you know how much I love and
appreciate my wife, Gayle. What I did should never reflect
in a negative way on her relationship with me. She has been,
and continues to be, incredible. The problem was not with her,
my children, or any of you. It was created 100 percent by me.

I have been permanently removed from the office of senior
pastor of New Life Church.

Until a new senior pastor is chosen, our associate
senior pastor will assume all of the responsibilities of the
office. On the day he accepted this new role, he and his
wife had a new baby boy. A new life in the midst of this
circumstance—I consider that confluence of events to be
prophetic. Please commit to join with [him] and the others
in church leadership to make their service to you easy and
without burden. They are fine leaders. You are blessed.

I appreciate your loving and forgiving nature, and
I humbly ask you to do a few things:

1. Please stay faithful to God through service and giving.
2. Please forgive me. I am so embarrassed and ashamed.
   I caused this, and I have no excuse. I am a sinner. I have
   fallen. I desperately need to be forgiven and healed.
3. Please forgive my accuser. He is revealing the deception
   and sensuality that was in my life. Those sins, and
   others, need to be dealt with harshly. So, forgive him and
   actually thank God for him. I am trusting that his actions
   will make me, my wife and family, and ultimately all of
   you stronger. He didn't violate you. I did.
4. Please stay faithful to each other. Perform your
   functions well. Encourage each other, and rejoice in God's

faithfulness. Our church body is a beautiful body, and like every family, our strength is tested and proven in the midst of adversity.

Because of the negative publicity I've created with my foolishness, we can now demonstrate to the world how our sick and wounded can be healed, and how even disappointed and betrayed church bodies can prosper and rejoice.

Gayle and I need to be gone for a while. We will never return to a leadership role at New Life Church. In our hearts, we will always be members of this body. We love you as our family. I know this situation will put you to the test. I'm sorry I've created the test, but please rise to this challenge and demonstrate the incredible grace that is available to all of us.

Ted Haggard

❖

On Sunday morning, when a spokesman read our letters to two packed services, every major news network had representatives in the building. Ted and I waited at home, pacing through the house as we wondered how it would go. Later, we heard that people wept as one of the overseers read our letters. People poured out their love through tears and supportive applause. Our son Marcus was in the crowd, and when someone pointed him out, the congregation gave him a standing ovation.

I wished I could have been there. I wished Ted could have felt their love and support.

Though young children had been dismissed from the service, the teenagers remained. Afterward, several high school members of our youth ministry expressed sympathy for Ted and promised not to leave the church. "Just because he messed up doesn't give us the excuse to run away," one fifteen-year-old told the *Colorado Springs Independent.*[1]

My hope of a spontaneous realization of our connection as sinners was not fulfilled. Nonetheless, people wept as they listened to our words.

I could only pray that they knew we were weeping with them.

You know of my shame,

   scorn, and disgrace.

You see all that my enemies are doing.

Their insults have broken my heart,

and I am in despair.

If only one person would

   show some pity;

if only one would turn and comfort me.

PSALM 69:19-20

7

THAT SUNDAY NIGHT, the overseers came to our home to say good-bye. I don't remember much about that meeting, but I do remember one of them stating that he believed our greatest ministry lay ahead. I also remember their praying for us.

That night, I wept as I got ready for bed. No surprise, really, because in those days I seemed to cry nonstop. I crawled into bed, rolled onto my side, and cried out to the Lord, "Wasn't it enough that I raised Jonathan? This is the thing I never wanted to face."

Perhaps I'd sensed what lay behind the wall Ted had put up to hide his problem. Even though I'd seen no obvious evidence, perhaps Ted's secret had lurked in my subconscious or in the marrow of my spirit.

With a prayer on my lips, I fell asleep.

At 4:30, I woke up and decided to go downstairs to pray. As I stepped into my closet and reached for my robe, I felt the Lord speak to me in that inner voice I've come to recognize as his:

I never intended for you to go through this alone. I have come to rescue Ted. I am going to rescue him from the fowler's snare, from the lion's mouth, and from the fiery furnace. I have a great purpose for you. Cling to me; I will carry you on eagles' wings.

I stood in the holy stillness and clutched my robe to my chest. Though I hadn't expected to hear from God in my closet, I found comfort in knowing he had heard me in my distress. He saw what I was going through, and he was answering my prayers. He had a divine purpose for us, and he was rescuing Ted.

Knowing that, how could I allow myself to feel hopeless?

Later that morning, after the rest of the family got up, we packed and headed to the airport. Some friends had rented a house for us on Captiva Island, in Florida, and we had arranged to stay three weeks. The children were coming with us, and I was glad to escape to a private place where we could process and heal, away from the hot glare of unrelenting media attention.

Once we were airborne, Ted opened a book by Stephen M. R. Covey, *The Speed of Trust.* He had bought the book a few weeks earlier and had stuck it in his travel bag. He read for a few minutes and then closed the book. I glanced over at him, curious about why he'd stopped reading so soon. Later, I learned that Covey's book contains a test to determine a reader's trustworthiness. Ted had taken the test and scored low, especially on self-trust, which is the basis for trustworthiness. If you continually fail yourself, you cannot meet higher goals in building trust with other people.

Somehow, Ted felt God speaking to him through Stephen Covey's writing. He knew that he had wrestled with a secret area of his life and had lied about it for far too long. He realized that the way to begin repairing his self-trust and my trust in him was through total and complete honesty. That's when he turned to me and said, "I'm going to tell you the absolute truth about everything. I will answer all your questions and not withhold anything from you."

With our children sitting behind us, I leaned toward Ted and asked him question after question. I needed honest answers, and I knew he needed to give them. I saw relief enter his eyes as he told me the complete, barefaced truth for the first time.

On that flight, I learned Ted's haunting secrets. I listened with mixed emotions—I was delighted that he was finally opening up and dismantling the wall between us, brick by brick; but I was horrified by what I discovered behind that wall.

I learned that Ted had been battling sexual temptations for years and that he had succumbed to those temptations involving sensual massages and other sexual sin. His dark thoughts had become obsessions, and those obsessions had led to compulsive behaviors.

Ted confessed that as the external pressures had increased in recent years, he had sought a way to escape. He went for massages—and in my naïveté, I had encouraged him to go. I had no idea that some of these massages culminated in sexual activity.

From the Denver masseur, Ted had also learned about certain drugs that purportedly would enhance his sexual experience. He gave in to this temptation and returned on several occasions to purchase drugs.

In a desperate attempt to control his compulsion and not involve anyone else, Ted searched for sexual gratification through pornography and these drugs. He never used drugs with any other person—not the masseur, and especially not me. Ted was engaging in this private behavior as late as October 2006. He honestly thought he was gaining control over his compulsive thoughts because his private practices did not lead to contact with other people. He was, in fact, only compounding his problem and becoming even more ensnared in his secret activities.

At the same time, he was begging God to help him overcome his sin. He had resisted at times through fasting and prayer. He had pored over the Scriptures; he knew his actions were a betrayal of his marriage vows and the Bible's instructions for righteous living. When he ordered the Covey book, he also ordered a correspondence Bible study course that focused on freedom and having control over one's thought life. He was grasping for anything that might give him victory over his compulsive thoughts and behaviors.

Ted also told me about his association with a man who attended our church. This man had come to Colorado Springs after being dismissed from a Christian college because he'd been involved in a homosexual relationship. He approached Ted for help because he wanted to be a pastor someday. I had known of this man's problem but hadn't been concerned. I knew Ted was trying to help him.

But Ted told me their relationship had eventually become inappropriate. Over time, the man intuited that Ted had similar struggles, which led to Ted's confiding details of his own battle. He even went so far as to tell the man how he had sought release from temptation through pornography and his "cocktail."

In hindsight, I think Ted had lost his bearings by that time—even though he was preaching some of his best sermons. I remembered him being extremely stressed and occasionally lashing out in anger at his staff, and sometimes at me. I'd observed him blocking out some of his close staff members in the same way he often blocked me.

"And then," Ted told me, "there was Cripple Creek."

I closed my eyes as my mind supplied the memory. In June 2006, as Ted's fiftieth birthday approached, he took a few days

GAYLE HAGGARD

off to fast and pray in the mountains. On his way back, he drove through the historic gold-mining town of Cripple Creek and decided to attend the Donkey Derby Days festival. He called and asked me to join him, but I begged off because I had a backyard party for pastors' wives that day. I was also busy planning his birthday party.

"What happened," I asked, my voice choked, "in Cripple Creek?"

"When you didn't come—" Ted kept his voice light, without a trace of reproach—"this man called me. As an impulse, I asked him to meet me at the festival. We decided to stay the night, and he went with me to the hotel afterward."

I closed my eyes, imagining the worst. *Why didn't I drop everything and go up there with Ted? I could have kept him from—*

"It's not what you're thinking," Ted said, interrupting my thoughts, "but it was still wrong. I should have come home that night."

Ted did not have a sexual relationship with that man, but he did masturbate in the dark with the man in the room—which was, of course, completely wrong. Ted confessed the entire incident to me on the flight to Florida.

Because I'd already come to terms with the reality of Ted's sinful actions, I was interested in finding out exactly what had been happening in his life. I wanted to know everything. I wasn't shocked or angry; more than anything, I was intrigued. The emotions associated with those revelations would hit me later. I'm like that—I tend to process things mentally before I process them emotionally. Plus, I was sitting in the middle of a very public commercial jet. Though Ted and I spoke in whispers, I was grateful that the man next to me wore noise-canceling headphones, or we could never have had that conversation.

I asked Ted about the occasions when he was tempted—what he would do; how often he would resist and overcome; how he would act out. I wanted to know if he thought of me when he was acting out; if he thought about our kids or our church. What would he do after he'd acted on his temptation, and how did he deal with the guilt? How could he preach the following Sunday?

Ted's answers were simple and direct: When he sinned, he would pray and beg God for forgiveness. He fasted and prayed. And when he'd preach, though he'd done his best to prepare himself by repentance, prayer, and fasting, he ultimately trusted that God would honor his own Word. "Whether you feel anointed or not," he used to tell his staff, "the Scriptures are anointed, and they have power. So preach the Scriptures."

As Ted and I worked through these issues, he answered all my questions, and we talked about the details. The conversation reminded me of an onion—we started with the top layer and kept going deeper, peeling back old issues and discovering new layers. The truth was so deeply buried that Ted needed time to sort through memories and recall some of the things he'd hidden away.

Though it was hard for me to hear the details, I wanted to know my husband fully. I wanted to know the truth, and I wanted Ted to tell me everything. If he could talk to me, and if I could listen without responding with condemnation, then he could safely face his own truth, confess it openly, and find healing.

Ted went over his entire sexual history with me. He was so thorough that later, when we had to do the same thing in counseling, his sexual history had lost its power to surprise or alarm me.

I know that some women might not want to hear details about their husband's infidelity. You might think my response was morbid or even perverse. But don't forget—for years, the cry of my heart had been to know my husband completely, to be his confidante and best friend. Ted had kept a private place he shared with no one, so once he decided to unseal that place, I wanted to be the one who heard his secrets. As painful as that listening was, I was thrilled that he had finally decided to trust me.

Perhaps most important, my listening satisfied Ted's need to confess and my need to forgive.

I understood the freeing nature of confession. I felt that half the battle was in facing the problem head-on. Secrets empower sin. The Bible teaches, "Confess your sins to each other and pray for each other so that you may be healed" (James 5:16).

Complete and honest confession released something in Ted. Though he had already admitted several of these things to the church staff and the overseers, for the first time he now allowed me an unobstructed look into his heart. He told me the unvarnished truth, and what I heard started a process that would forever change the way I view my husband, humanity, and the struggles we all face.

Even as my mind reeled with all Ted had shared, my heart yearned for wellness between us. This crisis had hurt us, and its resolution would undoubtedly bring more turmoil into our lives.

But we would find healing. Somehow, in some way, I wanted to find healing for my family, my church, and my world.

Before I could see healing within my family, I knew I'd need to see healing in my marriage. But where would I begin?

Had I suspected that Ted had problems before our crisis broke? Truthfully, yes. The disturbing memories that compelled me to pull Ted aside and question him before we went to see the attorney centered on two events that had occurred early in our marriage. Years before, Ted had told me that he wanted to speak to someone about struggles he was having with thoughts involving same-sex attraction, though he didn't use those exact words. He let me know that he needed to talk to someone about a problem in his thinking. Knowing that sexual thoughts and struggles are common problems, I prayed for him and encouraged him to talk to a pastor. He did so on several occasions. He continued to pray and fast and to develop into a dynamic and respected pastor. I thought he'd found a way to achieve victory over his thought life.

But though he had shared those concerns early in our marriage, I never realized the magnitude of the problem. On a few other occasions, I felt that something might be wrong, but there was so much *right* about our marriage that I couldn't put my finger on the problem. Even with the demands of our growing church and our children, our physical relationship was dynamic, and I knew we loved each other deeply. Ted was a great father and pastor. Because I couldn't see into his brain, I had no idea that unsettling thoughts lurked in his mind.

Yet when Jonathan was born, Ted feared that he might have passed along a sexually transmitted disease (STD) that had affected the baby. He came to me one afternoon after Jonathan's birth and confessed that earlier in our marriage, while he was taking a graduate course in another city, he'd had "an incident" after visiting an adult bookstore—a situation involving another male but *not* involving sexual intercourse. After he came home, he had visited a counselor and resolved never to return to the school or that bookstore.

His confession, even coming eighteen months after the incident, rattled me to the core. The day Ted told me these things was cold and rainy, and for a while I wondered if the sun would ever shine again. I literally shook when he told me what had happened because it was the last thing I ever expected to hear from him. But as the days passed and Ted went about his work, I told myself the incident was over and finished. After all, the bookstore incident had happened long ago. Ted had been young, and now he was extremely ashamed of what he'd done. Some might say I was in denial at that point, but I think I was young and naïve about the gravity of the problem. So though it was painful at the time, I reacted like the Shunamite woman—I tucked the episode away, sealed off the area, and moved on. I didn't know enough about psychology to be aware that that incident signaled a much deeper struggle.

I knew Ted resisted inappropriate thoughts, but don't most men struggle with lust? They are wired differently from women. I knew Ted had fought hard at a few points in his life, but I thought he had won his battles. Except for that one occasion in the bookstore, I never knew he had actually acted out. Sometimes I'd ask, "Is that area still a struggle for you?"

He'd say, "No, I never really think about it anymore."

And I believed him.

If I'd known then what I know now, I would have become more involved and encouraged him to see a counselor. At that point, I wasn't aware of what Ted was battling—I thought he was facing normal temptations. But if your husband is fighting a similar battle, I advise you to be patient, to encourage your husband to be honest and open, and to seek professional counseling. I'd also encourage you to walk through the process of therapy with him. As Solomon wrote, "Two people are better off than one, for they can help each other succeed. If one person falls, the other can reach out and help. But someone who falls alone is in real trouble" (Ecclesiastes 4:9-10).

A couple of years before our crisis, Ted and I had gone away for an overnight in Breckenridge, Colorado. We were enjoying our private time together when the topic turned toward marriage and intimacy issues. I'd spent a lot of time counseling women about their marriages, and I'd been entrusted with several stories about struggles with infidelity.

Yet I wasn't suspicious of Ted. Though, years earlier, he'd mentioned his struggle with "same sex" thoughts, he was obviously heterosexual. Furthermore, he'd never given me any reason to think he was attracted to another woman. Over the years, a couple of women had let it be known that they were attracted to him, but Ted had never given them any encouragement beyond the friendliness he demonstrated to everyone. In fact, after he recognized what I could clearly see, he learned to avoid being alone with those women. Armed with that knowledge, I had complete confidence that he'd never broken his marriage vows.

I remember telling Ted that our fidelity was the one thing I had total confidence in. Beyond all doubt, I believed we were both totally faithful to each other.

Still, I'd talked to other women who would have sworn that their husbands were faithful too. So in Breckenridge, when the conversation turned to the subject of marital faithfulness, I asked, "In our entire marriage, have you ever been with another person?"

Ted answered, "Absolutely not."

His assurance was a solid point of security for me, but when I discovered that my belief in our marital fidelity was nothing more than a mirage, I had to surrender that conviction. I could no longer feel proud or secure or confident in my performance as a spouse. I had to question whether some of the fault lay with me. Was I not attractive enough? Was I not fun enough? Was I not sexually satisfying enough? The idea that I just wasn't *enough* plagued my mind. Ted had kept assuring me that I was all those things and that the issue arose from within *him*, but now I faced the challenge of discovering which aspects of our marriage were actually real.

O God, you know how foolish I am;

my sins cannot be hidden from you.

Don't let those who trust in you

be ashamed because of me,

O Sovereign LORD of Heaven's Armies.

Don't let me cause them to

be humiliated,

O God of Israel.

For I endure insults for your sake;

humiliation is written all over my face.

Even my own brothers pretend

they don't know me;

they treat me like a stranger.

PSALM 69:5-8

8

THE MORNING AFTER our arrival on Captiva Island, we received a phone call from one of the overseers. He told us not to communicate with anyone from the church and not to have any contact at all with New Life staff members. The very idea stunned me. How were we supposed to heal if we were amputated from the body to which we were so strongly attached? I could understand if the intent had been to encourage us to stay out of communication in order to have time to rest and to focus on just being together as a family for a while, but his words sounded more like a permanent prohibition.

"These are our friends," Ted objected.

"No," the caller clarified, "they were your employees. You need to understand that."

Ted clicked off his phone, and we sat in shocked silence. My ministry to the women of the church had been called Women Belong, and I had just been told that I no longer did. "You belong to God, and we belong to each other, and you will never be alone, even in your darkest hour." How many times had I taught that precept? Yet when I was enduring my darkest hour, I felt that I was being forcibly torn from our friends and family at New Life.

As the family settled in at the vacation house, I called the residential school where Jonathan was staying. When I spoke to the administrator, she told me that she had been following what was going on with our family and that they were taking steps to shield Jonathan from the news. She said they had been cutting out all the articles about our crisis from the newspapers delivered to the school and were also ushering Jonathan out of the room if a television reporter began to cover our story. I could only imagine students reading from newspapers with large rectangles cut out of them.

Once, she admitted, Jonathan had walked in while a picture of Ted was on the TV screen. He had gotten all excited and was telling everyone, "My dad!"

We were comforted to know that the people at his school were protecting Jonathan. He was in a safe place, and we wanted to keep him there as long as we could. We were so grateful for the friends who donated funds to help us take care of Jonathan's special needs.

While Ted and I continued to engage in truth telling with one another, struggling to get to the core of what had gone wrong in his life, we worried that the church was being ravaged by rumors and confusion. Yet we felt powerless to do anything to help. We were beginning to discover that one of the worst consequences of Ted's sin was the authority it gave others over him, our family, our church, and our life's work. We completely lost our personal influence and our ability to serve and protect those we loved.

I felt like I was being ravaged twice. As the revelations from my husband tore open my heart, I thought I'd have the strength of the church behind me, but within the span of a few days, I lost my marriage as I had known it and also my church family.

When my mental fog began to lift, I realized that the overseers were serious when they told us we had to leave New Life for good. In the immediate aftermath of Ted's confession, I had heard them speak those words, but I hadn't fully grasped their meaning because the idea of a permanent separation from New Life was completely foreign to me. Yet as I clung to the Lord and the tattered remains of my marriage, something rock solid within me determined not to let circumstances define who I was or who I would be. No matter what pressures came against me, I would choose my response and who I was going to be. I wanted to be a woman who would remain faithful to the Lord, to my husband, to my family, and to our friends at New Life Church.

But how would I do that? *Could* I do that?

On the flight to Captiva, I'd been so grateful that Ted was finally being totally honest that I didn't dwell on the details of what he told me. But later, when his words began to settle in my mind, the truth hurt, and I realized that my own internal battle was only beginning. Though I will always prefer the truth to a lie, the truth took my mind places I never wanted to go—and yet I had to go there if I wanted to really know my husband.

I don't know if I can describe every emotion I felt as I adjusted to our new reality—pain, sadness, fear, repulsion, relief, despair, and even joy because my husband had finally opened up to me. As searing as the truth was, Ted was finally treating me like his safe place, and that's what I'd always wanted to be.

The metaphor that kept coming to mind was *surgery*: This process was painful; it involved cutting and removing, and some people wouldn't have the stomach for it. But I began to see how God had chosen to deal with Ted's sin.

During our first two weeks on Captiva Island, the kids went off to explore the nearby tourist attractions while Ted and I took advantage of the quiet to bare our hearts to one another. We talked, we wept, and we shared things we had never shared before. I felt as though we were getting to know each other all over again—and in some ways, for the first time.

On our second day at the beach, Ted and I went for a drive. I started in with the questions again, still wanting to make sense of what had happened. With sadness in his voice, he patiently tried to answer me—and then I went too far. I snapped and told him he was the stupidest, most selfish person in the world. "Weren't you thinking of anyone but yourself?"

A powder keg ignited inside him. "Of course I did!" he shot back. "And it made me feel like the worst person in the world. There, are you satisfied?"

In that instant, I felt unbearably alone. When we arrived back at the house, I took off down the beach, holding back my tears as I stalked away. When I had walked past the few beachgoers who had ventured out on that breezy afternoon, I had a heart-to-heart with God. I was as honest with him as Ted had been with me. I told him that I felt battered and empty and thoroughly ravaged but I was going to cling to him. I would hold on to him because everything else in my life had proven to be shifting sand. I told God that I didn't feel his nearness at the moment but I knew he was listening and that he cared. I begged him not to leave me and Ted, not now.

I walked until the beach ended at a rocky jetty, and then I moved into the sea grass in an effort to conceal myself from curious passersby. Amid the tall grasses, I sat with my head on my knees and sobbed. My grief was too great. Picturing what God had told me in my closet, I said, "Lord, I'm going to tie myself up under your wings and cling to you . . . because I don't know what else to do."

I didn't hear an answer right away, but I knew God had heard me. As I poured out the mixed emotions in my heart, I became aware of other people walking by. Some glanced my way, while others avoided turning in my direction. I'm sure they knew I needed to be alone, because no one stopped to ask if I was all right.

When I had cried to the point of exhaustion, I sat in the grass and waited. I had nowhere else to go. After a long while, I picked myself up, brushed the sand from my shorts, and walked back to my husband.

Over the next several days, Ted and I talked nonstop in that beach house. Sometimes we went for long walks on the beach and talked like two people catching up on a lifetime spent apart. We talked about our childhoods, our teen years, our most private thoughts and dreams, as well as the secrets that had created walls between us and kept us from communicating on this level in earlier years. Our conversation would usually turn to what was happening at the church. We felt that we were beginning to heal, but we were powerless to help the people at New Life. We knew that rumors were running rampant, but we couldn't address them.

For the most part, I found our conversations deeply satisfying and unifying. But there were other times when flashes of grief would rip through me like bolts of lightning.

As bad as I felt most of the time, Ted was in even worse shape. His misery was so overwhelming, so tangible, that it was as if another person—a dark and unrelenting presence—shadowed his every step.

I vacillated between feelings of compassion for the man in

despair and fury toward the man who had destroyed my beautiful world. "How could you?" I railed at Ted, unleashing my pent-up anger. "How could you do this to our children? Didn't you think about what this would do to them?"

But even as I heaped spadefuls of guilt onto Ted, I realized that the answer lay in the very nature of sin—it warps our thinking and makes us so irrational that we place our selfish desires above our concerns for our loved ones. Sin blinds us to consequences and tricks us into believing that our secrets will never be revealed.

After releasing my frustrations, I'd stand in front of Ted, trembling in every limb, and know that I needed to do what Jesus told me to do.

I needed to forgive my husband.

I kept thinking of the woman caught in adultery and of Jesus' instruction to the men who wanted to stone her: "All right, but let the one who has never sinned throw the first stone!" (John 8:7).

Then I'd think of what Peter asked Jesus: "'Lord, how often should I forgive someone who sins against me? Seven times?'

"'No, not seven times,' Jesus replied, 'but seventy times seven!'" (Matthew 18:21-22).

In the early morning hours, I would think about these things and fall to my knees in a quiet place. "Lord, I forgive Ted for all of this; help me to forgive him completely. I choose to love him. I choose to *keep* loving him."

When I had lifted my head after praying, I truly understood the verse that says, "Love covers a multitude of sins" (1 Peter 4:8). Like a mantle of pure, soft snow, love descends on broken earth and transforms the landscape, allowing us to see beauty where, before, we could see only dirt.

After such prayers, I'd manage to get a grip on my emotions, and I'd find myself feeling committed to Ted and forgiving his offenses. But emotions are fickle. An emotion that has been gently put to bed can awaken screaming in rage.

Then I'd find myself back in Ted's face. "You've always taught that things like this would happen when you sin. How could you have done this to yourself? to us?"

Ted would hang his head. "I understand. I hear you. I feel like the stupidest man alive to have done what I did."

I would hear him out, and then I'd go out on the beach and walk along the shore. The roar of the waves soothed my thoughts as I imagined the sea washing away all our troubles.

I kept a journal during our crisis. Because I was unable to talk to my friends, I poured out my feelings on its pages, often addressing my thoughts to God.

MONDAY, NOVEMBER 13, 2006

> I am married to a flawed man—a man as flawed as any other. Why should anyone be surprised? In our Christian world, we teach and believe the truths of the Scriptures and hope they will transform us, hope that goodness will grow in us and get rid of all the badness. But for some, for many, the realization of that hope in this lifetime seems forever distant. Occasionally it is brought near them, but then escapes them as they fall short of goodness yet one more time. Why, Lord?
>
> Ted has sought you with all his heart. Through pain, he has tried to press through—through fasting and prayer and resistance to his sin—yet, many times he has failed. That which he hopes for has eluded him.

Although disheartened, he has not given up. He tries again and again and again. Makes improvements and hopes it will work; that it will last this time.

O God, hear our prayer. We know you are faithful, that you are good and loving and kind. That you do not forsake us. My Father, hear my prayer. Pull the blinders off my eyes. Help me to stop being so naïve and to see clearly. Make my heart and my arms strong for the task to help my husband. He is yours! I know you love him. Show him your love through me. Empower me to help him win this battle against his flesh, his mind, and his calling in you.

"There is no greater love than to lay down one's life for one's friends." The isolation is cruel punishment for Ted and me. Being separated from the comfort, encouragement, and counsel of our friends has made the past twenty-two years seem devoid of substance. We have lived our lives for our friends. Where are they when we need them? A wounded limb of the body cannot heal if it is separated from the body. Does anyone have the courage to do the right thing? Or is everyone living in fear?

A few have had courage. They would be here in an instant if I asked them to come. Yet I want to be obedient to the overseers, so I will not compromise them. But where are those who could change all this? Where is _____? If he were in our shoes, Ted would not have hesitated to take a plane to find him—to honor the friendship and all he is and all he stands for.

We pray for the leadership of New Life Church every day. We love the church. Outside of the church, many are offering to lay down their lives for Ted; also many church members. Yet where are our closest friends?

There is so much secretiveness, secret meetings, etc.

Yet no one talks to Ted. No one talks to me.

As I worked through my tangled emotions, I couldn't help but think back to the many occasions when I'd counseled women at New Life Church. I've never considered myself a professional counselor, but as a pastor's wife and ministry leader, I've found that most people simply want and need to be heard. We all need the validation we feel when we know someone has heard our pain and listened to our story. And I'm convinced everyone has a story.

I've talked to many women and listened to their stories with tears in my eyes. When they finished telling me what they were going through in their marriages, or with their parents or children, or at work, I usually responded, "Thank you for telling me what they've done and how you feel, but now you have a choice. Who are you, and what kind of person are you going to be in this story? You can't do anything about the other person, but you can decide who *you* are going to be and how *you* are going to react. All of us have that choice."

Sometimes the response was a simple, wide-eyed stare. A lot of people are so busy staring at their problems that they never get around to considering a proper response to them.

"If you choose to face and climb this mountain," I'd tell them, "you may discover the marital intimacy you've been longing for on the other side. In the meantime, connect with other godly, supportive women. Women can affirm each other better than anyone else because we know what it feels like to be women, and we know what we need in the way of affirmation. Sometimes the men in our lives don't understand."

In our women's ministry, I encouraged women to go out of their way to support one another. I've always believed that women bring strength and joy to each other in their journeys, which can help to stave off loneliness for even the most neglected women. When we encourage one another in our tasks, we make those tasks a lot more fun. We help one another become better, more fulfilled women, which in turn can improve our marriages, our relationships, and our lives in general.

The night before our crisis erupted, I had spoken to a woman who was dealing with a physically abusive husband. I told her she needed to get to a safe place with her children. "You'll be no help to your marriage, your family, or even your husband if you're dead. Before you do anything else, you need to protect yourself and your children."

Then I brought the conversation around to my favorite question: "But who will *you* be in this story? Don't just react and let that reaction define you. Decide who and what you're going to be. Are you going to be forgiving and loving? Do you need to end this relationship in order to protect your children? You need to make those choices. If you have hope for your marriage and you choose to love and forgive, get to a safe place and seek professional counseling. You need to talk to someone who is equipped to walk you through this."

Now my own words came back to haunt me as I struggled to balance what my brain knew with what my ravaged heart felt. I kept asking myself the crucial question: Who am I going to be in our story? Will I be the woman who washes her hands of the situation and walks away from Ted, or will I be the woman who loves him and shows forgiveness? Will I cling to my status as a betrayed wife, or will I lay that betrayal at Jesus' feet and rejoice that God is blessing us through a severe mercy?

The choice was mine. A mountain stood in front of me, a difficult climb, and I didn't know what lay on the other side. But I knew I'd rather climb it with Ted than not face the challenge and walk away alone.

Did I consider divorcing Ted after the crisis broke? If he had been unrepentant, if he had persisted in his sin, or if he had been violent or abusive toward me or the children, I would have considered divorce for safety's sake. Adultery is a biblically permissible reason for divorce, but divorce isn't *mandatory*. Clearly, when reconciliation is possible, a healed marriage and family is the better choice. Besides, God wants families to serve as examples of his forgiveness and love, and most will face difficult circumstances in which they have to choose forgiveness in order to survive as families.

Many people expected me to abandon Ted; in fact, several people told me that I needed to be an example and leave him so other women wouldn't put up with that type of behavior from their husbands. They assumed that if I chose to do otherwise, I was weak and codependent. But why couldn't I be an example of Christ's love and forgiveness? Why couldn't I stay because I chose to be strong and do what I could to hold my family together? Why couldn't I choose to be Ted's closest friend in his weakness? I was willing to risk failure for the greater prize of getting to the other side of this crisis with my marriage and family intact.

"Think of your children," people said.

But I *was* thinking of my children. From my mom and dad I had learned that the greatest gift I could give my kids was to love their father. When we were growing up, my siblings and I lived in the security of knowing that our parents loved each other. To this day, that's what my kids care about most. "As long as you and Dad are okay," they'll tell me, "we're all fine."

I hope our story convinces people to believe in one true principle: The best thing you can do for your children is to love and cherish your spouse. My parents had modeled this concept for me, and now I hoped to model it for my children. Kids need to know that their parents love each other.

I knew that saving our marriage would be the best thing for all the Haggards, not just for Ted and me. Many betrayed women view their children as their first priority, but unless the marriage puts the children at risk of injury, that kind of thinking is backward. If you focus on your spouse, your children will reap the benefits of a restored marriage and a two-parent family.

Everything in me rejected the idea of divorce. If I left Ted, my life would be illustrating that some people mess up too badly to be redeemed and that some people are lost causes. And I don't believe that. I don't believe in throwing people away because they've sinned, because all people are valuable and loved by God.

I chose to stay and love Ted because commitment means something to me. Even during the heat of the struggle I thought, *This is my test. I am being tested on what I really believe.*

With God's help, I determined to pass the test. I kept going to the Lord and asking, "How do I do this?" I had no firsthand experience with marital unfaithfulness. I was enduring a situation I had hoped I'd never have to face.

While we were in Florida, I sought comfort in prayer, in journaling my feelings, and in the way Ted and I talked and clung to each other. But I also hoped to feel the support of our friends, and I waited expectantly for them to get in touch. I kept telling Ted,

"The brothers will come." I kept expecting to get a phone call or to see a rental car pull up. Ted had such close friends, and over the years he had done so much for so many others. To this day, he will do whatever he can to help someone out.

Even though before the crisis Ted and I had experienced an occasional emotional disconnect, he was one of the most compassionate men I knew. He would do anything for his friends—and often did. We belonged to a church filled with people who had endured horrific situations, and like a shepherd, Ted had taken care of many of them. He always saw people as works in progress, so I kept assuring him that the brothers would think of him in the same way. "You've rescued every one of your closest friends from some trouble," I reminded him. "They'll come now that you're in need."

But they didn't. No cars turned into the driveway. Ted's cell phone remained silent. The loneliness and isolation drove him into an even deeper despair. He felt that the nature of his sin had turned the stomachs of even his closest friends. I would like to have argued that point, but how could I? I had no evidence to prove otherwise.

In private, I walked along the beach and wondered why they stayed away. Was it because they thought his sin was too repulsive?

Ted was convinced he'd been ostracized because he'd committed a socially unacceptable sin. Because he had not told his closest friends about his struggle, he was sure they felt betrayed that he had kept a secret from them. I understood that anger—I felt it, too, at first. But I still thought compassion would soon bring those friends to Ted's side to ask, "Brother, what happened?"

In the week following Ted's public exposure, we received several letters and e-mails. Ted couldn't read them—he couldn't handle either the encouragement or the criticism. I read many of them and threw some of them away. For instance, one man wrote, "I have determined that you are a reprobate and without hope of salvation." How can one man make that judgment about another? He can't.

We also received many kind and supportive e-mails, but most of them came from faraway places.

Later I learned that in order to give us time to heal, the overseers had strongly instructed the church not to contact us. They didn't realize, though, that the deafening silence of our friends confused us and made our path toward healing much more difficult.

Ted's despair broke my heart and made me all the more determined to be not only a faithful wife but also a faithful friend. As I observed people heaping judgment and anger on my husband, I decided I didn't want to be like them. I wanted to represent the compassionate heart of God in how I responded to Ted. The fourteen thousand members of New Life had been discouraged from reaching out to their former pastor, but nothing would stop me from extending the tender care and prayerful support he should have been offered. Nothing stopped me from throwing my arms around him and weeping with him.

Every morning, we read the Bible together. At Ted's suggestion, we began to read Solomon's Proverbs, the favorite book of my youth. I knew Ted was familiar with all the warnings about sexual sin and being led astray by folly, but I didn't mind him getting a refresher course in the consequences of sexual immorality. We read a chapter a day together, and Ted would wince as he read verses such as Proverbs 5:15-17: "Drink water from your own well— share your love only with your wife. Why spill the water of your springs in the streets, having sex with just anyone? You should reserve it for yourselves. Never share it with strangers."

After reading that evil men are held captive by their own sins (5:22) and that a man "will die for lack of self-control" (5:23), Ted would say, "I am a fool." The painful realization deeply depressed him. One day he wryly remarked that he'd once heard that "the last thing you want to do is read Proverbs when you're a broken man."

I was glad the experience hit home.

After two weeks, our children flew back to Colorado, leaving Ted and me alone for another week. Once the kids had gone, Ted's spirits sank so low that I worried he might become suicidal. He grew quiet and visibly depressed. When he did talk, he said that he had ruined not only his own life but also the lives of everyone around him. He honestly believed the world would be better off without him. If he lived, all he could see ahead was a life of poverty and shame.

Nothing I said could lift his spirits for very long. I tried to be optimistic when I could; I kept in close touch with the kids and made sure Ted talked to them every day. And every night when we crawled into bed, I held him close until sleep claimed us.

One gray and cloudy morning, Ted went out to the beach and didn't come back for a long time. I kept glancing at the clock and walking to the window to look toward the beach, but I saw no sign of him. I worried that he had decided to start swimming until he drowned from exhaustion. Just as I was about to go looking for him, he came through the door, a look of resignation on his weathered face.

For a moment, I was so relieved to see him that I couldn't speak. Ted caught my gaze, and in his eyes I saw proof that I'd been right to be concerned.

"I was out there planning how to do it to make it easy for everybody," he said, speaking slowly. "But I'm not going to end it; I'm going to face it, though I don't have any hope for my future."

"You will get through this," I said, moving closer.

"But you should divorce me." His voice flattened as he sank into a chair. "I'm so toxic, Gayle, I'll ruin you. I'll cost you more than I've already cost you. But you and the kids could leave me. The church would take you in and help you."

I looked straight into his eyes. "I will not divorce you," I said, my voice breaking. "I am committed to you. I love you. We will get through this together. And I believe God has a purpose for you and me, even in this."

"I don't see it." He shook his head and hunched forward. "I can't pray. I can't feel God. My life might as well be over."

"Wait," I told him. "Just don't give up. Please, don't quit on me."

I didn't know how to change his perspective, but I did know that some situations can't be "fixed" in an hour, a week, or a month. Sometimes we have to be patient and let God work.

While we stayed in Florida, Ted got up every morning and went out running. Even though we were far from home, sometimes people recognized him because the story of our crisis had been reported everywhere. The media had portrayed Ted as an incredibly powerful personage in order to emphasize how far he had fallen. Newspapers and articles were filled with reports about Ted talking to President Bush once a week (not true); his regular meetings with government leaders (highly exaggerated); and how he had once considered running for Congress (barely). Though I doubt most Christians had even heard of the National Association of Evangelicals before November 2006, the press enhanced the importance of Ted's position as president of the NAE until it appeared he was some kind of Protestant pope. Nothing could have been further from the truth, but we could do nothing to counter those exaggerations because we had been ordered not to speak to the press.

One morning, as Ted was running, a woman pulled up beside him in her car. Ted tried to ignore her, but she idled along beside him and lowered her passenger window. "Excuse me," she called, "can I ask if you're Ted Haggard?"

Keeping his gaze fixed firmly on the road in front of him, Ted gave her a decidedly unfriendly answer: "No."

The woman didn't take the hint, but kept driving alongside him. "Well, *are* you Ted Haggard?"

Still keeping his gaze on the road, Ted finally answered. "Yes."

"Then," she said, ducking her head and smiling, "I'm here on vacation from Maine, and I want you to know our whole church back home is praying for you. Keep going."

With that, she drove away.

We might have been exiled from New Life Church, but God supported us through encounters with other believers. People slipped us notes of encouragement when we were in public places. Over and over again we were met by strangers who walked up to us and said, "We love you guys. Hang in there." Their encouragement kept us moving forward through some of the darkest days of our lives.

Have mercy on me, LORD,

for I am in distress.

Tears blur my eyes.

My body and soul are withering away.

I am dying from grief;

my years are shortened by sadness.

Sin has drained my strength;

I am wasting away from within.

I am scorned by all my enemies

and despised by my neighbors—

even my friends are afraid

to come near me.

When they see me on the street,

they run the other way.

I am ignored as if I were dead,

as if I were a broken pot.

I have heard the many

rumors about me,

and I am surrounded by terror.

My enemies conspire against me,

plotting to take my life.

But I am trusting you, O LORD,

saying, "You are my God!"

My future is in your hands.

PSALM 31:9-15

9

As Ted and I sorted through our feelings in Florida, we worried about our children in Colorado Springs. Marcus and his wife, Sarah, left their home and moved into our house to help the family. So while Ted and I spent another week working on our marriage, four of our children and our daughter-in-law gathered together at home. Jonathan remained at his school in Kentucky, where he was being sheltered from the disturbing news.

Later, we learned that our kids had several discussions in family meetings. Marcus and Christy took the lead in helping Alex and Elliott, our teenage sons, pull together and decide how they were going to stand as a family. I thought they did an admirable job. The world they had known had come crashing down, but they didn't let the disaster crush their spirits. They were all determined to stay committed to Ted and me and to our family.

I remember calling home and speaking to Elliott, our youngest. When I asked how he was doing, he said, "Not too good. I used to be the son of this really great preacher, and my dad was a great man. Now I'm just a nothin'."

I gripped the phone tighter and wished I were looking into my son's eyes. "This may be the best starting place for anybody," I told him. "What you had before may not turn out to be what will make you the kind of person you need to be. What you have now may be a better starting place for the rest of your life."

I honestly believed that. Though we'd tried not to spoil our kids, they had enjoyed a certain status as Ted Haggard's children. Now that Ted had been publicly shamed and exiled, they had to adjust to their father's infamy, but I knew they would grow stronger through the experience. After all, Scripture tells us, "When troubles come your way, consider it an opportunity for great joy. For you know that when your faith is tested, your endurance has a chance to grow. So let it grow, for when your endurance is fully developed, you will be perfect and complete, needing nothing" (James 1:2-4).

I was counting on that promise for all of us.

If you have experienced betrayal in a relationship, you are probably familiar with the wide range of emotions that crop up as a result. These emotions are not always predictable, and they can't be timed. Teri Garr, who played actress Sandy Lester in *Tootsie*, had it right when she beautifully delivered this profound line: "I'm going to feel this way until I don't feel this way anymore."

Throughout the first three weeks following the public accusations, I lived in the center of swirling emotion. Pick an emotion, any one you like, and at some point in the aftermath of our initial crisis I probably met it in the ring, stared it in the eye, and wrestled it to the mat. I took a few blows and had the breath knocked out of me a couple of times, but I survived.

Was I in denial? I was so determined to root out the truth that I don't think I entertained denial, yet I wanted the truth on my own terms. I wanted the truth to fit my understanding, and when it didn't, denial sometimes slipped in. Ted had to go through the process of determining why he had done what he did and discovering where those attachments and behaviors had originated. I wanted him to settle those questions based on our beliefs, but eventually I had to surrender my expectations and let him go through his own process.

When he would ask, "Am I gay? Am I straight or bi?" rather than give him a "spiritual" reply, I learned to say, "Only you can determine the answer to those questions."

Though I'm not a moody person, I did endure some low periods; but they didn't last long. I'm basically an optimist, so I never dwelled in despair if I could help it. A counselor would later comment, "You're a pull-yourself-up-by-the-bootstraps girl, aren't you?" She was right.

On several occasions, I morphed into a shrew who could do nothing but rage.

I remember driving down the road on Captiva Island and letting Ted have it yet again: "How could you do this to our children? What were you thinking? Didn't you know how much this would hurt them? how much you'd hurt all the people at the church?"

Most of the time Ted was patient and compassionate with me; he understood that I was going through a painful process, and he was sad that he'd caused it. But on a few occasions he grew weary of my questions, and his face flushed with irritation. "You don't think I've thought about that many, many times? Of course

I thought about it. That's why I tried to deal with it so no one would ever know. That's why I wanted it to stay a secret—I didn't want to hurt anyone else."

But Ted didn't fully understand how I felt . . . and how deeply rooted my feelings of rejection were. He didn't realize that I had an acute need to be his favorite person. I wanted him to choose me above everyone else. That's all I'd ever needed from him. That's why it hurt to imagine him being physically intimate with someone else. That's why I felt betrayed and so personally rejected.

I think my need for his affirmation was rooted in an experience I had in elementary school. In fifth grade, I was in a group of girls who sang to a combined group of fifth and sixth graders. Each girl had made a pretty paper flower, which we planned to toss to the boys in the audience as we sang our song. While we were planning our presentation, several of the boys called out, "I get Patti's" or "I get Lisa's," and soon every girl had been chosen to throw her paper flower to a particular boy. Every girl, that is, except one. No one said, "I want Gayle's."

Nobody chose me. I had formed the group, rallied the singers, and rehearsed the music, but no one wanted my paper flower. So I ran to the coat closet, buried my head in someone's wool jacket, and cried my eyes out.

When the other girls discovered me crying, they found a boy who would be willing to help me save face. But his offer came too late to relieve the pain of rejection. I'd been devastated to discover I was no one's favorite. Until that moment, I'd never imagined that I wouldn't be *someone's* favorite.

The story sounds trivial to my adult ears, but the experience didn't feel trivial at the time. Maybe I felt left out because my family moved so often; maybe no one had an interest in catching my paper flower because I was still a newcomer at the school. I don't remember the reason, but that experience taught me something profound: Rejection hurts at any age.

That experience stuck with me and played itself out in my life on several occasions. In my relationship with Ted, my driving need was to know I was his favorite. I admired the fact that he loved people; that's one of the things that made him an effective pastor. But I needed to know that I was the one he loved best. After our crisis, I again felt the acute pain of rejection—on an intensely personal level and on an incredibly public stage.

Ted repeatedly assured me, "I loved you so much and hated myself so much, I was afraid I would lose you," but his words did little to relieve the hurt I felt. His actions seemed to prove that he hadn't wanted to protect our marriage as much as I did. The fact that he had done something to threaten our marriage—and had potentially subjected me to diseases while I remained completely unaware of the risk—made me furious. My blood boiled when I thought of everything our children would face for the rest of their lives—the blogs they could read, the nasty jokes they would hear, the looks they might get when they gave their surname to a stranger. They didn't deserve that kind of scorn and derision. The people of New Life Church didn't deserve it. And neither did I.

Sometimes anger reared its ugly head when I least expected it. In those moments, I wanted to yell or hit something. I'm not the sort to break dishes or throw things, but I did punch a few pillows.

Once, I did something I never dreamed I'd do. At a particularly dark and lonely moment, I used the most vulgar language I could dredge up to attack Ted. I accused him of the vilest acts, and when he answered, I discovered that my dark imaginings were far worse than anything he had actually done. But after visiting that dark place a couple of times, I knew I didn't want to stay there. I didn't want to be an angry, accusing person, and vulgar language just isn't my style.

Imagination can be a woman's worst enemy. I couldn't help but think about what Ted had done, and those thoughts led to visualizing him in sinful situations. At some point, I had to learn how to stop obsessing about his sin and start reminding myself of everything that was good and right about him. The mental effort wasn't easy; it was hard work. But it was worth it because it helped me heal.

As I listened to attacks from others in the months that followed, I heard vile comments slip out of their mouths, accusations that were far worse than Ted's actual sins. All sorts of ugliness poured out of people's minds and hearts, but how could I blame them for imagining the worst? I had done the same thing. In my anger, I'd wanted to hurt Ted as much as he'd hurt me, and never in my life had I thought I would stoop to that level. But I did.

The thing I resented most was feeling like an object of pity. I don't like pity; it embarrasses me. Maybe it's my pride, or maybe it's old-fashioned self-reliance that prevents me from lapping up pity, but it's important for me to respect myself and to be the kind of person others can respect, just as I respect them. I don't think it's arrogant to work hard at living my life so others can respect me. I believe respecting oneself and others opens the door to trust.

In my role as a church leader, I cared far more about the function than the title. I didn't find my fulfillment in simply being on the platform; I loved leading by example. I had worked hard to live an honorable life, but when that life came to a standstill, I suddenly found myself in a pitiable position. I had to deal with hearing people say, "Oh, that poor woman," and I hated that.

When my emotions had calmed and the storms subsided, I would recall my own advice to the many women I'd counseled:

"Who are you going to be in this story? How are you going to be honorable?"

"And maybe," I could hear myself blithely saying, "on the other side of this mountain, you will find the intimacy you've been yearning for."

Now it was time for me to be tested on what I had been teaching others.

Later, Matthew invited Jesus and his disciples to his home as dinner guests, along with many tax collectors and other disreputable sinners. But when the Pharisees saw this, they asked his disciples, "Why does your teacher eat with such scum?"

When Jesus heard this, he said, "Healthy people don't need a doctor—sick people do." Then he added, "Now go and learn the meaning of this Scripture: 'I want you to show mercy, not offer sacrifices.' For I have come to call not those who think they are righteous, but those who know they are sinners."

MATTHEW 9:10-13

10

TED AND I left Florida a few days before Thanksgiving. When we returned to our home in Colorado Springs, we greeted our children and settled back into our isolated existence.

We were sitting in our family room one afternoon when the phone rang. When I realized that Ted was talking to the chief overseer, I motioned that I wanted to talk to him. He handed me the phone, and I spent half an hour pouring out my heart. If the overseers were still concerned about our desire to continue to be a part of New Life, I wanted to assure them that we were making progress and that Ted would not be a threat to the leadership. "This isn't about Ted vying for power; he's willing to mow lawns," I reminded the overseer. "This is about us wanting to heal with the church, and I think it's the only way to let the church really heal. Everything we believe is at stake here. Let us recover with the people who love us and know us best."

The man listened for thirty minutes, and then he asked,

"Well, Miss Gayle, have you bought your Thanksgiving turkey yet?"

I blinked. I'd just shared everything in my heart about my family, my marriage, and my longing for the church, and he wanted to know about our *turkey*?

Then Ted picked up the phone, and he and the overseer discussed the three prominent Christian men who had been chosen to oversee Ted's restoration process—a process of uncertain dimension and objective given that the overseers kept insisting that Ted must never again set foot on the grounds of New Life Church, at least not until some point in the future, probably years away, when they would determine him fit to do so.

I wasn't surprised to learn that one of the chosen restorers had declined to serve on the restoration committee. As I suspected, his schedule simply wouldn't allow him to participate fully. Instead, he had asked an associate to replace him, and that man was chosen to be our liaison with the other restorers, even though we didn't know him well. The overseer informed Ted that the committee planned to send us to a counseling center in Phoenix, a secular program staffed by Christians.

Ted accepted the plan with enthusiasm. He saw it as an opportunity to understand his problem. He had confessed his sin and faced it; now he was ready to be healed and restored to the life of the church.

I was equally eager. I saw counseling as a path to healing for Ted and to strengthening our marriage. As the chief overseer talked about professional counseling and oversight, we envisioned some sort of psychological program in which we'd be directly involved with the three men who'd been chosen to help us. Because Ted and I had been *giving* for so many years, I have to admit that I looked forward to *receiving* ministry in an environment where we could really gain understanding and better ourselves.

But that wasn't exactly what the overseers had in mind. "Personally," the overseer who called told us, "I don't believe in a lot of psychological mumbo jumbo; I think you just need a good deliverance session."

I raised an eyebrow—clearly, he didn't understand. Ted hadn't strayed from the Lord. For years he had sought deliverance and struggled through long periods of fasting and prayer to overcome his inappropriate thoughts. God had not miraculously answered Ted's prayers for deliverance from temptation, but perhaps he would now lead Ted to a path for healing.

"Like I said, I don't place a lot of stock in psychological mumbo jumbo," the overseer continued, "but to satisfy people, we're going to send you through a psychological counseling program."

Regardless of the overseer's skepticism, I felt nothing but relief at this news. If Ted hadn't been able to achieve victory with prayer and fasting, the problem might have psychological roots. We needed to discover what they were, and perhaps a licensed counselor could help us sort this out and shed some new light on the subject.

After all, if this overseer suffered from clogged arteries, he'd go see a cardiologist. If one of his children couldn't speak clearly, he'd take the child to a speech and hearing therapist. Why, then, did he seem to think that Ted's problem had to be solved by prayer alone?

Ted had believed that, too, and had once loosely held some of the same negative views about psychological counseling. He believed his problem was spiritual in nature. Yet, after trying for years to deal with his problem through spiritual methods (including confessing his sins privately to God, prayer, and fasting) with no lasting success, he knew he needed a new approach. Perhaps the answer to his prayers would come through the knowledge and skill of a professional counselor.

Jonathan also came home that week for Thanksgiving. He flew home on Tuesday, and I was feeling a little apprehensive when I went to pick him up at the Colorado Springs airport. I hadn't been out alone in public since the news of our crisis broke. I had a special pass to meet Jonathan at his gate, and as I walked through the wide hallway, a woman stopped me.

"Oh my gosh!" she screeched, drawing attention to both of us. "I've been praying I would run into you. My husband and I went through a similar situation a few years back."

With that, she broke into sobs. I tried to comfort her, but Jonathan's plane had arrived, and I needed to hurry to his gate.

The sobbing woman held on to me as the public address system blared throughout the concourse: "Will Gayle Haggard please come to the Delta desk?"

I lifted my head and saw people looking around—then all eyes seemed to focus on me. Again the loudspeaker blared: "Gayle Haggard, Gayle Haggard, please come to the Delta desk."

I promised to pray for the weeping woman and tore myself away. As I hurried toward the Delta desk, I saw people whispering and looking at me with sympathy in their eyes.

Jonathan was waiting when I made it to the Delta desk.

"Mom!"

I fought back tears as I hugged him. We held each other as we walked to baggage claim, and I avoided making eye contact with anyone. All I could think about was how we were going to tell Jonathan that New Life was no longer our church. He had grown up in those buildings; the church was like his second home.

As we drove back to the house, one of the first things he asked was, "When are we going to New Life?"

I knew we'd have to tell him sooner rather than later about what had happened. So many things had changed that he was bound to notice.

When we arrived at the house, Ted and I sat Jonathan down and told him that his dad was no longer the pastor of New Life. Jonathan became fretful; he couldn't understand why we didn't belong at New Life anymore. Again and again he asked why.

Ted responded, "We can't go there anymore because I messed up."

"Very bad?"

"Yes, Jonathan, very bad."

Each time Ted said that, I was reminded that our exile didn't make sense in light of New Testament teachings. We didn't go into details with Jonathan; we just kept telling him that Ted was no longer the pastor, but we must have had that conversation a dozen times.

We spent Thanksgiving 2006 with our children. I got up early that morning and went to the grocery store to buy a turkey and everything else we would need for the holiday meal. I was grateful I didn't run into anyone I knew. The year before, several New Life families had gathered around our table, so the house felt quiet by comparison. But we enjoyed our family time because we knew that Ted and I would soon be leaving for the counseling center.

For the next few days, Jonathan begged to go to church. On Sunday, we decided it wasn't fair to keep our innocent son away from New Life, so we called a friend who offered to stop by the house and take Jonathan to church. He was able to see all his friends and enjoy the place where he felt completely comfortable. Church was Jonathan's favorite place to be, and I could see no purpose in punishing him for a situation he couldn't even understand.

The friend who took him to church told us afterward that Jonathan was inundated with people hugging him, and they sent messages of love to us through our friend.

In a few days, Jonathan would head back to school in Kentucky, and we would be on our way to Phoenix.

In our remaining days at home, we learned that New Life Church had changed dramatically in the short time we'd been away. Friends who dared to call us said that within a week after the story broke, every picture of Ted and me had disappeared from the church walls, and every book and CD we had produced had vanished from the church bookstore. Though we had been spiritual "parents" to New Life Church, a purge erased all evidence of our involvement in the church's history.

We heard that some people were asking, "Where are Ted and Gayle?" In response, they were told that we had chosen to go away and heal in solitude. It's our understanding that they were instructed not to worry about us or try to contact us because we were under the attentive care of the overseers and restorers.

A few people ignored the prohibitions and stopped by the house to check on us. One gray, wintry day, an elder and his wife knocked on our door. Ted answered and said, "I'm sorry, but we can't talk to you."

"Why not?"

"Because you're an elder, and I'm prohibited from talking to the church leaders."

"Then I resign," the elder said, folding his arms. "But we've got to know how you and Gayle are doing."

We usually left the driveway gate open, but now we closed

it because we didn't want reporters slipping in and we weren't supposed to be talking to people from the church. But another friend parked his car on the road behind our house, tramped through the woods, and climbed a hill to get to our back door. He was a long-standing friend and an active volunteer in New Life's special-needs department, and he was determined to check on us.

Another day, we turned into our driveway after a snowstorm. We'd left the gate open as we drove away, and we came home to find a New Life member plowing out our driveway with the blade on the front of his pickup truck. He said nothing, but he waved good-bye as he drove away.

These unexpected acts of kindness never failed to lift our spirits. In our minds, those who reached out to us were courageous.

Even though we weren't supposed to speak to church staff or church members, we were not reluctant to speak to the overseers. In spite of the protocol outlined in the church bylaws, the overseers, whose original responsibility had been only to oversee the senior pastor, had joined with the trustees in modifying the church bylaws, giving themselves the authority to govern until a new pastor could be permanently appointed. Furthermore, spurred by rumors that Ted had seduced others in the church, they were questioning staff members in private interviews, asking if Ted had ever said or done anything inappropriate. Innocent actions and conversations were being viewed with suspicion. Everything was being scrutinized; everyone was being questioned.

What we heard from friends led us to worry that the atmosphere at New Life had changed from one of life and freedom to one of suspicion, fear, and control. On the New Life Web site, the overseers posted the following notice and provided a link to send e-mails to those leading the investigation:

To assist in both the process of Rev. Haggard's restoration and the protection of the Church itself, the Overseers are open to receiving current information relevant to either Rev. Haggard's recovery process or any concerns about New Life Church staff or its leaders. While they cannot promise confidentiality, the Overseers will handle any such information discreetly.[1]

New Life's actions did not go unnoticed, which elicited comments on hundreds of blogs, where it was described in such terms as "witch hunt" and "Soviet-style turn-in-your-neighbors pogrom." Our hearts broke when we heard about the interviews that were taking place—which some of our friends characterized as *interrogations*.

Ted called the chief overseer and told him that we wanted to be cooperative but we had to ask them to stop the witch hunt— and we wanted to be able to talk to church members we knew personally. We had invested our lives in the church, and our closest friends were church members—people to whom we had now been forbidden to speak. "At least let Gayle talk to her friends," Ted said. "This punitive thing is destroying people."

The overseer suggested that I find friends outside of New Life Church. He said I should contact women who had nationally known ministries, women who would be my "peers." He couldn't seem to understand that I didn't need a peer; I needed a *friend*—someone who had known me in better days and with whom I shared a history. The things I wanted to pour out of my heart were too personal to entrust to people I barely knew or to someone who would only see me in the context of the current crisis.

Meanwhile, the church investigation continued. Those in

charge compiled a list of accusations against Ted, but no one was safe from intense scrutiny.

During the overseers' investigation, the story came out about one young man who had run the church's 24/7 program, a spiritual boot camp for college-age men and women. The program was now being painted in salacious colors by some who focused on the physical-fitness aspect, but physical fitness was only one segment of an outstanding program to encourage spiritual, mental, and physical health for students of both genders.

Several years earlier, the young man had committed an indiscretion. He had called Ted immediately, and Ted had taken the time to talk to both people involved. After sounding out the situation, everyone had agreed that the indiscretion was a simple mistake, with no inappropriate intentions. Ted discussed the situation with both individuals, and they felt as though they'd both been honest and had forgiven each other. Everyone involved put the event behind them. But now the overseers had revived the years-old incident, and instead of allowing the original resolution to stand, they brought the staff member forward, embarrassed him, and then fired him. The 24/7 boot camp program soon faded into oblivion, another casualty of the fallout from Ted's sin.

Another young man from an underprivileged family had gone to Ted for counsel about homosexual tendencies. Believing that a fresh start might offer some benefit, Ted helped the young man get into a program similar to 24/7 at a sister church in another state. Because the young man had no money, Ted had used church funds to help him buy a sleeping bag, hiking boots, and other equipment he'd need. When the overseers learned that Ted had helped this young man, they sent word to the leaders of the program in the other state and recommended that the young man be pulled out of the program. He was subsequently dismissed and sent home.

Another young man, who had helped to build our dynamic children's ministry, also lost his job about that time. He was a great guy from a wonderful family, and he was engaged to a lovely Christian girl. However, a couple of weeks before the wedding, they had let their passion get the better of them. When the young man confessed this slipup during premarital counseling with one of the pastors, he was fired from his position.

In a church our size, a whole variety of mistakes and mishaps were to be expected. Our goal was to walk people through their difficulties and bring them to a place of health. These examples were not everyday occurrences, but they happened often enough that we had to be skilled in dealing with them. Even so, when they were compiled into a list, suspicions were raised far beyond what was reasonable.

That man's older brother came to our house, brokenhearted. "Ted," he said, "I know what you did for me, what you've done for all these guys, and nobody's defending you. I don't want to be part of this mess."

"Have your brother come see me," Ted said.

The young man came to the house, bringing his fiancée with him. Ted helped them process their failure, their disappointment, and their disillusionment. They got married, but that young man is no longer serving in an official ministry capacity.

One of Ted's most well-known sermons was titled "How Much Is Your Sin Going to Cost Me?" Ted was willing to accept that his sin had cost everyone around him plenty, but we were astounded that others were now extending the impact of his sin far beyond logical boundaries.

In reference to New Life, one of the overseers told me, "We have to get the fear of God back into that place." The leaders were reportedly on a quest to "get the sin out of the church," a task that may seem noble at first glance, but what does it mean in practice? If you completely rid the church of sin, you'd have to get rid of every sinner. If you got rid of every sinner, what would you have left? An empty building.

As wise Solomon once said, "Without oxen a stable stays clean" (Proverbs 14:4).

The overseers compiled a long list of Ted's alleged offenses, but he was innocent of most of them. Knowing that his word was no longer believed, he volunteered to take a lie detector test. In December 2006, he took three polygraphs, two in Colorado Springs and one at the counseling center in Phoenix. In each test, the examiners pointedly and explicitly asked about the sins he had confessed and the list of other accusations made against him.

In contrast to the results of the Denver masseur's polygraph, which had indicated deception, Ted's polygraphs revealed that he was being truthful in all his confessions and that he wasn't guilty of most of the accusations that had come from the investigation at New Life. His answers to those questions confirmed everything he had told me on our flight to Florida. He took a fourth polygraph in the spring of 2007 to verify his ongoing freedom from the sins that had brought him down. Each time, the results verified that Ted was telling the truth when he said he had not had a three-year affair with the masseur in Denver, nor had he had any sexual contact with any staff member or other members of New Life Church.

All the lie detector tests—administered by highly qualified technicians in Colorado Springs and Phoenix—also verified that Ted has had no inappropriate sexual or drug-related behavior since

October 2006. A single polygraph is reportedly 94 percent accurate. Ted passed *four* tests with no problems.

The examiners reported the results of Ted's tests to the overseers and a member of the executive staff of New Life Church, but those men chose not to respond to Ted or divulge the information to anyone else. I wondered why they didn't seem to value the truth revealed by the polygraphs.

Each time Ted passed a polygraph, I waited—and hoped—for some sort of acknowledgment from those overseeing his restoration. But even as late as June 2007, New Life's leaders were not differentiating rumor from fact in their interviews with the press. The overseers' and church leaders' unwillingness to denounce the ever-spreading lies was discouraging. I could understand that they wanted the church to move forward, but how does ignoring the truth about a situation help it to heal or make the wound any less painful?

Nearly every day, it seemed, I read or heard some variation of the lies that were circulating in the media, but no one publicly defended my husband—least of all, Ted himself. He was so ashamed of the sin he *had* committed that pointing out the ways in which his accuser had exaggerated their relationship felt like splitting hairs. So I sat in forced silence and listened to talk-show hosts and bloggers call my husband an "antigay minister" and accuse him of involving others in homosexual activity.

Ted has never preached hate or intolerance toward anyone. Earlier, I mentioned a video clip from the film *Jesus Camp* in which Ted made an unfortunate joke about blackmailing someone for money. Some people still use that snippet of video to illustrate how Ted Haggard's preaching was "horrible" and "hateful." But my husband has never been a hateful preacher. Ted taught the Bible, and the Bible condemns homosexual activity—along with adultery, stealing, greediness, drunkenness, cheating, and idol worship. But as Ted taught the Bible, he also preached compassion, in accordance with 1 Corinthians 6:11: "Some of you were once like that. But you were cleansed; you were made holy; you were made right with God by calling on the name of the Lord Jesus Christ and by the Spirit of our God."

Ted had always identified homosexual behavior as a sin, but he never condemned others. How could he, since he had succumbed to the power of his own tempting thoughts? "Jesus accepts everyone," he often said. "Anyone who comes to him."

The Bible quotes Jesus on this: "Come to me, all of you who are weary and carry heavy burdens, and I will give you rest. Take my yoke upon you. Let me teach you, because I am humble and gentle at heart, and you will find rest for your souls. For my yoke is easy to bear, and the burden I give you is light" (Matthew 11:28-30). Ted welcomed everyone and tried to help people who struggled with all kinds of issues.

While we went through testing, counseling, exile, and "restoration," the Denver masseur wrote a book and tried to parlay his newfound fame into an acting career. But Ted honestly felt grateful to the man because he was the instrument God used to stop Ted in his tracks. If the Denver masseur had not gone public, Ted might have become a drug addict and continued in his sexual sin. Though Ted emphatically repented in October 2006, not until he went through therapy did he gain the confidence to be able to walk out his repentance.

Writing these memories reminds me of a certain Bible passage: "It is shameful even to mention what the disobedient do in secret.

But everything exposed by the light becomes visible, for it is light that makes everything visible" (Ephesians 5:12-14, NIV).

Through the events of November 2006, God shined an intense light on Ted and me. And though it blinded and seared us, we learned to be grateful for its revealing work in our lives.

Troubles surround me—
too many to count!
My sins pile up so high
I can't see my way out.
They outnumber the hairs on my head.
I have lost all courage.
Please, LORD, rescue me!
Come quickly, LORD, and help me.

PSALM 40:12-13

I am not overstating it when I say that
the man who caused all the trouble
hurt all of you more than he hurt me.
Most of you opposed him, and that was
punishment enough. Now, however,
it is time to forgive and comfort
him. Otherwise he may be overcome
by discouragement. So I urge you
now to reaffirm your love for him.

2 CORINTHIANS 2:5-8

11

Because Ted and I wanted to cooperate fully with the overseers and heal completely, we packed our bags a few days after Thanksgiving and kissed our kids good-bye. I couldn't help feeling as if my shoulders were weighed down with a burden of sadness. We wouldn't see our kids for three weeks, and in the interim, they'd be miles away, trying to make sense of our family crisis on their own. Christy, who had thrown herself into a nurturing role to care for everyone in the family, drove us to Denver to catch our flight to Phoenix.

I thought a lot about restoration and church discipline on the hour-long drive. The Bible gives only one example of temporarily removing an unrepentant brother who has sinned, but even then Paul warns that his removal should not last long, lest he become discouraged (see 2 Corinthians 2:5-8). Paul writes to Timothy that church leaders who sin "should be reprimanded in front of the whole church . . . as a strong warning to others" (1 Timothy 5:20), but he also writes to the Galatians that "if another believer is overcome by some sin, you who are godly should gently and humbly help that person back onto the right path. And be careful not to fall into the same temptation yourself. Share each other's burdens, and in this way obey the law of Christ" (Galatians 6:1-2). If biblical discipline is handled correctly, rumors can be silenced and repentance made public. After that, the sinner should be forgiven, restored to fellowship, and allowed to rebuild relationships.

After all, we are all sinners. In an article for *Christianity Today* about scandals in the evangelical community, Mark Galli quotes Martin Luther as saying that a Christian is "at one and the same time a sinner and a righteous person. He is a sinner in fact, but a righteous person by the sure reckoning and promise of God that he will continue to deliver him from sin until he has completely cured him. And so he is totally healthy in hope, but a sinner in fact. He has the beginning of righteousness, and so always continues more and more to seek it, while realizing that he is always unrighteous."

"If we live in this hope," Galli continues, "we will not be puzzled or despondent when our public heroes fall or church disappoints or our own lives are as wretched as Paul's. Instead, we'll join him in saying, 'Thanks be to God through Jesus Christ our Lord! There is therefore now no condemnation (not from God, not from ourselves!) for those who are in Christ Jesus."[1]

The more I thought about it, the more I became convinced that our being severed from New Life was contrary to what the Bible instructs the church to do. Though I was grateful for the professional counseling, I had yet to hear a concrete plan about how the overseers and restorers planned to restore us—and to what: to the church? to ministry? So far, their plan seemed more about removing us from the church and keeping us quiet.

The Bible addresses how to confront a believer who's sinning and how to apply discipline if that person won't repent. But that wasn't the case with Ted. It wasn't just that he had broken down in tears before me, his staff, and the overseers, confessed his sin, and asked for help. He had also chosen to cooperate fully with the overseers, even though we didn't agree with the way they were handling the situation. And he didn't resist the idea of going to Phoenix for counseling. It seemed clear to me that Ted *had* repented.

I also think that, in the months leading up to the public charges, Ted had been silently crying out for help. Though I must have sensed it, I didn't see it.

What I did see was a man who got up in the middle of the night and drove to the church to pray. Later, I learned that Ted would walk through the dark auditorium and beg God to deliver him before he hurt anyone else. He knew he couldn't rescue himself. In September 2006, he begged God to do whatever was necessary to rescue him, even if it meant losing the church, his friends, and his family.

I knew that in October Ted had gone up to Praise Mountain to pray and fast. What I hadn't known was that while he was there, he made a decision never to participate in sexual sin again. He had thrown away the drugs he had and dropped facedown on the floor, declaring before God that those things would never again enter his life.

Then a sinister voice filled his ear: *All hell will break loose on you because of this.*

Ted started in surprise, but instead of being frightened, he felt reassured that God had heard his prayer and would soon take action.

A few months later, an article in our local paper about Ted and New Life Church included this line: "And in November, all hell broke loose."[2]

Many times I had heard Ted say, "Live your life as though there's no such thing as a secret." Yet suddenly, his secrets were put on display, thrust into the harsh light of public scrutiny and ridicule.

I knew he had battled these temptations before. He would wage war against them and think he'd won a victory. Then some pressure would serve as a trigger, and his troubling thoughts would reemerge. The more prominent he became, the harder he struggled to hide his problem; the more he struggled to hide it, the more virulent the temptations became.

In Ted's case, I honestly believe the Lord himself provided the most effective discipline. Ted suffered privately for months, and then he was publicly exposed, embarrassed, mocked, and humiliated. Because he confessed and repented almost immediately, the church's response should have been forgiveness and restoration of fellowship. Instead, Ted was held up as an example for exile. Instead of being comforted and drawn close, he and his family were pushed away and kicked out. He had served the needs of the church community for nearly twenty-two years, but when *he* became the person in need, no one in leadership stepped forward to help him shoulder the burden; no one defended him publicly; no one rejoiced that God had heard Ted's prayers and had provided a way out—albeit a painful one.

Just before we boarded our plane, I stopped by an airport restroom. I gasped in surprise when I turned the corner and met the wife of a prominent Christian leader. "Gayle," the woman said, her voice soft with pity. "Has Ted even broken yet?"

"B-broken?" I stammered, thinking of the tears that had been shed, the long talks, the suicidal thoughts, and the unrelenting media attention. "How could he not be broken?"

The woman murmured a soothing consolation and continued

out the door, but I stood as though rooted to the spot. What on earth was she thinking? Did she believe what she'd read in the paper or heard through the rumor mill? Did she honestly think that Ted was resisting help or fighting for his right to continue sinning?

Our side of the story, however, was not being heard. Very few people knew the reality of our situation, and we were cooperating with the requirement that we remain silent.

In Phoenix, we stayed at the lovely second home of some friends who offered their place so we wouldn't have to stay in a hotel while we attended counseling. I felt blessed by this kindness, but I continued to be troubled when I thought about our friends and family back in Colorado Springs. The story had not died in the media; in fact, it seemed to have taken on a life of its own. How were our kids handling the pressure?

When we arrived at the counseling center, Ted and I stepped out of the car and held hands as we entered the building. I wasn't certain what the staff had planned or how we would proceed, but Ted and I were both eager for help.

As it turned out, we were in no condition to appreciate the skilled counselors at the center. We were still numb, our emotions raw, from what had happened in November. We were operating in "just tell us what to do" mode. We showed up for our appointments on time, answered all their questions, and were as honest as we could be. At the request of the overseers and restorers, we signed several releases that gave the counselors permission to send reports of their assessment of us. We signed without thinking, blindly trusting that we were in good hands. That decision would come back to haunt us.

The counselors at the center tried to get to the root of our problems by dismantling our defenses, our rationalizations, and our coping mechanisms. In Ted's first meeting with the senior psychologist, the doctor listened to Ted's story then looked at my husband and smiled. "First of all," he said, "you need to accept that there is nothing wrong with you spiritually."

Ted broke into sobs. "How can you say that? I've made a mess of everything."

"But have you confessed your sins and asked for forgiveness?"

"Yes, of course. Always before God, and now before Gayle and several others."

"And have you repented?"

"Over and over again. I have memorized and meditated on Scriptures to help me in the process."

"And have you prayed and fasted about this problem?"

"Many times. I even built a world prayer center and a fasting retreat in the mountains. I was committed to those practices."

"And have you sought deliverance and inner healing?"

"Everything."

"Then it sounds like you've done everything you can do spiritually to solve this problem. So . . . how has it worked out for you?"

Ted shook his head. "I'm here, aren't I?"

"And that's how I know it's not a spiritual problem for you. It's not indicative of your walk with God. If you could have solved this through spiritual methods, you would have."

"Then I must be the biggest idiot on the globe."

The doctor gave Ted a small smile. "It's also not an intellectual problem. If you could have figured this out, you would have. The problem is linked to your physiology and your emotions. We can help you understand why." He clasped his hands and leaned forward over his desk. "We're going to give you a variety of tools you can use, if you choose, to grow in your freedom."

A few days later, after obtaining and discussing Ted's history, one of the therapists explained eye movement desensitization and reprocessing (EMDR), a form of trauma-resolution therapy, and why she believed it would work in Ted's situation.

I'm certainly no expert, but I've learned that EMDR therapy is frequently used to treat victims of post-traumatic stress disorder. The process, which achieves lasting results in a short period of time, involves guiding clients in revisiting traumatic incidents and reexperiencing their troubling feelings in a new way. It unlocks disturbing experiences that have been stored within the brain, along with all the sights, sounds, thoughts, and feelings that accompanied them. As clients reexperience the events, the therapists enable them to choose their *actions* as opposed to feeling powerless over their *re*actions.

Over the weeks, as Ted worked with his counselor and therapist, he offhandedly revealed that when he was in the second grade, he had been sexually abused by one of his father's employees, an adult male. Though the man was dismissed from his job after the incident, no one in the family ever spoke to Ted about what had happened. The experience was nonviolent, but the feelings it aroused confused seven-year-old Ted.

Throughout the next few years, Ted wet his bed at night and continued to wet his pants even through the sixth grade. He was humiliated and embarrassed when he had to wait on the playground for his mother to bring him dry clothes. As a child, he also wore thick glasses—another source of teasing that decimated his self-image.

His family had been well-off, living in a big house at the top of "Haggard's Hill," but when Ted was in seventh grade, his family lost everything. Ted's father had been a veterinarian and an entrepreneur, but after that financial loss he had to sell the family home and return full-time to his veterinary practice.

Ted had also been part of a group of boys who experimented sexually with each other in the sixth and seventh grades, the age when new neural pathways are formed and reinforced by behavior repetition.[3] This preteen horseplay, combined with Ted's unaddressed childhood trauma, only confused him further. These experiences left indelible impressions in Ted's brain, psychological neural pathways that would be triggered under certain conditions, including extreme pressure or emotional stress. Trauma-resolution therapy helped Ted unlock the negative memories and emotions, and then it helped his brain successfully process those experiences.

Counseling also helped him determine that he is not homosexual. He now calls himself "a heterosexual with issues," and I think that description fits, especially in light of the dynamic sexual relationship we've shared throughout our marriage.

Trauma-resolution therapy forced Ted's brain to deal with areas he had blocked off. The act of exposing and exploring those areas totally disempowered the impulsive behavior he had been struggling against. He felt as though trauma-resolution therapy gave him the tools to walk through his repentance—because, after all, repentance is an ongoing, progressive "turning away" from sin.

Our experience at the counseling center reminded us that medical doctors are equipped to deal with physical issues, pastors are equipped to deal with spiritual issues, and psychologists are best equipped to handle cognitive and emotional issues. The counseling center helped bring victory to Ted's life. Even though he had remained true to the commitment he made in October 2006, when he vowed, "Never again," trauma-resolution therapy gave him tools to make holding to his commitment far easier. As he says now, "It's no longer a white-knuckle struggle." As time has passed, the temptations have diminished, and the compulsions have disappeared.

Trauma-resolution therapy is not the answer for everyone who struggles with homosexual thoughts, desires, or tendencies. People who identify themselves as homosexual may have arrived at this conclusion for reasons other than trauma. Through ongoing study, researchers are trying to learn why same-sex attraction is such a powerful force in so many people's lives.

But for Ted, trauma-resolution therapy provided the ability to enact the repentance he desperately desired. The benefits of the treatment enabled him to find permanent and progressive relief from the unwanted, intrusive thoughts. In other words, Ted's healing is ongoing. He still sees a therapist because he doesn't want to allow any opportunities for a harmful pattern to develop and blindside him in the future.

I had chosen to love Ted no matter what, but trauma-resolution therapy gave me the confidence to hope that his long struggle might finally be easing.

The counseling process exhausted us mentally, emotionally, and physically. For three weeks we went to the office at 7:00 a.m. and usually didn't return to the house until 9:30 p.m. Though we were drained by the emotional workout we were getting in counseling, we couldn't forget that our church in Colorado Springs was being dismantled. I felt that in the overseers' hurry to cut Ted out of the picture, they had rushed us off to counseling before we had even regathered our wits.

I went through counseling and therapy sessions along with

Ted. Even though I hadn't been unfaithful in our marriage, the crisis had deeply affected me, and I needed answers. I wanted guidance on how to process all the pain I was feeling, because my emotions were still raw; but mostly I wanted to understand what had been going on with my husband and how we could heal our relationship.

In my first encounter with the lead counselor, I sank into a chair facing him and asked the question uppermost in my mind: "Is my husband the person I believe he is?"

The counselor smiled at me. "He is absolutely the person you believe he is."

I felt my shoulders relax. "Good. People are making him out to be a monster, but I've spent twenty-eight great years with him in a wonderful marriage. Certainly we have issues to work through, but our marriage is strong, and it's real. We have five children. And there's a church on a corner in Colorado Springs that fourteen thousand people call their home church. They're not stupid, and they wouldn't buy into a deceiver."

Other than Ted's secret battle, there was no other evidence of deceitfulness in Ted's life. In all other areas, he was known for his openness and honesty. That is why he described this struggle as being incongruent with the rest of his life. So I was really glad to hear the counselor's response.

I went through trauma-resolution-therapy sessions too. My therapist wanted me to understand what Ted was experiencing, so she used the same techniques to bring out the story of how I had felt rejected when I had no one to throw my paper flower to in the fifth grade. I'm a little embarrassed to name that story as my biggest childhood crisis, yet that incident led to another one involving my high school homeroom class. I was new at the school and had been assigned to a homeroom of mostly football players and a few girls. On one of the first days, the football coach stood at the front of the room and asked if anyone wanted to volunteer to be the homeroom representative. Of course, no one did.

In the security of my bedroom that night, I told myself that being the homeroom representative might be a good thing. By volunteering, I could serve my class and make new friends. Obviously, none of the football players wanted the position, so why shouldn't I take the job?

The next morning, when the coach repeated his question, I raised my hand. "I'll do it," I said, expecting to see grateful faces turn toward me.

"No! We want Brian!" One of the football players yelled out his preference, and in a heartbeat the other guys took up the chant. I slid lower in my seat as Brian grinned and accepted the coach's offer.

I felt rejected all over again. Different class, different school, different state, but the same awful situation, and it triggered a particular emotional response in me.

Another event I discussed with the counselors occurred when I was fourteen. During the time my father was stationed at Edwards Air Force Base, in the California desert, I had a horse that was kept at the base stables. One day, after I had bathed my horse and tied her to a hitching post outside the stable, I went into the tack room to get a sweat scraper. As I walked outside, the bright sun reflected off the blade and spooked my horse. She pulled the hitching post out of the ground and took off running, dragging the post behind her. The metal crossbar swung around and gouged her side and then cut through the hamstring of her hind leg.

I stood paralyzed as the event unfolded in front of me. I didn't rush to my horse's side when she began to spook and pull on the hitching post, because a boy from school was standing nearby and I didn't want to embarrass myself in front of him by running after my horse. But once I realized how wounded she was, I forgot about the boy and ran to help her.

I spent the rest of that day trying to comfort my horse through her pain. The vet came, but he couldn't save her, and we had to put her down.

Her death devastated me. I vowed that never again would I let embarrassment or what other people think stop me from rescuing someone who was in trouble.

Including my husband.

The most vivid experience I had with trauma-resolution therapy took place when my therapist asked me to imagine Ted in a sexual encounter with another man. I told her it was the most painful thought I could imagine, but she made me face it.

I drew a deep breath and closed my eyes. "Okay."

"What do you see?"

"I see—" I peered into the depths of my imagination. "It's like I've walked into a room, and I see Ted. He's looking at me with fear in his eyes, and behind him I see a dark figure."

"How does that make you feel?"

"It makes me want to scream at that figure."

"What do you want to scream?"

"GET OUT!" I shouted in the silence of the room as tears coursed down my face. "You will *not* destroy my husband!"

"And now what do you see?"

"I am watching that figure turn into a dark puddle on the floor."

"And then what happens?"

"Ted looks peaceful."

"What are you experiencing now?"

"I'm lying on a beautiful bed with a soft, fluffy white comforter, and everything around me is pure. I sense God's presence."

"And how does that make you feel?"

"Like everything is going to be all right." I caught my breath as a realization struck me. "Oh my . . . I feel like God is ministering to me and comforting me right now."

For me, trauma-resolution therapy proved to be a spiritual experience. No matter where we began, I ended up feeling as though God was ministering to me.

The counseling sessions didn't always end on a pleasant note. When I first sat down with one of the counselors, he wanted me to accept that I had known about Ted's problem and had unintentionally created behaviors to accommodate him because I didn't want to ruffle the waters. He kept looking at me as if I had to accept responsibility for Ted's problem because I hadn't kept closer tabs on him. But I've never wanted to be a suspicious wife who demanded to know her husband's whereabouts twenty-four hours a day. I insisted that my approach was healthy; he insisted that I had been Ted's chief enabler.

I told one of my counselors that I was using prayer and my understanding of the Scriptures to deal with our problem. I said I believed the Bible passage where Jesus says, "Anyone who listens to my teaching and follows it is wise, like a person who builds a house on solid rock" (Matthew 7:24). He kept telling me that I must be codependent (all pastors' wives were), and because I didn't have the strength to address Ted's problem, I had kept silent until the crisis.

I leaned forward and flatly told him that had I known about Ted's problem, I'd have been sure to address it. I was no doormat.

He kept emphasizing that codependence wasn't healthy, but aren't all relationships codependent to some extent? Husbands and wives *should* be able to depend on each other. They should *need* each other. Dependence is unhealthy only if it's detrimental to a person. This self-protective kind of thinking baffled me because it contradicted so many things I knew from Scripture: The person who loves lays down her life for another person. Husbands and wives submit to each other out of reverence for Christ. This isn't the way the world operates, but Jesus said his Kingdom is not of this world.

When I talked about the Lord, my counselor said I was using God as a crutch. He'd say, "You need to get angry at God. He can handle it." But I wasn't afraid of upsetting God; I just wasn't mad at him. He was our only source of comfort and hope.

One afternoon, while Ted was involved in a long session, I took the car and went back to the house. I had a brand-new worship CD from New Life Church, so I slipped it into the car's CD player as I drove. I listened, remembering how it felt to stand in the auditorium, surrounded by the beaming faces of my beloved church family. The voices on the CD were their voices, and though we were separated by time and distance, I felt united with them. Once I drove into the immaculate garage, I got out of the car, lay facedown on the carpeted garage floor, and worshiped God. I felt my weary spirit begin to revive. I returned to what was dear and familiar as I listened to the voices of those I'd known and loved.

That hour so invigorated me that it became my standard practice after difficult counseling sessions. Of all the things we did in Phoenix, those worship hours in that garage had the most to do with healing me. As I sang the songs and lifted my thoughts heavenward, the worship put me back in touch with God, and I felt normal again.

I cry out to God; yes, I shout.
Oh, that God would listen to me!
When I was in deep trouble,
I searched for the Lord.
All night long I prayed, with
    hands lifted toward heaven,
but my soul was not comforted.
I think of God, and I moan,
overwhelmed with longing for his help.
You don't let me sleep.
I am too distressed even to pray!
I think of the good old days,
long since ended,
when my nights were filled
    with joyful songs.
I search my soul and ponder
    the difference now.
Has the Lord rejected me forever?
Will he never again be kind to me?
Is his unfailing love gone forever?
Have his promises permanently failed?
Has God forgotten to be gracious?
Has he slammed the door
    on his compassion?
And I said, "This is my fate;
the Most High has turned his
    hand against me."
But then I recall all you
    have done, O LORD;
I remember your wonderful
    deeds of long ago.
They are constantly in my thoughts.
I cannot stop thinking about
    your mighty works.

PSALM 77:1-12

12

As THE DAYS passed, I began to regret our unthinking agreement to release reports of our counseling sessions to the overseers. Ted was making demonstrable progress, but the counselors seemed to want to put me in a box that didn't fit.

For instance, one afternoon they raised a new allegation that had come from New Life—information that came from the list of accusations they had gathered against Ted. Because Ted had been completely honest with me about the situation, and because we'd just spent three weeks in Florida discussing this and other issues, I didn't exhibit a strong reaction to the news. My counselors decided that my "nonreactive" expression meant I was in denial, so they wrote reports about me and sent them back to the overseers, reinforcing the prevailing opinion that I was deceived and not willing to face the truth.

The smiles and pleasantness we displayed with our counselors and the people in our group sessions earned us the label *seductive*, even though Ted and I thought we were only communicating friendliness and respect.

When they brought up embellishments to the story about the gay escort, I didn't react because I knew the new details weren't true. Ted had told me everything about the man in Denver, and I wanted to discuss this additional information with my husband before I shared my feelings with a counselor.

Though Ted and I had told our counselors about our truth-telling sessions in Florida, I'm not sure they believed us. Some of them kept expecting me to be more shocked; I think they wanted me to shout profanity and rage at Ted. They wanted to see more tears, more anger, more emotion on display, but we had already worked through a lot of those feelings.

The staff seemed particularly eager to see us express our anger. They kept talking about anger—how we had to feel it and why we needed to express it. "You need to tell Ted how you feel," they told me. "You need to tell him how angry you are and what you're really thinking and feeling."

I stared at them, wondering why they couldn't accept that we had already gone through this; we'd used up more than our share of explosive rage before we got to Phoenix. Still, if anger was what they wanted, I decided I would dredge up the remnants that remained in order to oblige them. As time passed, I discovered I had even more anger to process, and in keeping with the instructions I received at the counseling center, I expressed it to Ted. He had been counseled about the importance of letting me express my anger, but what amazed me was how patiently he processed it with me. Even on my worst days, though, I never returned to the level of anger I had felt in the early days, while we were on Captiva Island.

Our counseling program also included a visit to a medical

clinic. Both Ted and I went through a barrage of tests to check for HIV and other STDs. Ted was also tested for drugs. Our results came back after we'd returned to Colorado Springs; thankfully, every test for sexually transmitted diseases was negative, and Ted's drug test showed no evidence of any illicit drugs.

The doctor who did our physical exams warned me that we should expect more sickness than usual in the next several months. "When the body is under extreme stress," he said, his tone matter-of-fact, "your resistance lowers, making you more prone to picking up colds, flu, and other illnesses. I'm not trying to scare you; I just want you to be prepared." Yet neither of us experienced any illness during the two years following our crisis. Perhaps this is because we slept more than we had in our entire adult lives.

Each day at the counseling center drained us to the point of exhaustion, but we were grateful for the insights we gained there. One of our therapists helped me to understand the importance of properly ordering one's life. She drew a series of concentric circles on a sheet of paper and held it up. "See the inner circle, the small-est one?" she asked. "That's where you and God are. Put yourself with God in the center of your life. The circle just outside that one should contain your spouse. The next circle should contain your children. The following circles can contain your friends and work relationships. You can't have a healthy life if you have these circles out of order."

I was grateful for that simple illustration. I had built my life on the principles it represented, but I didn't think that Ted had. Before the crisis, he'd had too many people in his inner circle, and I had felt crowded out. The counselor explained to Ted that the inner circle belonged only to him and God. The second circle was my rightful place, and I should share it with no one else. She encouraged me to reclaim my place—or maybe claim it for the first time. Then she looked Ted in the eye and told him not to ever let anyone into the second and third circles except for me and our kids.

Jesus modeled this ordering of relationships for us. He chose seventy disciples, but he called twelve who walked more closely with him. From the twelve, three were intimate friends, but he reserved the center circle for himself and his Father.

The best part of the therapy was the time Ted and I spent talking and processing with each other during appointments and on the drive home. We went with an eager desire to learn, and we spent each night discussing everything we'd taken in that day.

Nonetheless, the more time Ted and I spent at the counseling center, the more we felt it was not a safe place. I was grateful for the tools Ted received, and we did take away some valuable insights, but because we'd signed those releases, reports were sent to people who had no context for what was said in our sessions and who lacked a full understanding of some of the terms used to describe us. I felt as if assessments were being made of us while we were emotionally vulnerable, and it seemed that everything we said was being used against us.

By the end of our three weeks, we were bone weary and eager to go home. The entire time we were in Phoenix, we worried about the church back in Colorado Springs. We wanted to get to the truth underlying Ted's problem, but we also wanted to get home because we feared for our church family. The last reports we'd heard were not good.

Our crisis brought me to a place where I had to do something I never thought I'd do: try to understand homosexual desires. I not only needed to understand them; I soon would go on national television and publicly defend a man who struggled with them.

Before Ted revealed his deepest problems to me, I wouldn't have wanted to touch the topic of homosexuality in any forum. I didn't want to even think about it. If someone had told me that her child or husband struggled with same-sex attraction, I would feel compassion, and I'd promise to pray for her. I wouldn't reject her son, daughter, or husband, but I wouldn't have wanted to invest myself in understanding the person's battle. I could give sympathy, but empathy? I didn't want to think about it that much.

But when I came to the place where I understood that I needed to support Ted as he worked through his struggles, I realized I was going to have to study and understand an issue I had avoided my entire life.

While we were in Phoenix for counseling, both Ted and I learned a lot about issues surrounding human sexuality. I had plenty of questions as a result of our crisis, and I discovered that I was in need of a better education on the subject. I wanted to know if Ted's actions were controlled by his will or by his physiology. How powerful are compulsive thoughts, and what causes some people to have them when others don't? Just how powerful is the unconscious mind? Is acting on our impulses really only a lack of self-control? If not, is it possible to control these impulses and compulsions?

Ted wanted answers too. Together we set out on a quest for more understanding.

I began to research sexuality, and I learned that if we solidify behaviors through repetition, we begin to identify with those behaviors—whether they involve eating, sexuality, alcohol, or drug use. The more we identify with those behaviors, the harder it is to abstain from them. Instead of accepting destructive behaviors as part of a person's identity, however, we need to find better ways to help people fight their battles and live healthy lifestyles. Most of all, we need to love people through their struggles.

At its core, Christianity accepts that human beings are flawed—that's a basic premise of the gospel, the Good News about salvation. We all struggle with some form of sinful behavior. The Bible says, "If we claim we have no sin, we are only fooling ourselves and not living in the truth" (1 John 1:8). Because humans are sexual beings, we are all capable of acting out our sexuality in any number of ways. Those of us who are in the church should not be shocked if brothers or sisters struggle in this area, because we live in a highly sexualized culture. Instead, we should offer a safe and supportive environment as they work through their issues.

I believe the church is equipped to offer forgiveness and hope to those who are trapped by sexual sin. The church should be informed enough to address issues of sexuality because so many people suffer because of them.

In recent months, Ted and I have received thousands of e-mails from people in the gay community, as well as from those who wrestle with homosexual attraction but do not accept a gay identity. Most of these e-mails are encouraging, the writers cheering us on to bring enlightenment to the discussion instead of simplistic categorization and exclusion.

"The brain has chemical-release mechanisms associated with pleasure centers," writes John DeCecco. "The experience of pleasure creates powerful, behavior-shaping incentives."[1]

"Unregulated sexual tendencies become habits, then compulsions, and finally something barely distinguishable from addictions," explains Jeffrey Watson. "Sexual fantasies may not be entirely erasable, but new, acceptable fantasies can be learned in place of the older ones. New behaviors can become more gratifying than the old ones; the power of the old behaviors can weaken and wither, although during stress old patterns are more easily provoked."[2]

"While a heritable gene may predispose a carrier toward physical height," Watson writes, "heredity does not require anyone to play for the National Basketball Association. Stated differently, even though a person may be born with a vulnerability toward manic depression or alcoholism, one's personal outcomes can be modified by choice and by experience. If a boy with a sensitive disposition is marked as 'different' by his father and is subsequently rejected by male authority figures, peers, and potential heterosexual partners, he may experiment with the temporary anesthesia of homosexual companions. What starts out as a relatively 'free' act can become less so over time because of the biological power of repetition."[3]

I believe most people can choose to change their behavior patterns, because we have the ability to determine the direction of our lives. Most of us can make choices about who we are and who we want to be in the face of difficult circumstances. The power to choose behaviors, however, varies from person to person. Some people have conditions (obsessive-compulsive and bipolar disorders, for example) that make compulsive behavior uncontrollable without the help of medication or treatment; so, sometimes, the ability to change a particular behavior is not related to making a choice or a decision.

Even in healthy people, following through on choices to change behavior patterns is not easy—ask anyone who's ever been on a diet—and this is where the problem lies. We have to be patient with one another during the process and offer encouragement as we allow the grace of God to transform our lives.

Ted's current therapist is absolutely convinced that Ted's desires were the result of childhood experience. Trauma-resolution therapy dealt with his compulsion to re-create the trauma he experienced as a child. His past life experiences created neural pathways and pleasure centers, and certain conditions and stress tended to activate these areas of the brain, triggering compulsive behavior. Trauma-resolution therapy, more specifically EMDR, dealt with the buried memories and helped Ted desensitize the triggers created by the trauma in his childhood. He had kept everything locked away, but when he went back and examined those episodes, he could deal openly with his problem and get on the pathway to healing.

In short, as Ted's therapist told me, "Ted experienced unwanted homosexual desires because of his childhood trauma. Since his treatment, he is no longer dominated by unwanted intrusive thoughts and compulsions."

In Phoenix, Ted told the counselors he had never been interested in a romantic relationship with a man. He did, however, have early sexual experiences that predisposed him to temptations in the area of same-sex attraction. I had found out while we were in Florida that, after we were married, Ted had been tempted to pick up magazines featuring gay porn, and we believe that experience started him on the path toward the sinful activity that became so destructive in his life. When he repented of those behaviors, he'd experience freedom for extended periods of time, but then something would trigger his buried traumas and he'd relapse.

The Bible says, "Temptation comes from our own desires, which entice us and drag us away. These desires give birth to sinful actions. And when sin is allowed to grow, it gives birth to death" (James 1:14-15).

Most people have thoughts and secrets they don't share with anyone, not even with their spouse. All our sins—whether pride, jealousy, envy, lust, or others—begin in the mind; but often we manage to keep them out of sight as we smile and move through our routines. When our sinful thoughts give way to sinful actions, however, it's hard to hide the shameful fruit of our thoughts.

That's why, as strange as it might sound, we can rejoice when our sin is exposed. As Jesus said, "The time is coming when everything that is covered up will be revealed, and all that is secret will be made known to all. Whatever you have said in the dark will be heard in the light, and what you have whispered behind closed doors will be shouted from the housetops for all to hear!" (Luke 12:2-3).

When Ted and I completed our time at the counseling center, we went home amid a barrage of news reports that Ted had been "cured" of homosexuality in only three weeks. Hundreds of tongue-in-cheek bloggers demanded to know the secret of this "de-gay-ification" center. Others participated in a "Bet on Ted" pool, in which participants placed wagers on whether or not Ted would "fall off the wagon" and we'd divorce. A consistent tone of ridicule and disbelief ran through nearly every article. People seemed to think that Ted must be gay and was foolishly thinking he could deny his true identity—all this despite the fact that he and I had been married for twenty-eight fulfilling years and have five children.

I find it interesting that this type of thinking never seems to be applied to the opposite situation. If a man who professes to be gay has sexual relations with a woman, does anyone chastise him and demand that he come out of the closet and admit his *heterosexuality*?

The truth is much more complicated, but it seemed that not many people wanted to hear it.

And our lips had been sealed.

❖

During our last week in Phoenix, we'd had to leave the home where we had been staying because the owners were coming back to town for a week. They offered to put us up at the Scottsdale Princess, a beautiful hotel, but we protested because we spent all day at the counseling center. "An inexpensive hotel close to the counseling center would be just fine," Ted told them. "All we need is a place to sleep. The rest of the time we are at the counseling center." Our generous hosts, however, insisted on putting us up in the nicer place.

One day, during a break in one of my sessions, I excused myself from the counselor's office and went to the restroom. While I was there, I became aware that voices were audible from the room next door. The walls must have been thin, because even though the counselor was in his office, I could hear everything he said. He was on the phone and in obvious good spirits, because he laughed several times.

As I washed my hands and prepared to leave, the phrase "They're staying at the Scottsdale Princess" came through the wall and halted me in my tracks. The counselor spoke in a mocking tone and went on to say that we wanted to be treated like royalty, so we were staying at the swankiest hotel in town. I bit back a rush of humiliation and anger. I wanted to storm into his office and set the record straight, but what good would it do? Reality dawned on me—people could say anything about us, form any opinion they liked, and we had no way to credibly defend ourselves.

Then I heard a voice I recognized over the speakerphone: "Even their family won't have anything to do with them." My cheeks burned because I knew the caller was referring to one of Ted's siblings who hadn't spoken to him since the crisis.

I dried my hands and was inwardly trembling as I reentered the office where Ted and I were in midsession with a different counselor. I told her I had overheard the conversation between her colleague and one of the men who had sent us to the counseling center. As I was telling her how I felt, the counselor I'd overheard walked in. Giving full expression to my emotions—the counselors should have been proud of me—I told him how upset I was and that I felt we were being misrepresented.

Although he appeared flustered, he waved my concerns away. He then informed us that one of the restorers would drop by that afternoon to see us. This would be the first time he'd met with us as a restorer.

We were thrilled to see Pastor Tommy Barnett's face when he walked through the door later that day. He embraced both of us with warmth and great kindness, which unleashed more of my emotions. I wiped away tears as we talked for a few moments, and then he mentioned he'd brought a letter that would ask us to move from Colorado. I was so shocked, my emotions so raw, that I burst into fresh tears and began to sob. "Please," I said, frankly begging. "Please don't make us move. Don't separate us from our church, from our community."

He tucked the letter back into his pocket and said he couldn't give it to us—at least not yet. He realized that we hadn't met with any of the restoration team and they hadn't yet heard from us in this process. He suggested we arrange a January meeting with all three restorers in Los Angeles.

After three weeks of intense therapy sessions and painful forward progress, the counselors cleared us to go home to be with our children at Christmas. While we were flying back to Colorado Springs, I looked out the window and thought that if the plane went down or if we died in the car on the drive from the airport,

I would be okay with that—and our children would probably be better off. I used to pray for safety every time I stepped onto a plane, but since the crisis I'd been praying, *If the plane goes down, Lord, I'm content. If you have no further purpose for us, let it be over. I'm okay if we die. I would never commit suicide, but an accident might be convenient right now.* . . .

Of course I wouldn't have wanted all the other people on the plane to die, but I was losing sight of the purpose I had always believed God had for Ted and me. I was beginning to wonder if the world *would* be better off without us.

But the Lord brought us safely home on Christmas Eve, and my heart thrilled to see the Christmas tree twinkling in the family room. The kids had decorated the house, done the shopping and bought groceries, and stepped up to do all the things I usually took care of during the holidays. Christy had even picked up Jonathan at the airport, so he was home where he belonged.

I bit back tears as I hugged each of my children, and I knew Ted was moved beyond words.

The next morning, after eating a Christmas breakfast and opening gifts, we held a family meeting, and Ted suggested each person in the room share their story. "This is how we get healthy," I added. I gave them a wry smile, well aware that I sounded like one of the counselors from Phoenix. We had learned our lessons well. "Lay everything out on the table, and let's deal with our feelings."

As we sat in front of the family room fireplace, I heard lots of anger expressed—but I was surprised to realize that our children weren't focused on their father's sin but rather on his having been away from home so much. All of the boys said that even though they knew he loved them, they felt as though he hadn't been available to them emotionally. They'd had to resign themselves to the fact that other people monopolized Ted's attention. But they also expressed hope. The change in our circumstances had given them back their dad, and they hoped they could now build the kind of relationships they wanted with him.

Imagine that—our kids were more concerned about Ted's busyness than about his sin. And we hadn't protected them from the details—they'd read the blogs; they'd seen the YouTube videos. They knew the most horrific things that people were saying about their father. But the issue they brought to Ted was their desire that he simply be their dad.

In my daughter's and sons' eager faces, I saw a reflection of my own yearning. To be his favorite. To be close to him. Looking at Ted through my children's eyes, I glimpsed the possibility that our family could become what I wanted it to be.

My eyes filled with tears as I looked around the circle at Christy, Marcus, Sarah, Jonathan, Alex, Elliott, and Ted. My family. My strength.

So how did I get through those darkest hours in my marriage and family? I made a simple choice—to love. To cling rather than separate. To bring everything out into the open, as opposed to remaining sheltered. And I remembered something I'd learned long before: Love isn't a feeling, it's a choice—a choice we make every day, sometimes every hour.

Ted and I continued to cling to each other right before falling asleep. Many times as we held each other, I'd think, *I have never felt closer to Ted than I do right now.*

I had learned that when one spouse has been unfaithful, the most common reaction from the other spouse is to be repulsed by the offending spouse's physical touch. But I've discovered that the godly response is usually the opposite of the human response. So instead of indulging my pride and turning away, I clung to Ted, and he clung to me. And somehow both of us felt safer.

After God created the woman from one of Adam's ribs, Adam realized that she completed him and made him whole. "Therefore," says the Scripture, "a man shall leave his father and his mother and hold fast to his wife, and they shall become one flesh" (Genesis 2:24, ESV). I discovered that my deepest yearnings were soothed when Ted clung to me.

I know that some people believe a wife shouldn't "reward" her husband with her physical touch at a time like this, that an adulterer needs to understand that there are consequences to his unfaithfulness. But I believed that if our marriage was going to heal, we needed to draw closer rather than pull apart.

Our children learned to cling to us, too, and we encouraged hugs and long embraces. We drew strength from each other in those moments, and we were able to stand tall as the storm raged around us.

Ted and I wanted to give honest answers to our children. When they came with a question, Ted answered them truthfully but not graphically. He chose his words with care because he wanted to respect their questions, but he knew they didn't want details. He was committed to openness, because the only way to earn trust is to consistently tell the truth. So he was truthful with the children, but he didn't give more information than they needed or wanted.

Our kids didn't ask a lot of questions. They were mostly concerned about the state of our marriage relationship. They wanted to know that we were working through our issues and that we were okay.

If I had chosen to separate from Ted, I think the children would have supported me; but because they would have continued to love Ted as well, they would have wanted to maintain a relationship with him. My decision to separate would have forced them to choose sides—do they comfort Mom or Dad?—which would have brought on a host of other emotional problems. They would have lost their security, and the effects would have rippled throughout their lives for years.

Instead, our children drew strength from the decisions Ted and I made together. And we drew strength from our children, far more than we would have imagined. My children won my respect as I witnessed their commitment to Ted, to me, and to each other. I took pains not to fall into a dependent role—I didn't want them to feel as though they had to take care of me. I've seen far too many children become caretakers of their grieving parents.

I don't want to belittle the pain my children endured. All of us went through a wide spectrum of emotions, including anger, sadness, confusion, hope, love, and fear. But we would have gone through far worse if I'd chosen to leave Ted.

My children's displays of emotion would have upset me more if I hadn't gone through the counseling-center program. That's where I learned that it's important for us to let those emotions come out. When people express their feelings honestly, they can work through their feelings instead of repressing them. Repressed emotions don't go away; they fester beneath the surface.

Through Ted's counseling experience, we learned the dangers of repressed emotion. If someone had known how to talk to him after he was abused as a seven-year-old, we might not have had to deal with this crisis.

Ted and I now gave each other permission to be completely honest and share everything. We talked and talked and talked, taking all the time we needed to deal with our thoughts and feelings. As we opened our hearts to each other, I gained the intimate marriage relationship I'd always wanted.

Ted also needed to confess, and I wanted to know my husband completely. I realize that everyone is different, but I would rather know the painful truth than be kept in the dark. Knowing the full truth led me to visualize things that were hard to deal with, but knowing the full truth voided other images that had filled my imagination.

And yes, I had to deal with painful images. Knowing the details put pictures in my mind, but this was a necessary part of my healing process. In the first few weeks after our crisis, I kept bringing up these images in my conversations with Ted, but I eventually realized I had to stop focusing on those images so we could move on. I had to redirect my thinking and stop scrutinizing my husband. He had been punished enough by his guilt, the media, and those who rejected him. He didn't need my punishment as well. More than anything, he needed my forgiveness. When God forgives us, he no longer holds our sins against us. That's what Ted needed from me.

That's when I fully grasped the power of love—and how it can cover a multitude of sins. After that, whenever I began to think those painful thoughts, I'd purposely silence them by telling myself, *I choose to love Ted and to no longer hold his sins against him.* Because I had committed to love, which I define as "preferring another person above myself," I had to let compassion and understanding replace the pain and fear those thoughts evoked.

One morning, as I was praying in the family room, one of those dark images rose up in my mind. I stopped and told myself, *I've got to stop harassing Ted; we've been over this.* As I continued praying, I asked God to help me heal from those tormenting thoughts so I could put them behind me once and for all. Immediately 1 Peter 4:8—"Love covers a multitude of sins"—came to my mind. As I contemplated what that meant, I remembered another Bible passage that provides a perfect description of love: "Love is patient and kind. Love is not jealous or boastful or proud or rude. It does not demand its own way. It is not irritable, and it keeps no record of being wronged" (1 Corinthians 13:4-5).

Love keeps no record of being wronged. The words struck my heart. Ted had experienced more than enough scrutiny and tallying of his alleged sins. News articles and blogs were daily reminding the public of his failures.

The many judgments against Ted did nothing to improve him or his accusers. I finally realized that I didn't want to be part of that critical group anymore. If I wanted to heal and wanted Ted to heal, my reminders of his sin weren't helping either one of us.

I believe we choose to see a person either through the grid of his failures or through the grid of his strengths. None of us wants to be scrutinized for *every* wrong we have committed. But when we feel loved and respected, we are more inclined to stretch to be our better selves.

I discovered that love is powerful enough to erase a person's sins. Love *is* forgiveness.

The rest of the familiar passage from 1 Corinthians filtered through my mind: "Love never gives up, never loses faith, is always hopeful, and endures through every circumstance" (13:7).

Those words became my aim and my path to healing.

O LORD, come back to us!

How long will you delay?

Take pity on your servants!

Satisfy us each morning with

your unfailing love,

so we may sing for joy to the

end of our lives.

Give us gladness in proportion

to our former misery!

Replace the evil years with good.

Let us, your servants, see

you work again;

let our children see your glory.

And may the Lord our God

show us his approval

and make our efforts successful.

Yes, make our efforts successful!

PSALM 90:13-17

13

AFTER THOSE STRESSFUL weeks of counseling in Phoenix, coming home felt like a welcome relief. We had our children with us for support, the familiar surroundings lessened our stress, and we loved being able to reach out and touch the comforts of home. I wandered through the house, running my fingers over the piano that Marcus loved to play, the cozy sofa in front of the living room mantel, and the tall, brick fireplace in the family room.

Our house was a great family home. It wasn't particularly lavish, but it had room enough for our five children and the church meetings we had often hosted. Still, it was an older structure and required loads of upkeep. I loved our home, but it seemed that every month something broke down and needed to be repaired.

As much as Ted and I loved our home, at the start of the new year we had to sit with pencils in hand and work out some serious calculations to determine if we were going to be able to keep it. Not only had Ted lost his job as pastor, but I had lost my salaried position as head of the women's ministry. The overseers had mentioned that the church would grant a severance package for both of us, but we did not yet know the terms of that agreement.

Ted had always been extremely attentive to the church finances, but when it came to our own, we were a little more relaxed. We just weren't that concerned about our retirement and thought more about investing in the lives of the people of New Life Church. Jesus said, "Don't store up treasures here on earth, where moths eat them and rust destroys them [and a recession shrinks them], and where thieves break in and steal. Store your treasures in heaven, where moths and rust cannot destroy, and thieves do not break in and steal. Wherever your treasure is, there the desires of your heart will also be" (Matthew 6:19-21).

We not only believed that verse, we also lived it. Ted's salary was way below par for other megachurch pastors, but we felt he made enough to comfortably meet our needs. Ted had never negotiated a pay package; in fact, he kept himself on the same pay scale as the rest of the staff. He believed that everyone who worked at the church was equally valuable, so every pastor who came on staff began at the same base pay level. Cost-of-living raises were distributed equally across the board, the same percentage to every salaried church employee. If Ted made more than the other pastors, it was only because he'd been employed the longest.

After giving at least 10 percent of our income as an offering to the church, most of what we earned went toward our kids' educations; so we were far from wealthy. We invested in our children, because all of them attended private schools—two were in Christian schools, two were in college, and Jonathan was in a special-ed institution. We happily paid those bills and felt financially secure.

I remember a time when New Life hosted a financial-planning

seminar for the church staff. When I mentioned to one of the executive staff members that I should probably go to the seminar, he replied, "Gayle, the church will always take care of you and Ted. You really don't need any of this."

After the crisis, we had to take stock of our financial affairs. We still believed God would provide for us, but we also knew we needed to be good stewards of what he provided.

Ted and I now took out a second mortgage, because we wanted to pay down our debts and consolidate. Because the church had stopped withholding taxes on Ted's severance checks, we also had to set money aside for income taxes.

After deciding to cut out any unnecessary expenses, we thought we should also sell my car, an adorable red Mini Cooper. I thought my parents might want to buy it, so I called them, and they agreed to take the car off our hands. We only had to drive it to their home in Palm Desert, California.

From the time I first called until the time we arrived in Palm Desert, my parents contemplated how they would react upon seeing Ted. Although they had been kind and supportive over the phone, they were still furious with him for the pain he had inflicted on the children and me.

When Ted and I finally pulled into their driveway, Mom and Dad stepped out of the house to greet us. I usually loved visiting my parents, but we'd never gone home under circumstances like these. I glanced at my dad and saw his stony expression—but he wasn't looking at me. He was fixated on Ted. As we approached the house, however, my father's features softened into a look of pure compassion.

Later, Dad told me how upset he'd been with my husband. But when he watched him get out of the car, he saw that Ted was a broken man.

"All of my anger vanished," Dad said. "It turned to sympathy."

Mom greeted us with a happy smile and seemed especially relieved to see me. She'd been troubled by my sad expression in pictures she'd seen of us in the media. She needed to see me in person to know I was all right.

That day, we had the most open discussions we've ever had with my parents. When we finished, Dad said that after talking with Ted, he had gained new respect for him. As for me, I relaxed and curled up in a corner of the couch, reveling in the safety and security I've always felt under my parents' roof.

Before we left the house, Dad told us he believed our future would be better than our past. We walked out feeling as though he had sent us on our way with a blessing.

Once Ted and I had completed the counseling program and set our marriage on the road to recovery, I wanted to heal our relationship with New Life Church. As the former director of women's ministries, I was naturally concerned about how that ministry had fared since Ted and I had been asked to leave. In time, through trusted friends, I learned that people were being told that they should not be in contact with me because I'd been deceived. Some went so far as to say I was living under the deception of a homosexual spirit and that Ted had led the church under that same spirit. They said that, under Ted's dominating leadership, I'd been forced to maintain tight control over the women of the church.

What?

Part of my continuing heartache concerned my three closest friends, the women I'd talked to right after news of our crisis broke.

By the time Ted and I retreated to Captiva Island, the overseers had forbidden me to talk to my friends. But after Ted's pleading on my behalf, they finally gave me permission in December to meet with them again. Ted and I had just come back from the counseling center, and we were still pretty raw, but I needed to vent and share my feelings with my closest friends. I was eager to see them, and when we met, I hugged them and felt I was in a safe place again.

That day, I poured out my anguish, unspeakably grateful for the freedom to share my heart with friends who knew me well. I told them about my grief over what New Life was going through and the decisions being made to separate us from the church. I told them about the talks Ted and I had had and about the trauma-resolution therapy we'd received at the counseling center. I told them everything, because I felt I could share freely.

Then, as an afterthought, I told them about a morning when I'd awakened in that fuzzy world halfway between dream and reality. "It was like the crisis hadn't happened, and things were back the way they used to be," I said, smiling. "I imagined standing before our women's class on a Sunday morning and saying, 'Good morning, ladies. Today we are going to talk about wisdom.'"

I knew it was only a dream, but it felt good to share it with my friends.

Without warning, one of my friends stood. "I can't hear this anymore," she said. "I have to leave."

I blinked in confusion. "I understand—I'm sorry for unloading all this on you. I know you are going through your own process."

She turned, gathered her things, and walked out the door, leaving me saddened and my other two friends stunned.

A few days later, we got a call from one of the church leaders.

"I heard about the meeting Gayle had with her friends," he told Ted. "You two have really messed things up for yourselves."

At first I was startled to discover that one of my friends had reported our conversation to a church official, especially because I didn't feel I had said anything wrong. Then I began to understand her position. She had become the director of women's ministries, so her loyalties had shifted. She felt a greater responsibility to the present church administration than to me, and she felt that she had to report my comments. Apparently, she had found what I said upsetting. She was also privy to discussions among the church leadership, which of course I wasn't, so I have no idea what red flags my words raised. Perhaps I shouldn't have shared some of the intimate details about what I was learning, or perhaps she thought I wasn't willing to give up my women's ministry role. Maybe the innocent retelling of my dream convinced her that Ted and I were planning to step back into our former positions at New Life, but a return of that nature was the furthest thing from our minds.

As I struggled to understand her perspective and her actions, I mourned the loss of her friendship. I thought longingly of the days when we were close friends and had spent so much time sharing our hearts and praying together.

Though part of me felt betrayed, I really didn't blame her. I blamed the "separate and silence" ideology that had come between close friends.

❖

As the world settled into January 2007, a new year and a fresh start, Ted and I flew to California for our first appointment with the three men who had been chosen to oversee our restoration. We were in good spirits and had high hopes for this meeting. Two years earlier, one of the men had visited our church, and during that visit he had said that Ted was like a son to him. We felt that a strong bond existed between them. I knew the second man as a loving, kindhearted pastor; and though I didn't know the third man personally, I knew he was highly respected and had experience working with pastors in trouble. I felt we were going to be in good hands. Safe hands.

When we met, the three restorers shared a document they'd received from the four overseers—a rough draft of a restoration agreement. We talked about several suggestions the overseers had made for our restoration: that we participate in regular prayer and Bible study, attend a life-giving church, write letters to revoke Ted's ordination and ministerial license, create a plan for a new career that did not involve any type of preaching or pastoral ministry, remain silent about Ted's work and ministry at New Life Church, avoid sexual immorality, and so on. The letter also stated that we would be prohibited from being on New Life Church or World Prayer Center property, attending any New Life meeting or small group, or communicating with any church employee, trustee, or elder unless the communication was initiated by the church's senior pastoral staff. Finally, the document required us to leave Colorado.

The restorer leading the meeting frowned at several of the clauses and struck them out, including the clause that required us to relocate out of state. "Perhaps you can move about an hour away," one of them suggested, "at least for a while. That way your sons can remain in touch with their friends."

The three men made other suggestions about changing certain restrictive conditions, and as the meeting wrapped up, the leader gave the marked-up document to Ted and asked him to type in the restorers' changes and e-mail it to each of them for approval. Then, as we stood in a circle with our hands on his Bible, the leader led us in a closing prayer.

Ted and I flew home, confident that we had settled the terms of our restoration agreement. Because we had never *stopped* praying and reading the Bible, the only stipulations that caused us real pain were those that separated us from New Life Church.

Because the restorers had suggested that we temporarily relocate an hour or so from Colorado Springs, we looked for another place to live. Our church had built a facility we called Praise Mountain, a mountain camp featuring several rustic cabins people could rent if they wanted to get away to fast and pray. After operating Praise Mountain for many years, New Life had sold it to a couple who planned to continue running it as a prayer and fasting facility. The husband had passed away, but his wife was still managing the place.

Because Praise Mountain was located a little more than an hour from Colorado Springs, Ted and I went to see the woman and her son-in-law, who was on her board, to ask if we could move into one of the cabins and live there while we went through our healing process. They told us they would talk to their board about it and let us know. Not long afterward, the woman called and gave us her answer: "I'm afraid not. I'm afraid it might hurt the ministry to have you all here."

Ted disconnected the call and crumbled before my eyes. "I have ruined *everything*," he said, his voice breaking. "I have destroyed everything I invested my life in."

Praise Mountain had been Ted's vision. He had led the way in developing the place, and he'd used it often for his own times of prayer and fasting. Even after the church sold the property, Ted had continued to promote and fund the facility.

I was disappointed too. Was anyone going to have compassion on my husband?

Our next idea was Fort Collins, a three-hour drive north of Colorado Springs yet still close enough for our boys to see their friends . . . and for any of our remaining friends to see us. We had talked about going back to school and thought perhaps we could attend classes at Colorado State University, so we drove up there to check out the area. We found a house we thought we could afford close to the high school and made arrangements to come back and see it the next day.

On our way home from Fort Collins, we received a call from one of the overseers, asking if they could come to our house that evening to present us with several documents. When the group arrived, we welcomed three of the four overseers and one of the restorers who'd been with us at the meeting in Los Angeles. We hugged them, and I ushered everyone into the cozy sitting area around the family room fireplace.

When everyone had been seated, one of the overseers cleared his throat. He began by assuring us of their love for us and their desire to do what was best for us and New Life Church. "I'm going to read you a letter," he said, "and I want you to feel the love in it."

Ted and I settled in to listen, expecting to hear a summation of what we'd discussed with the restoration team the previous week. Ted had done what they asked, typing up and e-mailing the revised document to each of the restorers, but we hadn't yet heard a response.

The overseer began to read a letter brimming with words of Christian concern, but it was the most devastating piece of correspondence I had ever received—ripping my family away from everything we'd held dear for twenty-two years.

"Our group of seven godly men," the overseer read, "feels it is in your best interest and the best interest of New Life for you to permanently depart from this area. . . . We do not feel your family can remain anywhere in the geographical region of New Life Church and the church heal without distraction. We also feel that a measured approach to local church restoration here over the next year or two could prove as harmful to you and your family as it could to individuals in the church. . . . Our recommendation, therefore, is that the two of you ask the Lord who is the pastor and local church you will relocate to that is totally outside the state of Colorado. Make a clean break right now with the faithful New Life believers you love so dearly. . . . Prepare yourself for some form of livelihood in addition to the support from willing friends and partners that you will surely receive from those outside this church.

"You will, of course, feel the awful consequences of sin and yet the loving embraces of the larger body of Christ simultaneously. . . .

"Thirty days should suffice to select another area and church. Sixty days will be a good target for relocating. One hundred eighty days could possibly be enough to sell your home.

"We trust that this communicates to both of you our final thoughts on this matter and that God gives you grace to submit, surrender, and obey. Your family and the body of Christ at New Life will be blessed by that decision."[1]

I couldn't lift my eyes to look at the men I had greeted so warmly at my door. For the first time in my life, I felt bitterness seep into my heart, and I hated that feeling. I resisted it, determined not to let it take hold, but I could not believe the things I was hearing. The words the overseer had described as "full of love" felt more like daggers going into my heart. I couldn't believe that the overseers didn't understand what these actions would do to the church, to Ted, and to my family.

After reading the introductory letter, the men presented us

with a restoration agreement and two separation agreements—
one for Ted, one for me.

Ted's restoration agreement, which had been signed by the
four overseers and three restorers, required him to submit to a
process of spiritual restoration that would include obeying the
restorers' and overseers' instructions communicated "in writing, whether by mail, e-mail, or text messaging from any one of
us." We could speak freely with any one of the seven men. Ted
would have to present a written plan for pursuing a new career
no later than April 30. He would have to participate in mental-
health therapy, a twelve-step program, and "spiritual direction
as we direct."

Much like the original draft of the agreement we had seen in
Los Angeles during our initial meeting with the restorers, the final
document stipulated that Ted and I and our dependent children
would relocate permanently outside Colorado. Our relocation
should be completed within sixty days. We were not allowed on
New Life or World Prayer Center property. We could have no "discussion or communication with any Church employee, trustee,
or elder." Ted could not engage in any ministry whatsoever. He
would have to sign documents requesting that the religious bodies that had ordained him or licensed him revoke their ordination
and any license or certification they'd given him. Because a person
is ordained for life, the seven men who authored and signed this
plan clearly did not intend for Ted to ever be restored to pastoral
ministry of any kind.

The agreement went on to state that Ted must not "engage in
any sexual immorality" and should comply with the terms of the
sobriety contract he had completed with the counseling center.

Another clause stated that Ted could quit the restoration process
at any time, but doing so would entitle the restorers and overseers

to publicly state that the process had ended without achieving its objectives.

"Ted," a final paragraph read, "our restoration process with you will continue until we determine that you have been restored. After that period, you will be subject to the terms of your separation agreement with the church and to the spiritual direction of your pastor at that time."[2]

An official separation agreement, a seven-page contract, accompanied the letter. Ted blanched when he saw it. "Please," he asked, "can't you deal with me as a brother instead of putting all these legal contracts between us?"

His plea went unheard. "We've never done this," one of the overseers said, "and we really don't know *how* to do this. There's no guidebook. So this is what we feel is best for all concerned."

Although I didn't say it at the time, I couldn't help thinking that the Bible was certainly sufficient to serve as the guidebook for restoration. After all, it gives clear instructions on how to conduct church discipline (see Matthew 18:15-17) and how and when a repentant brother should be restored to fellowship (see 2 Corinthians 2:5-11). The Scriptures also include specific instructions about how to discipline an elder (which would also apply to a pastor) if and when he falls into sin (see 1 Timothy 5:19-20).

After reading the separation agreement, our attorney declared he would no longer represent us if Ted signed the document. "As your lawyer, I cannot allow you to sign this," he told us at a later meeting. "It's legally unenforceable. If you sign it, I'll resign. Yet, I understand what you are doing and will continue to be your friend."

He was right; the terms of that agreement were atrocious. But if we protested or refused to sign, the overseers could claim that Ted was being unrepentant and rebellious.

In the separation agreement, the church leaders cited Galatians

6:1-2, which says, "Dear brothers and sisters, if another believer is overcome by some sin, you who are godly should gently and humbly help that person back onto the right path. And be careful not to fall into the same temptation yourself. Share each other's burdens, and in this way obey the law of Christ," and 1 Peter 5:1-10, which reads in part, "In the same way, you younger men must accept the authority of the elders. And all of you, serve each other in humility, for 'God opposes the proud but favors the humble.' . . . So after you have suffered a little while, he will restore, support, and strengthen you, and he will place you on a firm foundation."[3]

These seven men had set themselves up as Ted's authorities, but as I read the terms of the separation agreement, I wondered how exile and silence would ever allow us to be restored to our friends at New Life. I kept thinking of 2 Corinthians 2:5-8: "I am not overstating it when I say that the man who caused all the trouble hurt all of you more than he hurt me. Most of you opposed him, and that was punishment enough. Now, however, it is time to forgive and comfort him. Otherwise he may be overcome by discouragement. So I urge you now to reaffirm your love for him."

Ted had already repented. He had found the probable source of his problem and was seeking counsel and treatment. So why were we being permanently exiled instead of forgiven and offered the possibility of relational restoration?

C. S. Lewis once wrote, "We all agree that forgiveness is a beautiful idea until we have to practice it."[4] Jesus told us to forgive. Forgiveness doesn't mean that we excuse the sin or ignore the pain of it but that we welcome the errant person back into fellowship. Ted didn't want to reassume his position as pastor; he had never expressed that desire. But both of us yearned to be comforted by the people we had always considered our family. I knew they were hurting, but so was Ted.

As painful as some clauses were, the separation agreement also contained generous provisions. The agreement stipulated that the church would pay our salaries through 2007 and premiums for medical insurance coverage for the same period. New Life would pay for Ted's legal counsel and for the counseling services provided in Phoenix. They would reimburse our moving expenses when we relocated. But payment of all those benefits would be dependent on our public silence and obedience to the overseers and restorers. Ted's payment was tied to the church's fiscal health. If New Life's undesignated tithes and offerings for any month fell below 80 percent of the average amount, Ted's monthly severance payments would be reduced accordingly. For instance, if the church's income for a given month was 25 percent below average, our payments would be reduced by 25 percent.

The church offered to pay for professional counseling for our children and me. They agreed to contribute a monthly allowance toward the care of our son Jonathan. Other friends helped make up the difference.

The church also gave us the computer, cell phone, and truck Ted had been using in the ministry. Because neither of us had stepped onto the church property since November 1 (except for one night immediately following the crisis when Ted went to the World Prayer Center in the middle of the night to walk around the outside of the building and pray), someone gathered our personal belongings from our offices, boxed them up, and delivered them to a storage shed behind our home.

We were grateful for the generous financial aspects of the agreement even though we were concerned that our income might be unpredictable. But in the early days of the church we'd lived on little, so we knew we could do it again if necessary.

Other conditions of the separation agreements, however, gave us pause. The contracts prohibited both Ted and me from ever writing about our work or ministry at New Life Church. The terms also prohibited us from talking to the press about the events that led to Ted's removal as pastor. Furthermore, neither we, nor our "agents, designees, or attorneys should have any discussion with the press on any topic for three years."[5]

The agreement contained other clauses about nondisclosure, arbitration, confidentiality, the term (perpetuity!), enforcement, and contingency. We would not be allowed to discuss or admit the existence of these contracts, yet we read how others had publicly discussed them with members of the press.

When the overseers had reviewed all the contract details, I looked at the one restorer who was present. All of the overly restrictive clauses the restoration team had struck last week had reappeared, with none of the changes they had discussed with us.

He cleared his throat. "I know this appears disingenuous after our meetings last week."

I wanted to say, "Yes, it does," but I bit my tongue. What good would it do to speak up? Apparently the restorers had met with the overseers and had been overruled. They would be restorers in name only, because apparently someone else was calling the shots.

All this time, we had not been allowed to say a word. None of these men had even mentioned the church leaders' list of accusations or asked Ted which sins he had actually committed. While we were at the counseling center, the overseers had delivered the list to the counselor, and he had read it to us. To two-thirds of the charges, Ted had responded, "I did not do that." He had taken lie detector tests, he'd passed every one of them, and those results had been forwarded to the overseers. But they had never responded. And after reading the separation agreements, I was convinced they believed every horrible accusation and rumor that had been brought against Ted—and more—even though most of them were unsubstantiated.

"It doesn't matter," Ted had told me earlier. "They believe I'm a deceiver and a liar, so nothing I say matters. They don't trust me."

But I trusted Ted. After the plane ride to Florida, our truth-telling time in Captiva, and our rigorous counseling sessions in Phoenix, I trusted him unreservedly. I had glimpsed his soul; I had heard his prayers and held him while he wept. He had been so thoroughly broken and had lost almost everything. Why would he lie now?

Besides, what difference would it make to Ted's spiritual condition if every accusation and rumor *were* true? Ted had admitted he was in trouble and that sin had gripped him. But at what point does the gospel no longer apply? At what point is forgiveness beyond reach? At what point is restoration no longer possible?

A friend later put it this way: "Gayle, even if every horrible thing that has been said about Ted were true, *so what?* Those sins do not exclude him from God's grace."

I believe that, even though I am personally glad to know he did not commit all the sins he was accused of committing.

As we sat with those men in our family room, Ted's words replayed in my memory, and I realized he was right. Despite Western civilization's highly developed systems of due process and fair hearings in order to determine guilt or innocence, those systems and the biblical admonitions for proper communication were being ignored.

Ted had been walking in freedom from his sin since a month before our crisis, and the crisis had sealed his repentance and obedience. Yet this group kept insisting he was neither obedient nor repentant. If he protested their decisions, they treated him as if he were rebellious, angry, and manipulative, and they disregarded his views.

We had entered a battle we could not win with words. We knew other people hated what was happening to us, but they'd been told it wasn't godly to speak against their spiritual authorities. So they responded with deafening silence. No one stepped up to report that Ted had never been a hateful preacher or antigay. No one held a press conference to dispute the "three-year affair." While the press flayed us, the church leaders amputated us, and our friends in the church, who had to have been confused by all this, obediently remained silent.

As far as I could tell, the "restoration plan" consisted only of a series of steps to permanently sever us from New Life Church. If they wanted to cut us out of the New Life community, this was a solid step in that direction. They might even turn people's hearts away from us. But they could never erase us from people's memories, and that fact gave me hope.

As long as people remembered us, maybe we would eventually see some semblance of mercy.

With heavy hearts, we signed the restoration and separation agreements, and Ted signed letters that the overseers would send to the two ecclesiastical bodies that had ordained him. One group did revoke Ted's ordination, but the other party, a Southern Baptist pastor who had licensed and ordained Ted, refused to revoke his ordination. We were cheered by this bit of encouraging news because it proved that one person, at least, did not consider Ted unfit for future ministry. That pastor's courageous refusal gave us hope that God wasn't finished with us yet.

I write these things not because I want to disparage or embarrass anyone but because I want to explain why we remained silent for so long. We desperately wanted to speak to our loved ones at New Life Church. Ted wanted to apologize personally for the hurt he had caused, and we wanted to listen as others poured out their feelings. We wanted to answer their questions, but we were not allowed to speak to anyone or to step onto church property.

I worried that people at the church thought we were purposely remaining aloof or that Ted was caught up in rebellion and that's why he stayed away. I was afraid that people would interpret his silence as apathy or indifference, when nothing could have been further from the truth.

"As long as there is even one person in the leadership or membership who is offended by the thought of you[r] rejoining the ranks of the church, now or in the future," the chief overseer wrote in his letter, "we would err to force that issue."[6]

So . . . as long as one person in the congregation refused to forgive, we would be banished? The apostle Paul did not write, "Now it is time to forgive and comfort a repentant brother *unless someone is still so offended that he simply cannot forgive.*"

On Sunday, February 18, 2007, New Life declared a "day of hope." The board of overseers came to town to address the church and assure them that our family was under the loving care of the restorers.

To announce the special Sunday service, the acting pastor sent an e-mail to church attenders and told them that our family would relocate. Another pastor was quoted in the local paper as saying, "The process of restoration that's begun and the work that the overseers have begun with Ted has honestly been redefining the relationship between Ted and New Life Church. Make no mistake—we will never sever ties. The Haggards will always be part of the New Life family. We are committed to loving them, to praying for them, and to walking through this difficult transition together."[7]

During the service, one of the overseers stood on the platform to address the congregation: "Concerning Ted and his family, we have done extensive fact-finding into his lifelong battle with a 'dark side,' which he said in his confession letter has been a struggle for years. We have verified the reality of that struggle through numerous individuals who reported to us firsthand knowledge of everything from sordid conversations to overt suggestions to improper activities to improper relationships. These findings established a pattern of behavior that culminated in the final relationship in which Ted was, as a matter of grace, caught."[8]

I wish someone had discussed those "findings" with Ted, because that person would then have learned the truth: that Ted had denied most of the charges, that multiple polygraphs had verified his truthfulness, and that his counselor had dismissed the allegations as invalid.

I'm reminded of Proverbs 18:17: "The first to speak in court sounds right—until the cross-examination begins."

It is not an enemy who taunts me—
I could bear that.
It is not my foes who so
     arrogantly insult me—
I could have hidden from them.
Instead, it is you—my equal,
my companion and close friend.
What good fellowship we once enjoyed
as we walked together to
     the house of God.

PSALM 55:12-14

14

BECAUSE THE OVERSEERS hadn't specifically said that the boys couldn't come to church, and because my kids loved New Life and loved seeing their friends there, I drove the boys to youth meetings and dropped them off on the road outside the parking lot to remain in compliance with the contracts. After doing that a couple of times, I realized how ridiculous it was, so I actually drove into the parking lot and dropped the boys off at the entrance to the building. If anyone saw me, I'd wave and mouth, "Doesn't anybody else think this is ridiculous?"

In those freezing winter months when our hearts felt cold and empty, Ted would often go out to the barn to pray. He had a small heater out there, so he'd turn it on, settle in, and let God speak to him. Sometimes he would trudge up and down our driveway in the snow, praying. Those bitterly cold weeks were extremely dark and difficult for him, but he never stopped seeking God's will.

From time to time we would lie back on the bed and hold each other. Ted would say, "Let's remember what God has told us." We'd go back and forth—he'd recite Scripture or repeat something he'd felt the Lord had spoken to his heart, and then I'd recite a verse or share something I'd felt the Lord had spoken to me. That little exercise encouraged us and warmed our hearts during those cold months of exile.

I've sprinkled some of my favorite Scripture verses throughout this book. Another passage we particularly identified with was this one:

Hear my prayer, O LORD;
> *listen to my plea!*
> *Answer me because you are faithful and righteous.*
Don't put your servant on trial,
> *for no one is innocent before you.*
My enemy has chased me.
>> *He has knocked me to the ground*
>> *and forces me to live in darkness like those in the grave.*
I am losing all hope;
> *I am paralyzed with fear.*
I remember the days of old.
> *I ponder all your great works*
> *and think about what you have done.*
I lift my hands to you in prayer.
> *I thirst for you as parched land thirsts for rain.*
Come quickly, LORD, and answer me,
> *for my depression deepens.*
Don't turn away from me,
> *or I will die.*

PSALM 143:1-7

As we read Scripture together, we noticed things that had slipped past us on previous occasions. I've always enjoyed reading the Psalms, but for the first time I found myself underlining all the verses about having enemies and about being overcome with sorrow and crying out to the Lord in my distress.

As we read an account of Jesus' crucifixion, Ted pointed out a detail regarding the two thieves dying on the crosses next to Jesus. They were criminals, beaten and naked, and they hung before the onlookers in excruciating pain. Then Ted read the biblical account of what happened next: "It was the day of preparation, and the Jewish leaders didn't want the bodies hanging there the next day, which was the Sabbath. . . . So they asked Pilate to hasten their deaths by ordering that their legs be broken. Then their bodies could be taken down" (John 19:31).

When Ted lowered his Bible, he didn't need to explain what he was thinking. Two guilty men were dying in one of the most torturous executions imaginable. They were in unspeakable agony, but then the religious leaders came along and requested that their agony be *increased*—in order to avoid defiling the observance of the Sabbath. With their legs broken by a soldier's cudgel, the crucified men would be unable to pull themselves up for deep breaths, and they would soon suffocate.

I closed my eyes in silent understanding. I knew that Ted identified with those criminals, because he had been rightly declared guilty and he had accepted the consequences of his sin. But as he endured the myriad consequences—embarrassment, shame, public humiliation, the loss of his job, the destruction of trust in our marriage—it felt as though Ted's agony was being increased by excommunication and exile.

Ted and I sat quietly as reality descended on us. "If this weren't twenty-first century America," he said, "I think they would have burned me at the stake."

I reached for his hand and held it, offering what little consolation I could give.

In March, one of the New Life Church leaders called us. He hadn't spoken to us in months, so though we were happy to hear from him, our emotions were confused. In the course of the conversation, Ted asked why I couldn't come back onto New Life property. After all, I hadn't been involved in Ted's sin, so why couldn't I worship with the church I loved?

A week later, this church leader called us back on a Saturday night. He had talked to the senior staff, and they had said it would be fine for me to come to church the next morning.

Ted and I were sitting in the living room when the call came. When Ted looked at me and repeated what he'd just been told, I jumped out of my chair and started praising God and dancing around the living room. For the first time in months, my spirit lifted in absolute joy.

I called my daughter and asked her to go to church with me. Then I called one of my good friends and asked if we could sit together. What a blessing! I was excited beyond words and felt this was a significant step toward restoration. Even if I didn't say a word to a single soul, even if all I did was sit in the congregation, people would see me and know I was still the same person, I was okay, and we were healing. They'd know we were making progress and that we hadn't abandoned our faith or deserted them.

When the pastor who called told Ted that a church member who heads a well-known international ministry would be speaking in the worship service, Ted thought it would be a good idea to text the man and let him know I'd be in the service. "I don't want you to be caught off guard if you see Gayle," Ted wrote. "Such a beautiful picture of the gospel."

The man who would be speaking didn't respond to Ted's text, but within thirty minutes we received a long-distance call from one of the four overseers.

"You guys had better not try anything like this again," the man told Ted. "Stop scheming and trying to come up with ways to get back in the church."

"Wait a minute." Ted rose to my defense. "There's nothing in those documents to prevent Gayle from going to church at New Life."

"Then consider it added."

I stared at Ted as my excitement sputtered like a deflating balloon. "I should have known not to get my hopes up."

Ted shook his head and lowered the phone. "I'm sorry, honey."

The next day, my friend called me, upset. She told me that the speaker had preached a sermon on honoring the women in the church and how terrible it was that women at New Life hadn't been treated respectfully under the previous leadership. Yet this man had obviously called one of the overseers after receiving Ted's text, and the overseer had denied me permission to worship at the church I had helped to birth in our basement.

I felt as if history were being rewritten—that my work to bring honor and value to the women of New Life was being mischaracterized and that the people who had publicly lauded our work only months earlier were now working to remove any remaining traces of respect for the church's founders.

According to the original agreement Ted set up with the

overseers when he established their role, their authority over Ted ended when he resigned his position as senior pastor. After our crisis, he asked them to help him as friends and brothers in Christ, and he submitted to their authority as one brother submits to another. Once they assumed spiritual leadership of New Life Church (in a development that is still unclear to us), we continued to submit to them in order to demonstrate our cooperation with the restoration process.

But spiritual authority is not license for punitive actions. Proper spiritual authority, according to Paul, builds up; it doesn't tear down (see 2 Corinthians 10:8; 13:10).

Albert Einstein once said, "Unthinking respect for authority is the greatest enemy of truth." I *do* believe in obeying church authority, but when church authorities diverge from biblical practice, they should not be obeyed unquestioningly.

I firmly hold to the "priesthood of the believer," the doctrine that states that all believers have equal access to God. Believers can always go to the Bible and search for truth. They can pray and seek guidance from the Holy Spirit. They can wait on the Lord and trust that he will reveal his will at the proper time.

I love what John Piper says on the subject: "The ministry of the church does not belong to the elders; it belongs to the body, the flock, the saints, the believers. Overseers exist to equip and to protect and to guide; but all of this is done to liberate and empower . . . the priesthood of the believers."[1]

Ted and I said nothing about this heartbreaking incident. Because God had not shown us any other plan and Ted was still grieving over the loss his sin had caused, we decided to continue to quietly do our best to observe the terms of the separation agreement. I think a part of Ted felt that he deserved cruel treatment as a natural consequence of his sin—even though he hated the pain it caused me and even though pain and punishment are not part of the Bible's prescription for a repentant sinner.

In my deepest heart, though, I knew God had seen me dancing, and he knew my intentions were wholly honorable. I saw my attendance at church as an opportunity to worship and to help people heal.

I could only hope that God had taken pleasure in my momentary joy.

March was surrendering to spring when the four executive staff members to whom Ted had confessed visited our home. We were starving for the companionship of our beloved friends, and we had seen only one of these brothers on a few scattered occasions since our crisis erupted five months earlier. These men had been among Ted's inner circle. He had spent untold hours with them at the church, in executive meetings, and on trips to events away from home. They were so close that he called them to his side on that Thursday morning when he realized that his role in the ministry of New Life Church was about to vanish. They were the executive team with whom he'd wept as he gave his confession.

So I was overjoyed when they agreed to come to the house, even though they set stipulations on the visit. They would come, but they would only come together. They would come, but they would stay only two hours.

When we awoke that morning, Ted sat on the edge of the bed and told me he had a feeling it was going to be a bad day. From personal experience, I knew how grief landed a person on an emotional roller coaster: One day you're up, and the next you're bottoming out in despair. In those early days, I had very little control over my surging emotions, and sometimes all I could do was hang on, try to maintain my sense of balance, and pray for the ride to come to an end.

Ted wanted to ask if the guys could come another day. "I'm feeling really low," he told me. "I'm afraid my emotions will get away from me and I'll say something I'll regret." He called one of the men and tried to postpone their visit, but no, they had set their schedules and could come only at the appointed time. And only for two hours.

So we braced ourselves, and I hoped their presence would somehow lift Ted's spirits. Maybe they'd talk, and maybe this meeting would spread a balm of healing over these men who had once been closer than brothers. I began to pray, and the Lord filled my heart with a sense of peace. I had no doubt I could greet them with a smile and sincere affection.

When the doorbell rang, Ted and I looked at each other as a flood of unspoken anxiety and hope passed between us. I squeezed his hand, and we walked together to the front door. I greeted each of the guys with a hug, and so did Ted. Joy flooded my heart when I saw them, and the love I'd had for each of them warmed my spirit. We all moved into the family room and sat by the woodstove, the cozy spot where we had spent many hours laughing and talking. I sat in a chair next to Ted as the men looked to him for guidance, just as they had only a few months before.

As silence sifted down like snow, I remembered that two weeks before the crisis broke, these men had joined Ted on the platform at a men's retreat, where they participated in a forum on friendship. Perched on stools, they had each talked about the importance of being present in a friend's darkest hour. They'd testified to their deep friendship with each other.

Now that circle of friends had reassembled in our home. I was eager to see those abiding friendships in action.

Ted took a deep breath and attempted a smile. "I've learned that everybody has a story in this," he said, his voice wavering, "and I'd like you all to share some of your story. I'm ready to listen."

I was ready, too, and I waited, my heart full of hope, as I studied their faces. These guys had gathered in my family room more times than I could count. I knew their wives; I had attended some of their weddings. I had held their babies, visited them in their homes, laughed with them during backyard barbecues. A few months ago I had considered them part of my family . . . and wished I could talk with my husband as honestly and freely as they did.

I waited, holding my breath, and wondered who would speak first. Whoever it was, would he berate Ted? Would he comfort him? confront him? scold him? yell at him? accuse him? Whatever these guys wanted to do, Ted was ready and willing to hear them out.

But no one said a word.

Apparently they had come expecting something from Ted. No doubt they were hurting, but Ted had heard almost nothing from them in almost five months. They'd had many opportunities to talk among themselves and had probably agreed on what they felt they needed to hear from Ted, but they didn't tell us what that was. They simply sat, silently, waiting for Ted to deliver—what? More apologies? Ted thought he had apologized to them. He wanted them to talk to him. He was hurting too.

"Okay," Ted finally said, "then I'll start. I'll tell you what it's felt like to be me in this. I've felt like I've been abandoned."

Before he could continue, a storm erupted. These same men who had been mute a moment earlier suddenly had plenty to share.

"That's what we thought you'd say," one of them said. "It's always about you, isn't it?"

Their voices rose, cruel and harsh, and I blinked, stunned by the sudden outburst. I shook my head in disbelief—this was truly heartrending. In their eyes, Ted couldn't say anything right. He had apologized; he had repented; he had gone to counseling and was committed to continuing his therapy—what more did they want him to do, brand a scarlet letter on his chest?

Then one of them spoke up and said that he and Ted hadn't really been friends, that Ted hadn't hung out at his house like a real friend (even though he knew Ted's schedule and had spent plenty of time at our house). Another said that he and Ted hadn't "felt like friends for a long time." The others agreed. I listened in disbelief, realizing that these men, whom Ted had regarded as his close friends, were distancing themselves from Ted and in essence were saying, *We never really knew you.*

But they *had* known him, and Ted had served them as they had served him. And now they were seeing Ted as a stranger, instead of as a friend with a problem.

In hindsight, I can see that these men may have needed for Ted to personally apologize again for the hurt he had caused them. They obviously were not ready to hear him share his personal feelings of abandonment. He had mistakenly assumed that his repentance and numerous prior apologies, both public and private, were known and had been accepted by these guys.

At that point, I could no longer keep quiet. "On another note," I said, breaking into the tense silence, "I want to know something from you guys: Are you all okay with the way *I* have been treated in all this?"

I looked again at those four men—one was part of my extended family, two had lived with us for a while, three had gone with us on vacation, and all of them had worked alongside us and developed deep, trusting relationships with both Ted and me. They were like brothers to me, too. But again, all four were struck speechless.

Finally, one man who had been an especially close friend said that I was being treated in the same way as Ted because "it's always been you and Ted at the top, Gayle."

Bittersweet understanding dawned in my heart as I stared at him. Me and Ted at the top? Part of the ongoing struggle in my marriage had always been that these guys and others on our staff loved Ted so much that I felt an unspoken competition to be his closest friend. I had always felt pushed out of the tight circle of relationship. I had poured myself into the women's ministry because I'd felt I had no role at Ted's right hand.

But suddenly the circle had opened wide, leaving me alone by Ted's side. I had inherited the cherished position of my husband's best friend.

With startling clarity, I realized that I now possessed the very thing I had desired with my whole being. I would pay for it with every drop of my heart's blood . . . and I would cherish it with my life.

In that moment, I began to see God's purpose.

Even after this meeting, Ted would continue to send letters, e-mails, and text messages asking these men and others on our staff for their forgiveness. One particularly heartfelt letter he sent received a reply of "We are just not ready yet." A series of text messages sent more than a year after the crisis revealed that one man couldn't forgive because he didn't know if Ted was truly repentant. After all I'd been through and had witnessed in Ted, I couldn't believe what I was reading. This man had been present when Ted confessed with tears and brokenness. How could he judge the condition of Ted's heart? He was so far away and barely communicated with us, so how could he judge Ted's sincerity? He knew nothing of our process. Besides, who among us is in any position to judge another person's heart? According to the

Bible, only God can do this. What God tells us to do is forgive each other.

Only a week after our crisis broke, Ted had desperately wanted to communicate with the people from the church who'd been closest to him. Our trustees were all older, respectable, capable men whom Ted had handpicked to help him make corporate decisions for the church. Because he felt responsible for the painfully awkward position he had put them in, he had written them a letter in which he apologized for his sin and how it had affected them. He had asked for their forgiveness.

Because he'd been forbidden to contact the trustees directly, he had sent his letter to the overseers and asked them to forward it to the trustees. The overseers denied his request, saying they didn't feel the timing was right for Ted to send a letter.

Is there ever a *wrong* time to ask forgiveness?

Ted has said that he is grateful his struggle was against a visible sin. He could repent of an outward behavior. But what about those who sin by being high-minded, arrogant, and self-righteous? Many people are blind to those sins even as they commit them, because they feel justified in their judgments against others. But God looks at the heart. He sees the sinful thoughts arising from those dark places.

The Bible says, "The human heart is the most deceitful of all things, and desperately wicked. Who really knows how bad it is? But I, the LORD, search all hearts and examine secret motives" (Jeremiah 17:9-10).

One day, I overheard Ted's half of a phone conversation. The man on the other end of the line must have been berating Ted, because after a moment Ted said, "I feel like I am the unworthy sinner begging for God's mercy and forgiveness and you are the righteous religious leader."

Ted listened a moment more, then hung up.

I looked at Ted. "What'd he say?"

"When?"

"After you told him you felt like the unworthy sinner while he was the righteous religious leader."

"Oh." Ted shook his head as a sad smile crossed his face. "He thanked me."

As Christians, we are called to forgive. I don't understand the mind-set that says we can, on our own timetable, decide whether or not to offer forgiveness. Jesus makes it clear: "If you refuse to forgive others, your Father will not forgive your sins" (Matthew 6:15).

Before the four executive staff members left, our daughter Christy arrived at the house. She walked through the kitchen and stood in the doorway to the family room, taking everything in. Then she stepped forward.

"Before you all leave, I want to say something to you," she said. "You've been like uncles to me, and I'm so ashamed of how you've treated my parents in this process. All these years I've watched my mom and dad take care of you and work on your behalf. But a few weeks ago, when my parents were out of town and I was alone in my apartment, I had a lot of physical pain and felt like I was about to pass out. I needed help. But because of your response to my mom and dad, I didn't have the confidence to call you. So I called an ambulance to take me to the hospital. I had no one else . . . and I've never felt so alone."

She looked around the room at each man before she continued. "I want you to know that I've watched my dad go through this, and I believe he is still the most godly man I know."

I lifted my chin, forced a smile, and walked my guests to the front door. Their two hours had come and gone.

A short while after the four staff members left, two of the overseers stopped by the house. They'd come to town to check on the situation at the church and to check in with us.

I left one of them in the living room with Christy while I went into the kitchen to prepare lunch. Because she and Marcus would not be going with us when we moved out of state, Christy sat across from the overseer and poured out her heart, begging him not to separate our family, but to let us stay and heal with each other and with the church. She wasn't able to move him.

When she had finished, the man joined the rest of us in the dining room and mentioned what an intelligent young woman Christy was . . . but he never said a word about what she'd asked.

Meanwhile, Ted had been pouring out his heart to the other overseer. Ted pleaded with him, begging him not to make us move out of state; but the man only tinkered with his watch throughout the conversation, refusing to respond to Ted's reasoning.

Elliott, our youngest, also visited one of the overseers and begged him not to make us leave town. "Please don't make my family move," he said. "I'll have to leave my friends. I don't know anyone in Phoenix."

Elliott's entreaties also went unanswered.

Later that evening, the same two overseers returned to our home. We welcomed them, I gave them steaming mugs of hot cocoa, and we sat around the fireplace in the living room. I was still praying that I'd exhibit peace and grace.

The head overseer looked at me and said, "Sister Gayle, there's so much more peace in you now than the last time I saw you." Clearly, he assumed I approved of the way things were going, but beneath my pleasant expression I was thinking, *I hope so. The last*

time you saw me was in early November, just days after I was devas-
tated by news of Ted's sin and our developing crisis.

He asked us to kneel around an ottoman in the living room to pray, and I watched Ted surrender to the request. We were both eager for prayer and some evidence of a biblical process.

When the prayer ended, I thanked the overseer for saying that I looked like I had more peace. "I'm doing as well as can be expected," I told him, "but I want you to know that I believe it's wrong for you to separate us from New Life. This is a bad decision you're making; we need to heal with the church."

He dismissed me with a smile and moved toward the door.

Throughout that difficult spring, God continued to bless Ted and me through our children.

A couple of years before our crisis, as Ted was driving home from visiting a member of our congregation in the hospital, he saw a for-sale sign in front of a one-hundred-year-old downtown church. When he called to inquire about it, he discovered that a local business was preparing to buy the building, gut it, and turn it into a wall-climbing facility.

Ted was disturbed to think that a historic church building, in which people had prayed for years, was being sold to a local business. Those walls had heard so many prayers and witnessed hundreds of baptisms, weddings, and funerals. So Ted told New Life about the building, and many members made contributions so the church could buy it outright.

Once New Life owned the downtown church building, Ted thought it would be a perfect place for one of our young pastors to spread his wings and minister in that part of town. But when he offered it to the other New Life staff members, no one wanted to move downtown. The men didn't mind going down there to preach, but they all wanted to keep their offices at New Life, the main hub of activity.

Ted was a little disappointed. He had sincerely hoped someone would be willing to serve the people in that part of our city.

One afternoon, when Ted and I were talking in our bedroom, our son Marcus knocked on the door. At the time, he was a student at Colorado College, which was located only a few blocks from the newly acquired building. Marcus said, "Dad, I'd like for you to consider choosing me to be the pastor for the downtown church. I could move into the parsonage beside it and gather some of my friends and start meeting the people. We could start having services as soon as we get it cleaned up."

I was shocked. Marcus, twenty-one years old at the time, was majoring in international political economics, and we thought he was planning to spend his life encouraging economic growth in impoverished areas of the world. He had never preached a sermon in his life.

But if God was leading him to work downtown, who were we to discourage him?

He proved to be the man who would be willing to move into that neighborhood and invest himself in serving the people and building the church. The first Sunday he spoke, I sat in a pew and was deeply moved by his message. I was amazed at what a good speaker he was—he must have picked up a few things in all those years of watching his dad preach. Marcus's thoughtful and pragmatic message went right to the heart.

Because the church didn't have air-conditioning, they left the windows open during the services that first month. Everyone who lived close by could hear the worship music. Early on, Marcus went to visit an invalid who lived in the house closest to the church. She told him how beautiful the music had been and how much she had enjoyed listening to his sermons. She asked him to pray for her and said she wanted to become a follower of Jesus. She was his first convert after he became a pastor. A few weeks later, Marcus officiated at her funeral, his first as a pastor.

I was so proud of him. Soon people from all over the downtown area began to attend what Marcus called Boulder Street Church.

After our crisis, Marcus continued to pastor Boulder Street Church. He led his church through a beautiful healing process. Because the overseers did not permit Ted or me to attend any New Life services or small groups, we were unable to attend Marcus's church. However, my fiftieth birthday fell on Easter the year after our crisis, and I asked the overseers to please let me hear Marcus preach that day. They listened to my plea as a mother and gave us special permission to attend Boulder Street Church on that one occasion.

Marcus cried when he pointed me out to honor me on my birthday, and I felt tears well in my own eyes. Marcus was one of my precious gifts from God, and I was so proud of him.

The church welcomed us warmly and communicated how much they wished Ted and I could attend more often. Though young, Marcus had done a great job of leading his church in an understanding of the gospel.

Marcus resigned his position as pastor a year after our crisis. He decided it was time to go on to graduate school and leave Boulder Street Church in New Life's hands. New Life assigned a new pastor, and it continues as an independent church.

But I'll never forget that beautiful Easter morning when I watched my son lead his congregation and heard him preach . . . and remembered how richly God had blessed me.

❖

While we remained in Colorado trying to figure out how to sell our house, establish new careers, and relocate in sixty days, Ted told one of the overseers that he wanted to personally apologize to the man with whom he'd committed the indiscretion at Cripple Creek. This overseer had been particularly kind and thoughtful in his dealings with us and had demonstrated Christian love toward us. The overseer agreed to arrange a meeting, and Ted met the young man at our home. As the overseer, the man, and I sat in our living room, Ted apologized, with deep contrition and humility, for what he'd done and asked the man for his forgiveness.

The man brushed off the matter and said that Ted's apology was unnecessary; that of course he'd forgive Ted. "I knew that really wasn't you."

But Ted persisted. "I used you as a sounding board for my own sin," he said. "And that was wrong."

Then Ted took a basin of water, asked the man to sit down, and then washed the man's feet as the overseer and I watched. Afterward, we all prayed together, and the overseer made himself available to help the man work through his own issues.

Soon, however, this man began to call us. Whenever I saw his name on the caller ID, I took the call. We knew Ted could no longer serve as his mentor, so I encouraged him to find a counselor and get into therapy. A friend helped me find information on a successful ministry in New York, so I gave it to him, hoping he'd be able to go there for counseling. But still, time after time, he called the house, begging Ted to be his friend. I tried to explain that we were no longer in a position to help him and that he needed to go elsewhere for help.

I later learned that he did obtain counseling through New Life Church; but when the church stopped his counseling for some reason, he became upset and threatened to sue the church. He also told us that he'd saved incriminating text messages that Ted had sent during his troubled time in 2006. If we didn't talk to him, he'd give those messages to the press.

During one particular phone conversation in which he got through to Ted, he told Ted he was thinking about suing New Life. Ted asked, "Why would you do that?"

The man replied that he needed thirty thousand dollars to pay his school bills.

"Don't sue the church," Ted told him. "I'll try to help you."

But he didn't want Ted's help. Instead, he hired an attorney and formally threatened to sue New Life Church with exaggerated claims concerning his relationship with Ted. I heard about the pending lawsuit and spoke to him the next time he called: "Please don't do this."

He kept calling and threatening to further expose Ted. I was afraid he'd bring even more embarrassment and shame to our children. He kept calling and pleading, "I just want to be your friend. Please, can't I be your friend?" If I tried to hang up, he'd threaten to call the newspaper. He wore me down, leaving me so frazzled that I wanted to say, "I've had enough; don't do this to our children. Ted has apologized and you said you have forgiven him, so why are you still threatening us?"

I grew so weary of this man and the burden of his threats that I wondered if he existed only to inflict more pain on my family.

The church ended up settling out of court in 2007. An insurance company paid this man "compassionate assistance" of $179,000, with the stipulation that none of the parties involved discuss the matter publicly.[2] The story remained private until early in 2009, when Ted and I granted a series of interviews about the HBO documentary *The Trials of Ted Haggard.* Then the man came forward, and soon he was telling his story to anyone who would listen. The simple truth must have seemed lackluster, because I heard him tell Michelangelo Signorile, a radio host on the Sirius satellite network, a string of fabrications about Ted and me.

The interviewer asked whether I knew anything this man and Ted had talked about. The young man answered that Ted had told him that I was "a freak, too," and that I "would get high, too, with him," which is patently false. He then proceeded to embellish his story with colorful lies about my intimate relationship with Ted.[3]

In 2009, Larry King hit Ted with some of this man's charges during an interview on CNN.

"You know how we all dread seeing our sins revealed on Judgment Day?" Ted later said to me, half-joking. "Well, that's already happened to me. It happened on *Larry King Live.*"

I cry out to the LORD;

I plead for the LORD's mercy.

I pour out my complaints before him

and tell him all my troubles.

When I am overwhelmed,

you alone know the way I should turn.

Wherever I go,

my enemies have set traps for me.

I look for someone to come and help me,

but no one gives me a passing thought!

No one will help me;

no one cares a bit what happens to me.

Then I pray to you, O LORD.

I say, "You are my place of refuge.

You are all I really want in life."

PSALM 142:1-5

15

THROUGHOUT THE MONTHS of early spring, Ted and I wrestled with the inevitable: The overseers and restorers kept insisting that we leave the state within sixty days. If we wanted to submit to their discipline and restoration plan, we had to obey.

After Ted protested, the overseers removed the requirement that we sell our home within 180 days. I was grateful we wouldn't have to put the house on the market right away. Not only had the economy made it a tough time to sell, but I wasn't emotionally ready for a full move. The thought of packing up our memories overwhelmed me, and I wasn't ready for that kind of finality. Our home was a place of comfort and safety for our entire family. As long as we had a home in Colorado Springs, I felt that we had roots.

A few days before we left for Phoenix, the early morning men's prayer group from New Life knocked on our door in the gray light of breaking dawn. Ted and I answered the door in our bathrobes and ushered about twenty men into our family room. We didn't care about our early morning appearance; we were just so happy to see these men, some of whom we had known for many years. While Ted and I sat in the middle of this circle of friends, the men talked openly with us. Ted asked for their forgiveness, and they asked for Ted's, explaining that they felt they hadn't protected him enough. Then they washed our feet.

The warm water streamed over my bare feet into the basin, and I clasped my hands and bit back tears. *This* was an example of the loving concern and support we'd been missing.

After one of the men knelt and dried our feet, the men formed a circle around us, facing out as if they would battle the onrushing world on our behalf. With their arms locked in solidarity, they prayed for our protection. And as the warmth of their words chased away the chill from the damp morning, I remembered my heart's question from Captiva Island, and I felt God's Spirit whisper, *Here are the brothers.*

Those men will never know how deeply their words and actions touched us.

In those final days, four friends who had reconnected with us offered to help me pack what we'd need for our immediate relocation and get the house ready for our departure. Another friend offered to stay in the house until we made a decision about what we were going to do with it. We couldn't bear the thought of leaving it empty. It had always been so full of life, but Marcus and Sarah now had their own home, and Christy had her own apartment. Alex was going to stay with friends in order to complete his school year in Colorado Springs.

I think I found it hardest to leave Alex, even though we would only be separated for a month. He often plays the role of peace-maker in our family, and he's always been a source of strength to me. We share a similar sense of humor, so he can always lighten my burdens and make me laugh.

I hated that Alex had to go through this public crisis, especially during such a pivotal time as high school. We offered to pull him out and homeschool him for the remainder of the year, but he said as long as his friends from the church were going to school knowing that their pastor's crisis was being reported in the paper, he wouldn't feel right not being there with them. I was thankful the administrator of his high school demonstrated understanding and support, offering to give Alex all the time off he needed. In my opinion, Alex was a hero because he went to school with his head up and maintained his dignity while caring for his friends and comforting me. But the thought of leaving him for a month made my heart ache.

On April 18, 2007, Ted and I packed a U-Haul trailer and our truck and left Colorado Springs. We had already said good-bye to the other kids, and Alex came home from school to see us off. The only other person at the house as we pulled out of our driveway was a friend who had come by to help me clean. After twenty-two years of building relationships in the city, I found it incredibly sad that no one else showed up to say good-bye.

The hour of our departure was one of the darkest of my life. Ted and I felt unbearably alone as we drove through the gates, and we wept audibly as we pulled onto the highway. I glanced at the church through tear-filled eyes one last time as we stopped at the light near our home, but Ted couldn't bear to look in that direction.

Elliott rode in the backseat of the truck, and the pain he felt was visible on his face. He was inconsolable. He turned the air blue with cursing, venting every ounce of emotion and anger. I made no effort to reprimand him, because I understood how he felt. He was leaving his friends, his home, his brothers and sister, and the security of the only church he'd ever known. Like Christy, he had begged one of the overseers to let us stay. He felt safe with his friends. He needed their support. He was afraid of going to a strange place where he didn't know a soul but where everyone would likely see his family through the lens of our scandal and know nothing of our positive history.

After the tears stopped flowing, silence filled the truck, all of us lost in our sad thoughts as we rolled over the highway miles and headed south to Phoenix.

We had decided to settle in Arizona for several reasons. First, Tommy Barnett, one of the three men who had been chosen to restore us, pastored a church there, and we were trying to fulfill the terms of the separation agreement and remain in touch with him. Phoenix was also home to the University of Phoenix, and Ted and I had decided to return to school while we were still receiving our severance paychecks. We decided that I would finish my undergraduate degree in psychology while Ted worked on his master's degree. We thought the logical next career path for us might be in professional counseling, even though the restoration contract forbade this as a career choice. We were hoping that at some point that stipulation would be regarded as unreasonable and would be dropped. We thought that studying psychology and counseling would give us the opportunity to keep learning about our own situation and perhaps prepare us to help someone else in the future. We hoped to invest ourselves in something that would make sense of all we'd been through.

Finally, Phoenix had sunshine. Lots of blazing, searing sunshine. We hoped it would lift our spirits after a dark and dismal winter.

By the time we arrived in Phoenix, Ted and I felt like a pair of ragged limbs that had been torn from a body. Our emotions were raw, our thoughts clouded with sadness.

Once again, faithful friends stepped forward and provided a house for us to live in for a few months. They were away on a missions trip, and we were grateful for their generosity in offering us their beautiful home as we transitioned into life in Phoenix. The house was in a small gated community surrounded by a cinderblock wall. Ted and I were still apprehensive about being recognized in public, so we took comfort in the safety of this quiet neighborhood. Most of the other homes were empty because their owners had left for cooler climates before the arrival of the summer heat.

Elliott spent a lot of time in his room, playing games on a computer the owner of the house had provided for him, knowing he wouldn't have any friends in the area and Alex's arrival was still a month away. Occasionally, he joined Ted and me on our evening walks around the neighborhood. We walked after dinner, once the outside temperatures had cooled to below one hundred degrees. We enjoyed the casualness of wearing shorts and flip-flops as we spent lap after lap talking in the quiet of night.

We also discovered a golf course close by. Because none of us had ever golfed, one of the overseers urged us to take a few lessons. So, in temperatures above one hundred degrees, we ventured out on the course with our instructor, Ben, and tried to learn how to hold a club and perfect our swings. In those first few weeks, Ben was our only friend. We were grateful for his patience as we tried to summon up some enthusiasm for learning the game. We discovered later that he knew who we were, but he didn't let on. He just met with us lesson after lesson and encouraged us to have fun.

One evening, while Elliott played computer games in his room and Ted talked on the phone, I went into the living room and sank onto the sofa.

My mind drifted back to the cares I had been trying to avoid. I was thinking about our marriage when a new thought dawned on me—an idea I'd been too busy or preoccupied to consider in the last six months. I had always drawn security from Ted's faithfulness. His fidelity and loyalty had given me great confidence and stability. But I no longer had those things, did I? Ted had been unfaithful.

A creeping sadness darkened my thoughts. I was alone, sitting on another woman's sofa, living in another woman's house. I felt disassociated and unattached, as though I didn't belong anywhere.

Ted came into the room. He saw my expression and immediately asked what was wrong.

"I was thinking," I told him honestly, "about how much security I used to draw from my sense of your faithfulness. I don't have that anymore. So what am I supposed to do now?"

Ted sat next to me and propped his arm on the back of the sofa. He didn't speak for a moment, and I was glad he hesitated. I didn't want a glib answer or an automatic response.

I closed my eyes and listened to the sound of my breathing. I felt hollow, as if I were empty inside. Ted had lied to me and eroded the basis of my security. With loyalty and fidelity gone, I had to figure out how to start over, how to rebuild our relationship, and how to learn to trust my husband again.

"I'm groping for a foundation," I told him. "We need something to build on. If our foundation isn't faithfulness, what is it?"

"I'm sorry," Ted finally said. "And I'm sad that I've destroyed something so precious. I know I can't fix what I've done in the past, but I do want to fix things for our future. I don't want you to be afraid. I want you to trust me again."

I shifted to face him, pensively waiting to hear what he had to say. I knew Ted was worth my effort, and I knew our marriage was worth rebuilding. I had chosen to love him, but now I needed to discover *how*. "How do I do that?"

Ted lifted one shoulder in a shrug. "I can help. I can set up systems."

"What kind of systems?"

"For one thing, I won't go anywhere or do anything that makes you uncomfortable. And if I ever have the opportunity to travel again, I won't travel alone. From now on, I won't go anywhere without you, one of our children, or someone else you're comfortable with. You will always have free rein to look at my e-mails and text messages. You can ask me anything, and I will answer you truthfully. My goal is to make you feel safe. I want to earn your trust again."

I leaned back and studied him, measuring the commitment in his eyes. "You'd do all that?"

He nodded. "I'll do it for you. For your peace of mind."

As Ted promised what he would do for me in the future, I realized what I could do for him. For years I'd taught women who struggled in their marriages to take a new look at their husbands. In order to rebuild trust, they had to focus on the things they could trust *now*.

In that moment, I knew I could trust Ted's love for me.

I could trust that Ted and I were equally committed to making our marriage work.

I could trust Ted's sincere repentance.

I could trust Ted's great love for our children.

Since that day, Ted has come to me on several occasions and asked, "What can I do to make you feel safe?" That question, and the willingness behind it, have done a great deal to restore my trust in him.

Later, as I was reading the book *Fighting for Your Marriage*, I came across the following quote: "Trust builds slowly over time. Trust builds as you gain confidence in someone being there for you. Deep trust comes only from seeing that your partner is there for you over time. . . . The best thing that can happen is for a considerable amount of time to go by without a serious breach of trust."[1]

I knew I could trust Ted . . . one day at a time.

Not long after our arrival in Phoenix, our friends returned from their missions trip, and we left their home and moved into another house. Though we didn't know the owners of the new place, the arrangements were made through a mutual friend, the woman who was living in our home in Colorado Springs. We soon discovered why the homeowners had fled the state—because of the heat! The temperature outside rarely dropped below 100 the entire summer, and we endured a string of days where the mercury consistently hit 117 degrees.

Many evenings were too hot for a walk, so sometimes we got up at one or two in the morning and took a stroll on the golf course. Those are precious memories for me. We would lie down on a grassy hill and gaze up at the stars while we wondered what the future held for us. Sometimes Ted used that time to pray; but because I prefer mornings for prayer, I was content to simply lie beside him and listen as I stared up at the night sky.

One morning, the passage I happened to be reading was Jeremiah 29, which contains the prophet's letter to the Israelites who were in exile. One section practically jumped off the page as I read, "This is what the LORD says: 'You will be in Babylon for seventy years. But then I will come and do for you all the good things I have promised, and I will bring you home again. For I know the plans I have for you,' says the LORD. 'They are plans for good and not for disaster, to give you a future and a hope'" (Jeremiah 29:10-11).

I had heard this verse used many times as a passage for encouragement, but never had it been as meaningful as in that moment. I felt as if God were speaking directly to me. I was reminded of the night when I'd heard the Lord speak to me in my closet; when he had told me he had a purpose for what Ted and I were going through . . . and he kept telling Ted to watch him.

I felt a blanket of comfort settle over me. God hadn't forgotten us. He still had plans for us. All we had to do was wait and watch him work.

While we lived in Phoenix, we attended the church pastored by Tommy Barnett, one of our restorers. He and the congregation welcomed us with warmth and compassion, but I couldn't help but see the irony in our first service there, when the pastor taught on the forgiveness and reconciliation available to us when we fail.

At the conclusion of the service, Ted and I looked at each other, both thinking the same thing. The pastor had preached a great sermon on forgiveness and restoration, a message we believed, but those conditions thus far had eluded us. Why wasn't that lesson being applied to our situation?

The leader of the women's ministry, Pastor Tommy's daughter, invited me to come to the women's meetings. She had her father's warmth, and she offered her support. And while she encouraged me to come and enjoy the meetings, she also said that whenever I wanted to teach, lead a small group, or connect with her leadership team, she would love to facilitate that.

After that conversation, I decided I needed to get involved, so I went to a meeting and slipped into the back row, hoping to go unnoticed. As the women began to worship in music, tears began streaming down my face. Immediately I was overcome with memories of the women worshiping at New Life . . . and I realized how desperately I missed them.

Even though the women of the Phoenix church generously offered to let me help in their women's ministry, I knew I wasn't ready to commit to another program. But occasionally I would attend and simply listen—and I was always blessed. The meetings featured some of the most dynamic women's speakers I've ever heard; every time, I was struck by the depth and wisdom of their teaching. Yet I still wasn't ready to let go of what I had left behind. In other circumstances I would have enjoyed the welcome of these women and would have seen the value of jumping in and building new relationships, but these circumstances didn't seem right to me. I almost resented being forced to start over.

After Christmas, however, I decided to make another attempt at becoming a part of the women's ministry at the Phoenix church. The ladies were beginning a new Bible study, so I picked up a copy of the book to prepare for the class. As I read through the first chapter, one word spoke to me because it called to mind all the things God had done in my life. As I read it, I felt God speak into my spirit: *Remember.*

Since the crisis, I had only been able to focus on my sadness in being separated from New Life Church. But now I felt God leading me to remember every good experience, as well as the positive messages he had spoken into my heart in all my years there.

My mind flooded with memories. I remembered the vibrant feel of Sunday morning services—the halls and foyer brimming with happy people as they flooded into the auditorium. I remembered weaving through tables in the café between services and greeting people, some of whom would smile at me without speaking because they'd just taken a bite of a doughnut or bagel.

I remembered how the auditorium filled with the presence of God as we began to lift our voices in worship. I remembered how the young people would surge forward and crowd the area around the platform, greeting each other and joining in the songs of praise.

I remembered Ted's preaching. How he made people laugh. How he made so much sense. How he always gave us such intelligent and reasonable applications of Scripture. And how his words penetrated our hearts and we would feel the Holy Spirit revealing truths to our minds.

I remembered the New Life women's meetings and the sense of friendship and joy I had felt among those women. I remembered the eager faces of the young women as I taught them.

I remembered all the summer staff meetings in our backyard, the feel of the grass under my bare feet as we sat at tables on the lawn, and the taste of the Schwann's ice-cream sandwiches we always passed out for dessert. I remembered the playful bantering and the discussions about everything from deep theological questions to how to minister more effectively in our areas of influence. And laughter, lots of laughter. Our friends were smart and funny, delightful men and women.

I remembered the annual Day for Women we held at New Life and our luncheon tea. We'd assign volunteers to tables and give them the freedom to decorate their tables any way they wanted. When their guests arrived, they'd see a veritable feast for the eyes: Victorian tables, African tables, Christmas tables (in August!), and color-themed tables. We'd hear from a speaker or watch a movie together; and through it all, we'd bond as sisters.

I remembered attending productions of *The Thorn*, New Life's version of a passion play. Each year we presented the musical drama over the course of Easter week, nearly fifty thousand people would come to see it. I would go every night and be deeply moved by the production, because every night was like seeing it for the first time.

I remembered pool parties in our backyard, defending scores of screaming girls from the boys who wanted to throw them into the water, and riotous water basketball games between competing youth ministries.

I remembered baptismal services, when we'd rejoice at the public testimony of more than four hundred people who had come forward in an evening to be baptized as a symbol of their decisions to follow Christ.

I remembered standing down front with Ted after the service, talking to people who stopped by and lingering until the building had emptied. I remembered Ted's joy in being with people, and how they smiled at him in appreciation.

I remembered . . . and felt God comforting me.

Though I loved and appreciated the Phoenix church, it didn't feel like home. The members treated us with kindness, but we shared no common history. Yet I will forever sing the praises of those people, because they did what they could to make us feel welcome and loved.

Still, our church family—the people in whom we'd invested twenty-two years of prayers, tears, and joy—remained in Colorado Springs. We knew their strengths and their weaknesses, many of their secrets, and most of their dreams. New Life was a lively and unique congregation, and one of the things I loved most about our church was our people's rich compassion and mercy. People recognized that we are all on a journey toward maturity in Christ. Ted and I yearned to heal among our church family. Worshiping

in Phoenix, as pleasant and reassuring as it was, felt a bit like opening presents with someone else's family on Christmas morning.
Lovely, yes; home, no.

I don't want to sound ungrateful for the kindness we were
shown, but everything about Phoenix just felt wrong. Our hearts
remained in Colorado.

Our crisis and its aftermath deepened me in ways I never expected.
Prior to that awful day in November 2006, I usually felt that the
lines of communication between God and me were always open.
I was keenly aware of God's presence, and I often felt him prompt
me and speak to my heart.

But those feelings faded as I worked through my emotions
and struggled to come to terms with what had happened. I never
stopped praying or studying the Bible—and I knew God was with
me no matter what I *felt*—but I began to question whether everything I believed about God and the church was really true.

During those empty, arid days, I looked around and saw darkness
everywhere—even in the hearts of people I loved. People now seemed
cruel; relationships and friendships I would have described as full of
life and light had become mean and suspicious. I could no longer see
anything that looked wholesome or good, and the absence of light
shocked me. I asked the age-old question: "Is anything good?"

Before the crisis, I had been an incurable optimist. I would
have described everything in life as good in one way or another.
Maybe I was a Pollyanna, but that's how I felt. After the crisis, I
found myself insisting that nothing and no one was good. I shifted
from optimist to pessimist with no hesitation in between.

That transformation first hit me in Florida, when Ted told me about the secrets in his past. I kept trying to imagine how this could have been going on with Ted while everything else seemed so wonderful.

After that revelation, everything I had previously considered good seemed to have a shadow cast over it. The church had been full of light and life, but now it seemed overshadowed by an atmosphere of fear, suspicion, and mistrust.

From the few friends who dared to call us, we learned that the open-door policy at New Life had been replaced with secretive, closed-door meetings. Programs that had once been lauded were being viewed through a dark lens of mistrust. Though, in his letter to New Life, Ted had described himself as a deceiver and a liar in regard to his private sin, people were now regarding his entire public ministry with skepticism and doubt.

Friends and leaders who had been joyful and loving around us were now angry, accusatory, and apprehensive. Cooperating with the new mode of operation, they turned innocent comments and programs into targets of suspicion.

The media and bloggers were painting word pictures of us and our church in dark, foreboding colors.

The emotions that warred in my spirit, even after I forgave Ted and decided to stick by him, seemed to have more evil intent than good. I agreed with the psalmist: "No one does good, not a single one!" (Psalm 53:3).

Worst of all, I had always told our children that life was good and the future full of promise. I had dozens of wonderful lessons and concepts to share with my children, but I didn't trust those things anymore.

The bottom had fallen out of my world.

I felt as though everything I had done and everything I believed were under attack and no one was defending me. I wasn't angry with God, but I kept wondering, *Have I been wrong all this time?* I could easily shake off my doubts and talk myself back into my faith, but in those hours I realized that I didn't know as much about God as I thought I did. I could quote Scripture—I'd read it all my adult life, and I'd taught thousands of women—and still, everything on earth seemed disappointing to me. I wondered whether I had spent years being wrong about how good life and people were and if all goodness was really reserved for heaven.

But whenever I experienced seasons of doubt, eventually I would remember how God had spoken to me in my closet. How he had comforted me with his words and his presence. How the only light I could find, the only hope, I found while reading his Word, the Bible. Then I would remember the many miraculous encounters I've had with God's Spirit throughout my life and the discoveries Ted and I were making as we read Bible passages that were coming to life for us as never before.

When I compared my memories with the alternative—life as mere happenstance, an accident dependent on what you make of it—I knew God was real. Life is so much more than mere existence. Faith lifts us above simple existence and gives us true meaning and purpose, *especially* in times of suffering.

I chose to believe—not as a result of blind faith, but because of the evidence I saw around me and within me. The magnificence of our vast universe speaks of God's glory, as does the minute atom. Countless historical records of people's experiences with God have been preserved in the Bible, and I had my own experiences to convince me that God is who he says he is.

Instead of making me lose my faith, my doubts compelled me to learn more. I yearned to fill the gaps in my knowledge so I would understand why I had doubted . . . and how I could reinforce my faith during tough times.

I had never been tested like this. I had heard that a person's faith grows deeper in times of trial, but my life had been relatively carefree until our crisis. I hadn't experienced that deeper growth. Not yet.

One morning in July 2007, I woke up in Phoenix and began to pray. I had begun to feel spiritually arid and wondered if my prayers were traveling any higher than the ceiling. But that morning, God surprised me. He spoke to my heart, and I fell silent, stunned to hear his inner voice after so many months of empty silence.

Do you trust me?

My response caught in my throat. "Yes—yes, of course I trust you."

Then trust me—it had to happen this way.

Eight months had passed since I'd heard the Lord promise to deliver Ted from the fowler's snare, the lion's mouth, and the fiery furnace. Now he was speaking to me again, and I still didn't understand exactly what he meant. I didn't know *what* "had to happen this way," but I rested in one affirmation: Despite everything, God knew what was going on in our lives, and he was directing our course.

I found confirmation of my conviction in Psalm 139:16: "You saw me before I was born. Every day of my life was recorded in your book. Every moment was laid out before a single day had passed."

Nothing we had experienced—no sin, no event, no emotion—could surprise God.

❖

My stomach churned in a strange combination of anticipation and anxiety when I enrolled in the psychology program at the

University of Phoenix. More than twenty-five years had passed since I last sat in a college classroom. Loneliness heightened my anxiety. Though Ted, Elliott, and now Alex were with me in Phoenix, beyond them I still felt friendless. Out of all my friends in Colorado Springs, only a few still kept in touch. Conversations with them tended to be awkward because I was never certain about what they knew, what they'd heard, or what they believed.

Ted and I felt completely cut off from Colorado Springs, and we didn't know if we'd ever go back home. But I was back to being an optimist, and I decided to look at my situation as a new adventure. I tried to give myself little pep talks. *We are entering a new phase in life*, I'd tell myself. *God has brought us to a crossroad and led us in a direction we never expected. So you might as well get focused, Gayle, and learn what you need to learn.*

What I needed to learn in the fall of 2007 was psychology.

Ted and I had received valuable information from the Phoenix counseling center, but we learned even more from our professors at the university. Soon after our arrival in Phoenix, Ted had enrolled in a graduate program for counseling, and I started my classes in August. We were both taking psychology, and we pored over our textbooks together. As we studied the various psychological theories and schools of thought, we discussed our own ideas. Understanding how the mind works helped us understand ourselves.

In one of our classes, we discussed the importance of never making a decision about a person without that person present. The guiding principle is "no decisions about us without us." We loved that—especially because we'd just come out of an experience where too many decisions about us were made without our participation. We knew how demeaning and dehumanizing it felt to be left out when others were making decisions about us without involving us in the process.

In one of my first classes, the professor asked each student to come to the front of the class and explain why he or she had chosen to study psychology. When it was my turn, my thoughts raced as I stood and walked to the front of the room. This would be the first time I'd spoken to a group of people since the crisis. Would I even be able to do it, or would I be too emotional?

I turned and faced the group, scanning my fellow students' faces. All of them were adults, but all were younger than I was. Still, I felt a connection with them, and as I began to speak, I discovered that I still felt passionate about people. I could do this.

"The first fifty years of my life were pretty wonderful," I told them. "I married the man I loved, we raised five beautiful children, we had many friends, and we did the kind of work we enjoyed and found tremendously fulfilling. But just before my fiftieth birthday, something terrible happened to us, something that destroyed my life as I had known it. As a result of that experience, I learned something I didn't know before. I learned . . . that people are stupid. We all are. We judge and categorize each other without ever really seeing or hearing each other. And in doing that, we cause a lot of pain."

You could have heard a pin drop in the room. "Now," I continued, "as I'm entering the second half of my life, I've decided I don't want to do that anymore. I want to really *see* people; I want to really *hear* them. I want to understand more so I can help more. I want to listen to people with greater understanding. I think that by studying psychology I can gain some insight into how people's minds work and what makes them do what they do. Then, perhaps, I may be able to help and not hurt my fellow man."

When I finished, I looked around the room. What I'd said wasn't much different from what most psych majors would say about their motivation for studying in the field, but I saw tears in people's eyes and realized that my words had touched something in their hearts.

In that moment, I felt my new life beginning.

My psych professor divided our class into learning teams, and I found myself grouped with several other women, two of whom remained with me throughout the program. All of them were younger than I was, and none would have identified herself as an evangelical Christian. One described herself as a Universalist, and another was involved in a lesbian relationship. Others who trickled in and out of the program represented all varieties of worldviews. We worked on our papers and projects together, and those relationships helped fill the "friendship void" in my heart.

As I worked with the women on my team, I often alluded to the major crisis I had experienced—a horrific event that completely redirected my life. I never explained further, and though I caught a couple of curious glances passing between my teammates, they never probed.

At the end of the term, the girls on my team approached me with a question. "You've got to tell us your story," they said. "Can we hear it now?"

I looked at them and smiled. I wanted very much to tell them my story. Over the course of the year, I had grown to love these women. They were friends, and I felt like I'd been keeping something from them, though I liked the fact that when I was with them I could forget about the past and focus on trying to understand Freud and Skinner and what motivates us to do what we do.

"Okay," I said. "Why don't we go to lunch this Saturday, and I'll tell you what you want to know."

So the four of us—my two friends, the newest member of our team, and I—went out to lunch, and I told them what had happened to my family. One of the women said she remembered Ted's name from the news but never dreamed I was connected to that scandal. They listened intently as I told my story. When I finished, I discovered tears in the eyes of my three young friends, and they asked me to pray for them.

In that moment, I discovered something: I had changed.

In all the years Ted and I pastored New Life Church, we had welcomed everyone. I felt we were as merciful and compassionate toward people as we could be. But we didn't know what it felt like to be the person in need of mercy and compassion. Without realizing it, we saw ourselves as *us* helping *them*.

But as I shared with my friends—a Universalist, a lesbian, and one who described herself as "really messed up"—I realized that I'd become part of a "we."

We need help.

I wasn't telling them how to make their lives like mine. Instead, I found myself saying, "Look at God's faithfulness to me in my darkest hour." After hearing that, they were touched.

One of those women still writes to me from time to time. I'm happy to call her my friend. Those women taught me about Jesus, because after talking to them, I was finally able to understand why the Lord shared so many lunches with tax collectors and other so-called sinners instead of with the religious leaders.

I'm so grateful to my teammates for asking me to share my story. I thought I was merciful and compassionate before our crisis; but since then, I've come to see myself as someone who's desperately in need of mercy and compassion. I am as human as the next woman. God's faithfulness to me is proof that he will show mercy to anyone who comes to him . . . and a reminder that I need to be compassionate and merciful to others.

My suffering was good for me,

for it taught me to pay attention

to your decrees.

Your instructions are more

valuable to me

than millions in gold and silver.

PSALM 119:71-72

16

TED HAS ALWAYS advised new Christians to align themselves with a Bible-believing church. "When you join a church, find a place to serve right away," he says. "Find out what the pastor's vision is, and see if you can serve that vision in some way."

Pastor Tommy Barnett's most cherished vision was the Dream Center, a halfway house for prison parolees, former prostitutes, recovering alcoholics, and drug addicts on the rough road to sobriety. He had established a highly successful facility in Los Angeles and was working to develop a similar program in Phoenix. In August 2007, the staff at the Phoenix Dream Center invited Ted and me to visit the facility, so we went on a tour. We immediately fell in love with the work they were doing. For one thing, we felt like we fit. We were in trouble, just like everyone else there, and we were all trying to put our lives back together.

While we were there, someone on the Dream Center staff asked if Ted and I would like to be involved with their ministry.

They envisioned Ted counseling the men and me counseling the women. Our hearts stirred, and the next morning we woke up wondering if we might be able to get involved with the halfway-house ministry and help support the vision of our new pastor. We talked about the possibility of moving into the Dream Center facility with our boys and serving in whatever capacity we could—cooking, cleaning, or facilitating meetings. Our boys liked the idea, so we called Pastor Tommy to ask what he thought of the possibility. "Best idea I've heard yet," he replied. He promised to call the overseers to see if he could get our move to the Dream Center officially approved.

We were still praying about the possibility of the move when our Phoenix church held their annual donors' banquet. Pastor Tommy invited us, and after the meal he addressed the crowd. "I'm happy to announce," he said with real enthusiasm in his voice, "that Ted and Gayle and their two boys will soon be moving into the Dream Center."

As the other guests gave us a standing ovation, Ted looked at me and grinned. "Well, I guess that settles it."

I nodded and smiled, thinking that perhaps this was the confirmation we'd been praying for. Summer was almost over, and we needed to move out of the house where we'd been living because the owners would soon be returning. We needed either an apartment to rent or some alternative . . . and now it looked as though the Dream Center might be our answer.

Afterward, we asked Pastor Tommy about the overseers' response, and he said they had all approved the move. We were set.

The Dream Center building is an old hotel, and the staff agreed to renovate a few rooms so our family could have a small apartment. Ted and I sat down to figure out how we could handle our financial obligations in light of this new opportunity. Because we were both still in school and our severance payments from New Life would end in three months, we knew we'd need some sort of financial support if we were going to feed our family while we worked as volunteers at the Dream Center.

Ted jotted down the names of thirteen friends who had previously mentioned that they'd be willing to offer financial support if we needed it. He wrote an e-mail detailing the ministry of the Dream Center and then added an afterthought: "If you know anyone else who might be interested in supporting this ministry, feel free to pass this request along."

This sort of solicitation isn't unusual in the world we had been living in—college students frequently use such letters as a means of raising money for missions trips, and most missionaries would be unable to serve in the mission field unless they were financially supported by regular donors. We had responded to fund-raising letters many times throughout the years, so I didn't see Ted's letter as unusual, improper, or in violation of our contract with the church or the overseers.

In the e-mail, Ted said, "It looks as though it will take two years for us to have adequate earning power again, so we are looking for people who will help us monthly for two years." He added that during that two-year period we planned to work toward our degrees while we served at the Dream Center. He concluded the e-mail by saying that once he graduated, we would no longer need outside financial support.

When Pastor Tommy heard about the e-mail, he contacted Ted and suggested that he adjust some of the wording, so Ted did. One of our friends forwarded his copy of Ted's letter to a news station because he believed lots of people would want to support us if they knew about our need. Not long afterward, the news reporter who had received the e-mail contacted Ted to let him know he was posting it on his Web site, so Ted e-mailed him the updated version.

Word of the letter traveled fast; within twenty-four hours, news of Ted's fund-raising letter hit the Colorado Springs newspapers. Articles pointed fingers, and editorials seethed with indignation as people demanded to know why Ted and Gayle Haggard dared to ask for money. People seemed to have the idea that we had millions tucked away somewhere. Worse yet, some people were upset that we were volunteering to serve in a ministry. As the story spread nationwide, bloggers joked about "Ted Haggard—the story that keeps on giving."

Within a few days, the overseers committee did an about-face and rescinded their approval.

Pastor Tommy called us into his office, where we were startled to learn that the overseers and restorers had issued a press release, saying it was "premature" and "inappropriate" that we should try to minister or counsel anyone. We also learned that because New Life Church had recently installed a new pastor, some people were speculating that we had somehow staged the Dream Center drama in order to draw attention from New Life's newly elected leader.

I sighed at this news. We hadn't planned on any media attention at all. If anything, Ted's e-mail message demonstrated that we were trying to settle down in Phoenix. It had nothing to do with New Life or the new pastor.

I found it ironic that some in the Christian community had written articles stating that what Ted needed to do was go work quietly in a humble place, caring for the needy while he worked to rebuild his character and credibility; but when we found precisely that kind of opportunity at the Dream Center, our willingness to serve was maligned and snatched away from us.

On that day, in that hour, an elemental part of my personality shifted. For the first time I said, "Let them flap all they want; I don't care anymore." This latest accusation had finally pushed me over the edge. I used to care deeply about what people thought of me and of Ted. I used to value a good reputation. But when I heard people attacking us for trying to get our lives back on track, I surrendered. I told Ted, "Let the world rage against us; let others suspect our every motive and action. Let them criticize, let them malign, let them gossip. Let them imagine evil intentions where none exist. Let them credit us with schemes too grandiose and complicated for our combined intellect. Let them ignore our plight and imagine the worst; I don't care."

From that moment on, criticism stopped going straight to my heart. I had come to a crossroad, and I was turning a corner. I would no longer consider what other people said about us. God knew we were willing to move into the Dream Center. He knew our hearts and our motives. He knew *us*, and he was ultimately the only one we desired to please.

He also knew that by closing the door on our opportunity to work at the Dream Center, we would have to throw ourselves into finding some other kind of full-time employment. Our severance benefits were coming to an end, but we still had bills to pay and groceries to buy. And we would have to find an apartment to rent.

God used the Dream Center fiasco to teach me an important lesson: I can't please everyone, even when I'm doing things "by the book." Christian people are still people, so I no longer expect more of them than I do of anyone else. I stopped trusting people I would have trusted with my life before our crisis. I no longer expected them to care about us or to protect us as brothers and sisters in Christ.

That's when I realized the full meaning of John 2:24-25: "Jesus didn't trust them, because he knew human nature. No one needed to tell him what mankind is really like."

I didn't stop caring about people; I simply stopped caring about their judgments of me. And I learned that one doesn't have to trust people in order to love them.

❖

On Sunday, December 9, we had just stepped into our small apartment when my cell phone rang. I dropped my purse on the kitchen counter and answered the phone, curious as to who might be calling so soon after church.

The caller was a good friend from New Life, whose husband worked at the church. Her voice trembled. "Gayle, there is a shooting going on at New Life. My husband's there. He's hiding under his desk. The shooter is in the building."

Shock siphoned the blood from my head. There was a *what* in the church? Did she say *shooter*?

"Please pray," she said, and then she hung up.

I looked at Ted, who obviously saw the concern in my eyes. As I began to tell him what my friend had said, he hurried over to the television in the living room and turned it on.

"She thought we needed to know," I finished. "She knew we'd pray."

Already the national news channel was airing reports of the events taking place at New Life. The somber newscaster reported the tragedy as "still ongoing."

I began to pray, lifting my thoughts heavenward as I struggled to make sense of what was happening. We sat in front of the television and watched, horrified, as the story unfolded. A family had been shot in the parking lot, where people were getting into their cars after the worship service. The gunman, who carried two handguns, an assault rifle, and more than a thousand rounds of ammunition, had entered the building through the east entrance and moved through the foyer.

Jeanne Assam, a petite blonde who attended the morning service and volunteered as a security guard during the later service, saw the armed man coming through the doors and took cover. She would later tell the *Denver News* that she "came out of cover and identified myself and engaged him and took him down."

"God was with me," she said. "I didn't think for a minute to run away."[1]

New Life's pastor would later credit Ted for having the foresight to put a security team in place, but our brother-in-law, Lance Coles, had actually been the driving force behind the idea. The fifteen or so volunteer security guards who patrol the grounds are church members, and the security team members who carry weapons are licensed to do so.

We had never experienced an incident that required armed intervention. Though we were saddened by the plight of this young man and his family, we were grateful that Jeanne Assam was willing and able to stop the gunman before he could inflict more damage.

Our phone rang off the hook for the rest of the day as people called and asked us to pray. Many of the calls were from people we were hearing from for the first time since our crisis. They were calling to tell us what they'd seen and experienced. I understood the urge to reach out—they wanted to vent, to lessen their trauma by sharing it with someone who would understand.

I completely identified with those feelings.

The worst part of the tragedy for us was feeling helpless because we were so far away. We watched as the news unfolded, we listened as people poured out their fears over the phone, and we prayed. Later, we grieved for the wounded and for the family of the two teenage girls who were killed, and we felt frustrated because we couldn't be with our church family at this time of tragedy.

Later, we heard news reports describe dozens of terrorized church members, some running for the entrances, pushing each other through doorways as they struggled to reach safety. We heard more reports of people huddling under desks, in restrooms, and in closets, desperately attempting to hide. Several church members needed counseling after that terrible event.

The next morning, as we heard the full story on TV, we saw the church's new pastor face the cameras. Ted and I had never met him, and we were impressed by his demeanor. In the midst of tragedy and terror, he showed himself to be a strong leader. "This will secure the new pastor in the hearts of the people as he leads them through," Ted said, nodding at the screen.

Both of us wanted the new pastor to succeed. Despite the heartache of the past few months, we still loved the church and prayed that it would heal and thrive.

When 2008 arrived, we still had no financial security. We owned a home (or part of one, anyway, since the bank held mortgages on the property), but it was miles away in Colorado Springs, and we weren't allowed to return to it.

After the Dream Center fiasco, we realized that a lot of people believed we were independently wealthy. Newspaper articles reported that we received royalties for our books, so we *couldn't* be hurting financially. But those articles didn't report that our books had stopped selling after the crisis. Many bookstores, including the one at New Life Church, now refused to carry Ted's books. And because most Christian book-publishing contracts have a "moral turpitude" clause, we weren't even sure if our publishers would continue to *print* our books.

We'd been in Phoenix for about five months when the time came for us to move into an apartment. We'd appreciated the hospitality extended to us by friends who had offered their homes during our transition, but we knew we couldn't take advantage of people's generosity forever. We rented a modest apartment for the four of us, though the rent payments would have to come from the second mortgage we'd taken out on our home in Colorado Springs.

Ted decided to stop his graduate studies so he could go on the road selling health insurance, but he encouraged me to stay in school. We were hoping he could make enough to allow me to be a part-time student and full-time mother to Elliott and Alex.

For the first time, Ted and I experienced what other people go through when they are let go from a job. After hearing that someone had been laid off, we used to think, *Oh, he can easily get another job*, but we didn't realize then how it feels to be so traumatized that you can't figure out how to start over. We didn't know where to begin. During the first year after our severance from New Life, we were so dejected we could barely function. We were still caught up in grief. We learned that it takes time to get your strength back and figure out a new way to earn a living.

Despite Ted's work experience in the church, where he'd done everything from driving busloads of students to youth events to leading major ministries, we didn't know how his job skills would translate outside the church world. The overseers kept telling him, "You'll get a job in no time, you're so gifted." People outside New Life would tell Ted, "Don't worry. You'll be fine." But there's no way to know how difficult the process is until you live it.

I thought about the few people we had let go from our staff over the years, and I grieved that we had not been more understanding of their plight.

Now when I see unemployed people on the news, my heart aches for them because I'm familiar with that struggle. If you lose your job in a tight economy, it's hard to pick yourself up and feel certain you can provide for your family. People think it's easy to quit one job and get another, but it's not. Especially when you have invested years of your adult life in one company or position.

Nevertheless, God took care of us, and for that first year he provided for us through our severance packages from New Life Church. Most severance packages are considered rewards for years of faithful service, but ours came with dozens of strings attached.

Still, Ted and I were grateful for the financial help the church provided. Ted made several attempts to find work that year, but none of them panned out. With January 2008 fast approaching, we were serious about scraping out a living on our own. Ted applied for and was offered a job as an admissions counselor at the University of Phoenix, but at the same time, a friend offered him a position selling health insurance. Ted has always been a "people person," so he thought he might do well in sales.

But that was a difficult job—lots of hard work for very little return. My heart ached every time I thought of how much Ted had invested in the Kingdom of God, yet every morning I watched him get up, put on a tie, and go out to try to sell insurance. He was a castaway, adrift on a sea of uncertainty, and few people seemed to care.

❖

After a long and frustrating year away from our older children, our home, and our church family, Ted and I decided to approach the overseers and again ask them to drop the contracts between us.

We'd made the request many times over the previous months. Once, three of the overseers flew to Phoenix to meet with us, and we pleaded with them to drop the agreements. They kept saying, "Why are you fixated on the contracts?" We kept trying to explain that legal agreements weren't the best way to handle a situation between Christian brothers.

One of them remarked, "Why are you so worked up about the contracts? They're just words on a page."

Words on a page . . . like the Constitution and the Bible are just words on a page? Words on a page *mean* something, so we took them very seriously. Besides, the words on our contracts were legally binding. They kept us from what we believed we should be doing.

At one point, Ted asked, "Don't you think it would be a good idea for us to speak on the phone at regular intervals?"

"Oh, that's already being done," one of the men replied. "We have a conference call every week."

We were stunned by his answer. They talked *about* us every week, forming conclusions and making decisions, yet we were excluded from having any input. We were keenly aware that plenty of decisions were being made "about us without us." Ted and I believe that people—*all* people—should be respected enough to be brought into the dialogue, particularly when it affects their lives.

One day in September, right after the Dream Center episode, Ted went off to train for a career in insurance sales. That day was one of my lowest. Not because Ted would be selling insurance instead of pursuing the calling God had placed on his life, but because I felt that nobody cared. Ted had been the beloved pastor of a church of fourteen thousand. People all over the world had respected him, and he'd done so many great things, yet very few stepped forward to be his friend in his time of need. We'd spent months in exile, where one day melted into another in an endless stream of loneliness and disillusionment.

I sat at home and wondered if anybody cared at all. Ted was one of the brightest minds in the evangelical community. Not only had he founded New Life, but he had invested himself in helping leaders around the globe develop their churches. He'd had such a positive impact on the lives of so many, yet thousands of people had written him off because he committed a sin—a sin he didn't embrace but desperately resisted.

I wept most of that morning and sat in silence most of the afternoon, my thoughts haunted by the awful memory of the day we left Colorado Springs for Phoenix. But God had not deserted us, even in the darkest hours. I couldn't always feel his presence, I couldn't always hear his voice, but I knew he was watching over us.

One day in December, as Ted drove from Phoenix to Flagstaff for an insurance call, he sensed the presence of God with him, in much the same way he had years earlier when he first felt God call him to Colorado Springs. He sensed the Lord speaking to him in his heart: *When you were twenty-eight years old, I called you to Colorado Springs, and no man has the authority to remove that call from your life.*

Startled, Ted focused his attention on the voice within him.

When you were twenty-eight years old, I called you to Colorado Springs, and your sin *does not have the power to remove that call from your life.*

Ted waited, his hands gripping the steering wheel.

When you were twenty-eight years old, I called you to Colorado Springs, and you do not have the authority to remove that call from your life.

Ted pulled to the side of the road and bent over the steering wheel, overcome with emotion. Sobbing, he picked up his cell phone and called me. With a trembling voice, he told me what he felt the Lord had just said to him. I felt my spirit ready to explode within me. I believed the words Ted had heard were from God. "We need to go tell Pastor Tommy," I said. "He needs to know what God is saying to you."

I didn't question a word Ted said. Years before, after an intense time of fasting and prayer, he had heard God speak to him about several specific ministries in Colorado Springs, and every one of those promises had been fulfilled. Ted has always had a close prayer relationship with the Lord, so I had no reason to doubt him.

We made an appointment to see our pastor, Tommy Barnett, and in his office we shared what Ted had heard. Pastor Tommy listened intently and then nodded. "I believe that was God; he is telling you to go back to Colorado Springs. I'll see what I can do to get the contracts dropped so you all can move back home."

Prior to that, Ted had talked with two of the overseers, and once again he'd asked them to drop the contracts. "These are not legal," he told them. "They keep me from being able to fulfill my call, they've hurt my family, and they'd never stand up in court. More to the point, they have nothing to do with biblical restoration."

In January 2008, apparently in response to Pastor Tommy's request, the overseers agreed to drop the restoration contract, but they did not declare Ted "restored."

On the last day of January, we received a hand-delivered letter from the overseers and restorers. "Dear Ted," they wrote, "one year ago, we began working with you in a process of spiritual restoration. We all knew it would be difficult, and it has been. You recently spoke to [two pastors] about ending the restoration process. We have discussed it, and we accept your decision.

"You are hereby released from any further obligation set forth in our January 27, 2007, letter to you. New Life Church will send you a letter regarding your continuing obligations under the Separation Agreement. Our primary concern is that you live a life of holiness and that you and your family are well."[2]

Even though we'd been freed from the restrictive restoration agreement, the leadership of New Life Church made it clear that our obligations under the separation agreement remained in place in perpetuity. We were still forbidden to publish anything related to New Life Church; communicate with the press; speak against the church, the overseers, or the restorers; or disclose that the separation agreement existed. Only one stipulation was not perpetual—the requirement that we abstain from engaging in ministry within one hundred miles of New Life Church for at least three years.

The church issued a press release, outlining a brief history of our situation and concluding with the following statement: "New Life Church recognizes the process of restoring Ted Haggard is incomplete and maintains its original stance that he should not return to vocational ministry. However, we wish him and his family only success in the future. Because spiritual restoration is necessarily a confidential process, the church does not anticipate that it, or its overseers or restorers, will make further comment about it."[3]

And so the overseers and restorers officially terminated the restoration that wasn't a restoration at all. I refer to it as an amputation. Ted calls it a divorce. We managed to save our marriage, but the leadership of the church chose to divorce us.

After reading those last letters, I wondered again what the over-seers and restorers wanted from Ted. Repentance? They had had that on the first night. Turning from sin? Ted had turned his back on his sin a month before the story broke. Counseling? He got it, and we're grateful for it. He's still seeing a therapist to help him avoid blind spots so he can prevent trouble from developing in the future. Most of the trauma he deals with now stems from the aftermath of his crisis, our separation from the church.

Did those men want Ted to endure years of humiliation and shame? We lived under those conditions for two years, and even now we wake up to new blogs and newspaper articles that use Ted's name as though it were synonymous with *pervert, hypocrite,* and *liar.*

What did the church leaders want from him? And why did they feel it necessary to issue a press release stating that they hadn't been satisfied?

Because I wasn't sure I could find a clear answer, I pushed those questions aside. No matter what the overseers and restor-ers intended, I was watching God work in my husband. He was becoming healthier and stronger each day. He was so much more solid, he had reclaimed his integrity, and his voice and clarity of mind were coming back. With every passing day, I saw Ted becom-ing a better man.

I was stronger, too, but I still had to sort out my feelings about the decisions others made for us during our most critical months. I am no longer angry at the people who made the decisions. I think the group honestly believed they were acting in everyone's best interest, though I believe they were misguided. Some of them as individuals were kind and helpful, and I will always appreciate their kindness. Even those who weren't as helpful are my broth-ers in the body of Christ, and I've always appreciated being in a family with opinionated brothers. I don't mind occasionally say-ing, "Knock it off, guys," or "I think you're wrong on this point," or "Maybe we should rethink this proposed solution."

But I need to be *heard*. Being honest and direct is always better than pretending everything's all right or covering things up.

What I want to be heard is my challenge to the flawed ideas that were used to determine a response to Ted's sin. More than one life was at stake—those ideas affected the lives of a family, a church, and all who watched the unfolding events. The world desperately needed to see the gospel message in action.

As painful as the truth may be, I would rather get it out on the table and deal with it than live a lie.

Yes, I was disappointed and hurt to know that some of these leaders allowed so many lies to be believed, both about Ted's sin and our "restoration process," even though they had access to the truth. To this day, I run across articles that mention Ted and repeat three-year-old falsehoods. But I dismiss them; I've moved on by the grace of God. I freely forgive all those who hurt us, and I hope to continue a dialogue that will lead to a better response in the future. Even so, our family still feels the effects of Ted's sin and the resulting slanders.

A father can do one of two things for his children, Ted says: bring them honor or bring them disgrace. Even though our family has pulled together and our children love their father deeply, Ted will always regret having brought pain into their lives.

Once we were free of the restrictions found in the restoration agreement, we weren't sure what we should do next. We wanted to go home, but we weren't sure about the timing. By that point, Christy had moved to Phoenix because she wanted to help us out. She moved in with us and got a license to sell insurance. Soon she had pitched in to help Ted in his new business.

Some people in Dallas contacted Ted about a job with a wealth-management firm. Ted and Christy went to check it out, but I stayed in Arizona until Alex and Elliott completed their school year. When the boys finished in May, we knew we had to make a decision about which direction to point the U-Haul when we left Phoenix. Should we drive toward Dallas or Colorado Springs? We prayed about it, and on May 14, we learned that the wealth-management company had split and one faction was preparing to sue the other.

Ted saw that development as our answer. "We're not going to be a part of that," he told me. "We're going home."

Help me, O LORD my God!
Save me because of your unfailing love.
Let them see that this is your doing,
that you yourself have done it, LORD.

PSALM 109:26-27

17

IN EARLY 2006, before our crisis, Ted and I had met Alexandra Pelosi, daughter of House Speaker Nancy Pelosi and a self-described "New York liberal Democrat." Four years earlier, Alexandra had made a documentary called *Journeys with George*, an Emmy-winning film about George Bush's 2000 presidential campaign. In 2006, she was filming *Friends of God*, a documentary on American evangelicals, so she came to New Life Church to interview Ted.

Ted had an open-door policy at New Life. Members of the media were welcome to film anything they liked, anytime the church doors were open. Ted met Alexandra and liked her, so he allowed her to follow him on a Promise Keepers road trip. She also interviewed other evangelical leaders, but Ted gave her more freedom and more access, so she spent a great deal of time with him and our family. Even though she had strong ties to the political left and would never call herself an evangelical, Ted enjoyed her honesty and straightforwardness, and he trusted her.

Alexandra later gave an interview to *The Advocate*, a gay news-magazine, in which she told the interviewer, "A lot of New York liberal Democrats who go to the megachurches come back talking about how scary they are, and I never say that. I have nothing but admiration for these people and respect for them. I don't think they are dangerous or trying to take over the country like a lot of people think they are. . . . I'm not afraid of them, as most New York liberals would be."[1] She went on to describe Ted as a "really nice guy."

"Living in New York," she said, "my caricature of the religious right is they are these Holy Roller Jesus freaks. Meeting Pastor Ted, he changed my impression. That's why I stuck with him. He was reasonable. . . . He wasn't a hater."[2]

Ted and I invited Alexandra into our home and introduced her to our children. I had to laugh when she mentioned her mother and then looked at my kids and rolled her eyes. "And you think your dad embarrasses you?"

She spent countless hours following Ted with her camera and said he was the most interesting of the evangelical pastors she'd talked to. Unfortunately, our crisis broke only a few days after she had finished her work on *Friends of God.* She was also expecting a baby, so she was under a lot of stress before Ted's story shifted the focus that had been directed at her film.

Alexandra told *The Advocate*, "If this movie had aired before Ted Haggard's fall, [evangelical Christians] would have loved this movie, and shown it in their churches, and been proud to make it to secular television in prime time. But since the fall of Ted Haggard, they are very embarrassed by him. The only complaints [about] Pastor Ted [were]'He fell from grace—can't you edit him out before this airs on television?'"[3]

"When I heard [about the scandal]," she told *Christianity*

Today, "it was just stunning. I was shocked and confused. We knew Ted. We trusted Ted. It was just a total disconnect from the Ted that we knew."[4]

Alexandra tried to phone us in late 2006, but we couldn't talk to her because we weren't allowed to speak to anyone from the media. Her husband, Michiel Vos, called Ted and asked if they could talk as friends, but Ted said, "I'm sorry, but you can't come see me, and I can't talk to you."

But later, in early May 2007, Alexandra and her husband were visiting Alexandra's sister in Scottsdale and heard that we lived nearby. So Michiel called Ted, and Ted invited them over. They offered to bring lunch and came over with their new baby, and we sat around the patio table, eating sandwiches and talking. After a few hours, we ordered pizza and talked some more. To her credit, Alexandra kept her camera in her diaper bag the entire time. We ended up talking for nine hours.

Alexandra and Michiel were shocked by what had happened to us. We felt we were with friends, not media people, so we shared what we'd share with any friends who came to visit.

The faith elements of our story were not lost on Alexandra. "Look at what's happened to you because you believe," she said. "Just a few weeks before your scandal, it was like 'Ted Haggard's the man, we love this guy,' and now, everyone's gone."

I knew what she meant. Ted is a people person; his greatest joy has always been investing in the lives of others. He has always been approachable, and people loved him for that quality. Alexandra knew that; she had witnessed how the people loved him.

"What happened?" she wanted to know. "I've lost faith in humanity over this. This is really hitting me at a deep place. It's horrific that everyone's gone silent in your life."

"Not everyone," Ted assured her. "My family is still with me."

Alexandra and Michiel remained silent for a few moments; then Alexandra dipped her chin in a decisive nod. "We are confident that you're going to resurrect. You are going to come back. You can't help but come back. But all that's out there right now is this horrific scandal."

Ted spread his hands in a helpless gesture. "What are we supposed to do? We're prohibited from talking to anyone, so we can't present our story."

"Let us at least get some video of you," Alexandra said, "so when you make your comeback, you'll have a record of the process, the in-between time. It'll be footage for you, for your own records."

At first we said no—a film would be a violation of the contracts we'd signed. But both Michiel and Alexandra convinced us that the footage would not be publicly shown without our permission. It would be our own personal record of our process.

Ted looked at me, a question in his eyes.

"I think," Alexandra said, "someday you'll be glad you have this. Michiel and I can get some footage every time we visit Phoenix."

So that's what she did. She and Michiel visited us several times over the next few months, and they even traveled with Ted on some of his insurance sales trips. Michiel shot footage of Ted waking up in a hotel room and reading Scripture on his PalmPilot. Alexandra filmed Ted and the boys moving boxes in and out of the U-Haul and sweating as he drove the truck in the Arizona heat. She got footage of our boys claiming bedrooms in a borrowed house and of Ted and me lugging clothes up a flight of stairs into our rented apartment.

She later told an interviewer, "Ted never seemed to really care that I was filming. He probably never thought anything of it because he didn't really think anybody would care to watch him. Over a year and a half, we filmed him from time to time."[5]

"The big moment for me in the movie was when he was moving into this little second-floor tiny apartment with his kids. It was October 5, 2007. I said, 'How do you feel moving to your new house?' And he gives me this look like, 'Just be quiet and leave me alone. Let me just die in peace.' And then he walks away, and he turns around and says, 'I just don't want my family to be poor.'"[6]

Alexandra filmed us sporadically throughout the year of our exile. She caught Ted's despair and, in some scenes, his desperation. She caught his optimism; but most of all, she caught his faith.

In the fall of 2008, Alexandra called and said she was compiling the footage for a film tentatively called *The Trials of Ted Haggard*. "I want to show it to HBO," she told us, "but the film's not going anywhere without your permission. I'd love for you to consider letting HBO air this movie, though, because it's horrific what people are believing about you."

Ted and I promised to think and pray about it; then we'd let her know our decision.

After we disconnected the call, Ted asked me if we really wanted a permanent record of everything that had happened over the last year.

"What more can they do to us?" I answered, shrugging. "The truth is not as bad as what's out there."

Yet we still weren't sure what to do. We were still bound by the terms of the separation agreements we'd signed, and we knew that if we violated any terms of the contract, the church could sue us. We took this threat seriously. Even though we were not going to receive any money for the documentary, we weren't sure the film was worth the risk of getting sued by the church. Yet we also felt that at some point we'd have to reclaim our right to speak out. After all, we're Americans, and we treasure the freedoms our forefathers gave their lives to win. We also believed that God was restoring us to spiritual health and had a purpose for us. God had taught us so much as a result of what we'd been through—surely at some point he would open the door for us to share with others what we'd learned.

As Queen Esther said when summoning her courage to commit a forbidden act, "If I must die, I must die" (Esther 4:16).

I looked at Ted and said, "Let them sue."

When we spoke to Alexandra again, she asked us to come and see the film before making a decision. "HBO is willing to fly you to New York," she said. "They think it's a terrific documentary, but I won't give it to them without your okay."

I have to admit, we were curious. What could she possibly have done with footage from those dreary days? I wasn't sure I wanted to relive a single minute of that time, but I agreed that we should at least watch the movie.

So Ted and I flew to New York City. Once we reached the HBO offices, one of the division heads pulled me into the ladies' room. "Honey," she said, "I am a self-professed pagan. When it comes to Christianity, you're the real deal. You make me want to read the Bible."

I smiled as my thoughts whirred. What was in that documentary?

Alexandra Pelosi echoed this woman's thoughts. She later told an interviewer, "I'm not a really religious person. We consider ourselves to be Catholics, but we think of it more as a cultural thing. But what I love about Ted's story, at least about Ted's family, is that the Bible got them through. They read the Bible. They would read these passages, and it moved me. I went out and bought a new Bible. When I was making *Friends of God*, everybody quoted the Bible, but I was never inspired to go buy one. But this experience with Ted turned me onto the Bible in a whole new way, because he would read these passages and it would really inspire me. . . . Gayle and the kids read the Bible a lot, and they weren't doing it for me. They got through all of this with the help of the Bible."[7]

Ted and I went into the HBO "awards room," a space lined with shelves holding the many Emmys the company had won for various films. In walked Richard Plepler, copresident of HBO. He told us he had taken the movie home and watched it with his wife. He spent forty-five minutes talking to us about portions of the film that had deeply affected him. He called it "the human story" and told us he felt other people would be powerfully moved by it as well.

"Ted," he said, leaning toward us, "if you are willing to let us air this documentary, in January I would like to present it to the television critics in Los Angeles as our featured documentary."

We were dumbfounded. We still hadn't seen the film, and we couldn't imagine what in it inspired this sort of enthusiasm. So they put on the film, and we settled back to watch it for the first time.

My first thought was that the documentary definitely wasn't a puff piece. Segments of it were embarrassing; other clips were emotionally painful. Ted had never seen any of the news interviews in which the overseers from New Life spoke to the media, so for the first time he saw one of them tell a reporter, "We instructed him . . . he just needs to disappear."

When the film ended, Ted and I sat in silence for a long moment. Though we had mixed emotions, we both felt as though it was an important piece about a very human journey in God, and for the first time we understood the power of its message. Could Alexandra's film bring a message of healing to the multitudes that needed it?

We told the HBO officials that we would consider giving our permission, but our children would have to make the final decision. The movie would reignite public discussion about their father and our family. If it aired, those discussions would bring up all the issues they'd already processed.

So HBO offered to fly our entire family to New York to see the documentary. After the kids saw the film, we asked them to weigh in with exactly how they felt. Every one of them agreed that the movie was important and should be aired.

"People need to see it," Marcus said, "because they have so many misconceptions."

The other kids agreed, though Christy was the most outspoken. "I'm tired of all the lies that have been put out there," she said. "People need to know the truth."

In early 2009, with our children's approval, HBO aired *The Trials of Ted Haggard* as its feature documentary.

❖

Though some have speculated that Ted is a "media hog" who can't resist a camera, the honest truth is simple and plain: We saw Alexandra's documentary as an opportunity to speak for ourselves and challenge some of the misinformation circulating about us. We also saw the media interviews as public opportunities for Ted to confess and apologize to the national audience that had learned about his sin.

How did we cope with the prospect of seeing some of our weakest moments aired on national television? The same way we coped with our crisis—with prayer and a dash of humor.

Any parent who has ever dealt with a crisis will tell you that one of the best coping mechanisms is laughter. You can see traces of our family's humor in *The Trials of Ted Haggard*. You can see it in Ted's quick grin, the boys' comments, and my wry smile.

Ted and I have always enjoyed laughing together. In raising Jonathan, an experience with many anxious moments, we discovered the healing balm of laughter in difficult times. In situations where we could have cried, we chose to laugh. Sometimes we did plenty of both, but we learned not to take ourselves too seriously.

I'm fortunate to have a family in which everyone has a well-developed sense of humor. Sometimes, when we were caught up in a trying situation with Jonathan or in some development related to our crisis, different ones of our kids would volunteer a humorous observation. Their quip—and its unexpectedness—never failed to momentarily dispel the pain.

My children's humor and adventurous approach to life helped us endure those early days of the crisis, especially when we were hounded by the media. As we drove by the house on that first Thursday night and saw blankets hanging over the windows, I forgot my pain for a moment and marveled at my kids' ingenuity. When a news van chased Alex and followed him to a friend's house, we all laughed. I think my kids enjoyed the challenge of handling reporters—not that they'd want to do it every day, but they didn't let it ruffle them.

When we walked through the airport and prepared to fly to Florida, we passed newsstands where Ted's picture blazed from the front page of every newspaper. People were pulling out their cell phones and snapping photos as we walked by. Instead of being offended, my kids laughed at the surreal experience.

I remember telling my kids that shame is destructive, but we weren't going to be destroyed by our crisis. "We're going to walk through this with our chins up," I told them. "We're going to maintain our dignity because we know who we are. We're in a shameful situation, but we're not going to be ashamed."

No matter where we went or what we encountered, my kids stood tall. They weren't proud; they were respectful of people. They defended our family without becoming arrogant or oversensitive.

Alexandra Pelosi gave us a tip that helped us handle the public pressure. She recommended that we never read any of the press articles about us. The idea that we didn't have to read everything was incredibly liberating. We have learned that we can live peacefully without being aware of all the bad press out there. Plenty of people are quick to weigh in with their opinions, but a lot of those opinions are based on untruths or half-truths. Those comments can quickly become burdensome, so for the most part, we ignore them still. Every once in a while, we'll go online and look around. We're always amazed at how people have built entire cases against Ted based on things he never did.

I remember our family being together one night in Florida. The children were back from wherever they'd gone that day, and someone had turned on *The Jerry Springer Show*. We were laughing at the ridiculous situation depicted on the show when someone pointed out that in comparison, our family had no problems at all!

We realized that we Americans are so self-focused. When we stopped to consider what families in Darfur, Rwanda, or some of the former Soviet states have endured, our problems paled in comparison. We learned to count our blessings.

One day, Elliott was feeling particularly low, and I could see that he was angry. I pulled him into his room and looked him in the eye. "Well, Elliott," I said, "who knows? Maybe we're all going through this for you, so God can prepare you for something you'll need to do later in life."

The storm in his eyes cleared as he grinned. "Maybe."

Humor even helped us during our counseling sessions. We had our adult kids come to Phoenix for counseling because we wanted to be sure they had the option if they needed it. During one of our family sessions, we uncovered some raw emotion that hadn't yet been discussed. After airing that emotion—sometimes with anger, sometimes with tears—we'd sit back, laugh, and say, "Okay, we got through that one. Next?"

Humor. It was one of God's best gifts to us during our time of trial.

I chose to forgive Ted early in our crisis—actually, I started working on forgiving him the first day. But the thing that helped me truly and completely forgive him was something that occurred months later.

In April 2008, while I remained in Phoenix with the boys, Ted and Christy went to Dallas, trying to decide if we should move there to live and work. Ted connected with the guys he was working with at the time, and they invited him along on a Christian men's retreat. He knew there'd be a lot of private time for fasting and prayer, in addition to time for open conversation with the other guys. I was thrilled for him to go.

I flew from Phoenix to Dallas to meet him on his return. I was hoping the retreat had been a healing time for him.

He knew I would be in Dallas to greet him, but I wasn't prepared for the man who met me. These guys had been away from civilization for several days, and I don't think a man among them had packed a razor. I was watching the bus, waiting for my husband to step off, when suddenly a bearded man in dark glasses and a cowboy hat grabbed me from the side, threw me back, and kissed me on the lips. After my surprise, I yelled, "Hey, I'm married!" The other men hooted and slapped their legs while I tried desperately to push the guy away. "I am *not* your woman!"

Then my assailant removed his glasses . . . and I realized the man who held me was Ted. I'd never seen him in a beard before.

Overcome with delight, I melted into his embrace.

That night, Ted took me to dinner. After we ordered and the waiter had cleared the menus away, Ted looked into my eyes. "I know I've apologized to you before," he said, "and I know you've forgiven me, but I wanted you to know I've realized how much of a jerk I have been to have treated you this way."

I studied him as his words sank into my heart. I've known that a person who says, "I apologize" can often mean little more than *I'm sorry you're upset.*

The next level is "I'm sorry," meaning *I regret what I did.*

But "I've been a jerk to you" is taking ownership and recognizing how the action has violated or betrayed the other person.

In that moment, I felt I could completely forgive my husband. When Ted recognized the destruction he'd caused in my life and took ownership of it, I didn't have to work so hard to forgive him.

I thought Ted had apologized as deeply as he was able to, but when he told me that he'd been a jerk, I realized that's what I needed to hear. Waves of forgiveness flooded my heart.

Forgiveness doesn't mean that you forget the wrong. It doesn't mean you won't continue to hurt for a while. It doesn't mean you won't still need to grieve your loss. It *does* mean, however, that you're willing to let go and that you'll no longer hold the wrong against the other person.

Make no mistake: Forgiveness will cost you something.

My forgiveness of Ted cost me my church, my life as I knew it, many of our friends, financial security . . . and the right to make him suffer more for his wrongs.

The authors of *Fighting for Your Marriage* say, "Forgiveness is 'a decision to give up your perceived or actual right to get even with, or hold in debt, someone who has wronged you.'"[8]

No feeling comes close to the lovely release that comes with genuine forgiveness. But when interviewers ask me if I'd forgive Ted if he fell into his sin again, I have to be honest. "I'd like to think I could once again practice the teachings of Jesus and respond to Ted's sin with love and forgiveness," I say, "but to tell you the truth . . . I'm not sure I could handle betrayal a second time."

I hope my heart is never put to the test.

I love the story of the Prodigal Son. A family has two brothers, and the youngest leaves home, wastes his inheritance on foolish choices, and ends up in a pigpen. When the errant son comes to his senses, he says, "I will go home to my father and say, 'Father, I have sinned against both heaven and you, and I am no longer worthy of being called your son. Please take me on as a hired servant'" (Luke 15:18-19). Yet when he returns to his father, his father has been waiting for him and greets him with open arms. When the broken and contrite son confesses that he has sinned and is not worthy to be called a son, his father refuses to bestow second-class status on him. Instead, he says to the servants, "Quick! Bring the finest robe in the house and put it on him. Get a ring for his finger and sandals for his feet. And kill the calf we have been fattening. We must celebrate with a feast, for this son of mine was dead and has now returned to life. He was lost, but now he is found" (Luke 15:22-24).

After someone falls, sometimes we, as Christians, do not comprehend the depth and breadth of our Father's love. We tend to take the same approach as the Prodigal Son: "Yes, I am forgiven (or you are forgiven), but now I am (or you are) demoted to the status of a servant in the house." But that is not how the Father practices his love.

I've always felt that Ted and I needed to go home to finish our story. After twenty-two years of wonderful, productive work, I didn't want our story to end with a scandal. After all, there's something to be said for centering your work in one location. Ted and I thought it was important to go back to Colorado Springs and finish our story in the city where our work began.

We didn't announce our homecoming, but the newspaper did. When we returned in the summer of 2008, the local paper ran an article featuring quotes from the new pastor of New Life Church. "[Ted] could be here six months or sixty years," the pastor told *The Gazette*. "He's free to do whatever he wants, but he will have no affiliation with this church."[9]

We didn't go home with the intention of becoming re-affiliated with the church, but we did feel a need for some form of healing between us and our former church family. We didn't know how the Lord would work that out, but we were willing to wait for his direction.

Once we settled back into our home, we were amazed at the warm welcome we received from church people we met as we went about our daily lives. We'd meet people in grocery stores and restaurants, friends who would come up, hug us, and tell us how happy they were that we'd come home. When generous, anonymous patrons paid for our meals in restaurants, my heart warmed as though I'd just experienced a little miracle. Only a few months before, I wouldn't have believed we'd ever witness such kindnesses in Colorado Springs again.

In June, we celebrated Ted's birthday at the Royal Gorge, a spectacular national park about fifty miles south of Colorado Springs. The park features a train that travels through the deep granite canyon, so we rode in the dining car to celebrate Ted's special day. Apparently, a few of the waiters recognized him, because several of them came by to greet us. An accordion player moved through the car as he played, and when he reached our table he leaned over and said, "Welcome home, Pastor Ted."

Later, as we traveled through the canyon in the open car, the accordion player stood next to Ted and played "Amazing Grace." Tears came to my eyes as I listened. What a special treat for my husband's birthday.

As nice as those assurances of friendship were, the best thing about being in the Springs again was knowing that we'd come back to the place where God had planted us. We'd come home.

You have allowed me to suffer
  much hardship,
but you will restore me to life again
and lift me up from the
  depths of the earth.
You will restore me to even
  greater honor
and comfort me once again.

PSALM 71:20-21

18

One Saturday night in July, only a month after our return to Colorado Springs, Ted and I received an emergency phone call from Jonathan's residential school in Kentucky. Jonathan had to leave, the headmaster explained, because he had set his socks on fire. They would put him on a flight to Colorado Springs early the next morning.

I knew Jonathan was still having a hard time because of all the changes in our lives. He didn't know what to do with his turbulent emotions, so sometimes he acted out. The staff at the Stewart Home School had always been wonderful about working through his outbursts, but playing with fire was an infraction that could not be tolerated. An out-of-control fire could be disastrous and endanger many lives.

On Sunday morning, Ted and I got into the car and headed for the Denver airport. On the way, I called a friend who had told me about a ranch in northern Colorado for people with special needs.

I called the ranch to explain our predicament. As the Lord would have it, we caught the ranch director as she was passing through the office that morning. When we explained what had happened, she said, "You'll be halfway here when you pick Jonathan up at the airport. Why don't you come on up and look us over?"

That's exactly what we did. We picked up Jonathan and continued on to the ranch. We discovered that the facility had just built a new home, with room for one more rancher. We thought it was a perfect fit for our son.

Ted and I love having Jonathan closer to us. We weren't able to visit Kentucky very often, but now we're often able to drive up to the ranch to see our son.

And though Jonathan is not able to comprehend all the changes in our lives, he understands the basics. One day I saw him signing a message to Ted: *Dad, New Life, out! Me, Stewart Home School, out!*

I'd say he understands enough.

Over the years, we've received several letters about our ministry from people who feel they've received impressions from God while praying for us. We received a flurry of letters and e-mails after our crisis, and many of those included erroneous details that had been reported in the press. Because they were neither truthful nor helpful, we disregarded them.

But we had received one particular letter *before* November 1, 2006, and later it shocked me with its accuracy. I found the message, written by one of our church members, in Ted's suit pocket. A woman had brought it to him the Sunday before the accusations came to light, and he had simply tucked it away.

"Are you sure," the letter began, "it's a secret? The thing you have tried so hard to hide; you've been so careful to cover your tracks, to destroy all the evidence? Are you certain it remains undisclosed? Oh, child, do you not know it is really not a secret. I see all, I hear all, I know all. . . . You need to simply confess your sins, even those you think are hidden—and turn from the path of destruction. . . . Come to me to receive my mercy. Come willingly and receive forgiveness and freedom."[1]

After reading the message, I asked Ted what he'd thought when he read it.

"I thought it was meant for the congregation," he answered, shrugging. "I never thought it applied to me."

I stared at him, amazed. The message fit his situation perfectly, but his sin had blinded him so completely that he didn't realize he held an exhortation from the Lord in his hand.

A week after the crisis hit, we received a letter from a Florida woman who had been praying for Ted. It comforted me, even as I was amazed at the insights it contained:

He did not merely stumble, it wasn't as though on some
bright sunny path a rise in the road caught him off guard.
It wasn't because he was wearing the wrong shoes that
were too big, too far reaching so the terrain was more
than he and his shoes could take. It wasn't an accident.
He wasn't pushed from behind. Nevertheless, he fell. And
the weight of his body hitting the earth that day sent
tremors to faraway places. . . . The outrage of his collapse
was plastered across the front pages of newspapers in big,
bold letters that reminded me of a branding iron. All that
was missing was the cry from the one being burned. He
should never have listened to those voices. The ones that
called to him from the shadows over and over again till

finally he turned and abandoned the bright, clear, sunny way for the ever-darkening trail in the deep woods where the sirens sing. He chose wrongfully. Ultimately, it rose to the surface from the murky depths. Who could have known or guessed that the dark trail was an artery, a heart condition?

Who could have imagined that the deep woods where the sirens sing came from within? He was sick and nobody knew. His smile had fooled them all. Even his wife. But he didn't fool God. . . . You see, that is impossible. The surgeon looked at his dying patient with eyes brimming with compassion. He knew he couldn't wait another minute. It was time. First a gentle sleep, then with precision he opened the heart. A bleeding, pumping spectacle, the surgeon worked quickly, perfectly; after all, there was a life to save, and not just any life. For, you see, the surgeon held in his hand the heart of his son.

The dark trail would be removed as his son lay in full surrender. The deep woods and sirens who lived there would be discerned by the gleaming surgical sword and cut away till even no residue would dare to remain. . . . And He who has begun a good work . . . will perform it . . . will bring it to completion. The son slept well that night, better than he had in years. The only voice he heard was the voice of his Father. The only wind was the warm breath of his older brother, who watched over him, and the song that played was a melody coming . . . would you believe, from his heart.[2]

Even more amazing was a letter I found while packing for our move to Phoenix. The letter was dated March 1998—*eight years* before our crisis—and was addressed to Ted. In it, one of our church women told Ted about a vision she'd seen while praying for us:

> [I saw] a chess board and all its pieces. The "king" represented you and the "queen" represented Gayle. The pieces that surrounded you represented the people that are presently around you. As this vision continued, I saw many of the "people" fall away for various reasons that I do not know. I began to weep as I was watching . . . but the Lord said I was not to worry. It was very clear that you and Gayle stood, and that He would uphold you. The Lord also showed me something interesting regarding Gayle.
>
> If you know the game of chess, the king is an important object; but it is the queen that [protects] him. . . . The Lord wanted to reveal that Gayle has begun to step into a place that she may not have walked before this time. . . . He will cause her to grow in great strength; because you will need that in the days ahead and God will use Gayle more and more to speak great truths to you.
>
> The Lord showed me in another vision that He is going to pierce your heart, even to the depths of your soul. In the days ahead, what God is getting ready to do in you will be a new thing. Because of the new thing that God will put in your heart and display in your life, it will become a stumbling block for many. There will be Christians that will speak out against you because of it. In the days ahead, the thoughts of many hearts will be revealed—and yes, you will experience great anguish; but the Lord said you are not to fear. After you have suffered

a little while, He himself will restore you and strengthen you and cause you to stand firm and steadfast.

The Lord then showed me a third vision. I saw you bent over, carrying on your back a heavy load. The Lord said it was there because you have walked in fear to some degree without really even being aware of it. He said that He will begin to throw off your yoke as you begin to place those areas you have struggled with in Him and trust Him in a way that you have not known. Again He will restore you and you will be bent over no more; but instead, He will enable you to stand.[3]

It is only now, in hindsight, that I fully understand and appreciate these letters. They have been a source of comfort and encouragement to us.

About a week after our trip to New York with the kids to preview the HBO documentary, we received a call from a close friend who was part of the New Life staff. We'd had very little contact with him during our exile, but he asked if he could come over for a visit. We readily agreed.

He dropped by and stayed seven hours. We talked about everything that had happened to us, and we asked about what he'd been through on the church side of things. We really wanted to know how he and his family were doing since the crisis.

During the conversation, Ted mentioned that we had decided to go public with our story—we had no intention of hurting the church, naming names, or exposing painful details, but we were tired of the mischaracterization of Ted and the judgments people had formed based on misinformation. We felt it was time for Ted to give a public confession and apology. By this time, *The Trials of Ted Haggard* was in the works, but we thought it would be premature to talk about the documentary.

A week later, one of the recently hired associate pastors at New Life came by the house as a photographer was taking pictures that HBO planned to use in promo pieces. We stopped to greet the pastor on our front porch.

"I don't want to interrupt," he said, glancing at the photographer, "but the senior pastor would like to come by sometime and meet with you. Would that be okay?"

We assured him that we'd be happy to meet with New Life's current pastor. In fact, we'd been disappointed that he hadn't tried to contact us since assuming his new role and had declined when others tried to arrange opportunities for us to meet. We invited him and the associate pastor to our home for lunch the next week.

When the senior pastor arrived and took a seat in our dining room, the first words out of his mouth were, "I just want to apologize for the fact that you were forced to move from your home, and that you were dealt with through an attorney and legal contracts. I felt that was wrong."

His ready apology surprised us, but we thanked him sincerely and had a great discussion over lunch. We enjoyed what I thought was an uplifting and positive conversation as we got to know each other and briefly discussed where we were in our process and how our insurance business was going.

Then the pastor cleared his throat and changed the subject. "I understand that you've decided to go public."

Ted nodded. "Yes, we feel we've been silent long enough, and our silence has led to a multitude of mischaracterizations and misconceptions about us and the process we've been in for two years. I'd be happy to tell you everything, but you hold a legal contract over me, so I don't feel the freedom to speak openly. If you get rid of that contract, however, I will tell you everything, and I think we could do this together. It could be a positive experience for both of us."

At one point, I took the opportunity to speak up. "I want very much to be restored to the people of the church," I said, "but I'm not interested in standing on the platform as a token of a 'well-done restoration.' Ted's situation was not handled well, and many people were needlessly hurt. I want to be reconnected and restored to the church body, but I don't want to have to act as though the past two years didn't happen. There's more to this story, and it needs to be discussed openly."

The pastor nodded in apparent understanding of my strong opinion. I was happy to have been heard, and Ted and I thought the meeting had been fruitful. We hugged the pastor and his associate as they left, and we thought we were finally heading toward honesty and healing for the people we had once pastored. The pastor had impressed me, and I felt he exemplified courage and strong leadership.

A couple of weeks after that lunch, the senior pastor called our house. Because Ted was on another line, I took the call and heard that we'd been released from all the contracts and were no longer bound by them. A staff member would soon deliver a letter to that effect.

I thanked him exuberantly.

Ted and I exhaled with relief. We could now enjoy the simple freedoms most Americans take for granted: We could speak to the press, we could move without getting permission, and we could talk and write about our experiences.

To keep his end of the verbal agreement, Ted called New Life's senior pastor and told him about Alexandra Pelosi's documentary. He also explained that HBO was planning to send us to the Television Critics Association meeting and had lined up an interview on a nationally televised talk show. Because Ted has always believed that the circle of confession should be as large as the circle of transgression, he was ready to confess his sin and ask forgiveness before a national audience. His sin had been reported all over the world, so he felt his confession and apology should be just as public.

In early January 2009, the senior pastor and two New Life staff members visited us again. The conversation began cordially enough, but then the pastor said he'd brought a letter outlining a new procedure for "restoration," another process that would put us under a new set of regulations and the authority of another group of men who barely knew us.

We patiently explained that we'd already done that. After all we'd been through, we would not agree to that kind of arrangement again. Besides, our experience had taught us that God was handling our restoration process. If the original overseers' goal had been to restore us to a Christian lifestyle—prayer, Bible study, and righteous living—well, we had never deviated from those things. We had done everything the first set of restorers had told us to do, though most of their requirements had more to do with separation than restoration. One of the restorers had been virtually absent in our lives; we hadn't spoken to him since our initial meeting in January 2007. The only restorer with whom we'd had encouraging contact since that first meeting was Pastor Tommy Barnett, but he was powerless to do anything of real significance because of the contracts and the consensus reached by some of the others.

Our "restoration process" seemed to have little to do with

correcting Ted's problem and more to do with keeping us quiet and out of sight. The only affirmation we received from the group of overseers and restorers was the news that they "felt good in their spirits" to hear that we had moved to Phoenix and were pursuing a career in insurance sales. So what was the point of placing ourselves under the authority of another set of virtual strangers?

By this time, we had reached the realization that being "restored to New Life" no longer held the same meaning for us. The buildings were the same buildings, but since our return to Colorado Springs, we'd become increasingly aware that the church now meeting in the New Life worship center was not the same church we'd pastored. New Life was under new leadership and had developed a new church polity. Thousands of people had left in the two years we'd been away, and many new members had joined. We were grateful the church was doing well, but reconnecting with the present church wouldn't accomplish what we'd hoped for a few years earlier. We were not interested in stirring up controversy or pastoring the church again. We had wanted to heal with and eventually be restored to fellowship with the people we'd led, but that exact group no longer existed. We wouldn't be reconnecting with the same people. The offer to go through a new restoration process with the goal of possibly at some point reconnecting with New Life Church was too little, too late.

Not only had the church changed, but Ted and I were no longer the same people. As I listened to New Life's pastor, I realized I was no longer the pastor's wife I'd been two years before. I'd been forced out of my happy church life and thrust into the world. I'd been shocked, angered, dejected, and driven to despair. I'd vented, stormed, and wept. I had doubted my husband, my God, and myself.

And I was stronger for the experience.

I gave the pastor and his companions a careful smile. I tried to be gracious, but I wasn't sure they could understand what I wanted to say. "While I appreciate your offer to restore me to the life I once knew and cherished," I began, "after being ripped from that life, I think God is leading me toward something new. I used to live in the world you're living in. I used to be happy in that world, but that world was totally annihilated for me. I don't think my idea of being restored to the people in the body of Christ would look the same as yours. You're thinking of putting me back into the world I clung to even as every last shred of it was ripped away; but I can't go back. I no longer fit there. I see things differently now, and I've accepted the fact that I no longer belong."

I looked at Ted and knew that we were in agreement. "I'm beginning to think God has something new for us—something that isn't confined to that world."

Ted grinned. "We think God is calling us to a broader audience that might include people who've been kicked out of their churches. You wouldn't believe how many people I've met who would put themselves in that category. We have a huge box filled with thousands of e-mails from people who feel they're not welcome in the church."

The pastor's face clouded. He informed us that he could not support our decision to air the documentary or to do public interviews.

I remained silent, keenly aware of the gulf that existed between us. Ted and I believe that every follower of Christ has equal access to the Bible and guidance from the Holy Spirit. But the overseers and restorers had insisted that *they* knew better than we did what was best for Ted—they had determined that something like selling insurance was God's will for the rest of his days. But they didn't understand God's call on Ted's life. They hadn't considered Ted's gifts and how he'd been equipped to serve the body of Christ. They hadn't considered the possibility that God might have a purpose in what we had been through and a plan for us. They hadn't considered the possibility that God had been speaking to us and guiding us all along. The Scriptures say that God disciplines those he loves (Hebrews 12:5-6). Ted had surely been disciplined, but God had welcomed him back with open arms.

God can use anybody or anything he wants to use to carry out his purposes. Ted and I believe God used a gay masseur to rescue Ted from the sin that was destroying him. God could—and has—used the devil to accomplish his will. He has used pagan kings to fulfill his purposes. He's even used a donkey to speak his truth (compare 1 Chronicles 21:1 and 2 Samuel 24:1; see also John 13:27; 2 Chronicles 36:22; Numbers 22:28). So perhaps God could use a broken, repentant sinner—a son whom he had rescued, forgiven, and healed. And what man could make that judgment? What man has that authority over the calling of God?

The meeting didn't go as well as we'd hoped, but we hugged the men as they left. And as Ted and I stood at the living room window and watched them drive away, we realized that God had quietly weaned us from New Life Church, just as a mother weans her child from the breast.

The procedure wasn't pleasant, and we still yearned to promote healing among the people Ted's actions had wounded, but we trusted God to show us a better way to proceed.

When publicity about Alexandra Pelosi's documentary began to hit the news, the man from our church with whom Ted had had an inappropriate relationship went public with his story. Once again, the editorial pages of the Colorado Springs papers were filled with letters about our crisis, though to us the incident felt like ancient history.

Not long afterward, we received an e-mail from a woman at New Life. "Why are you trying to hurt the church?" she asked. "Why would you open these wounds again?"

I thought her question was well put. If wounds can still be opened, then clearly they haven't healed. Why *don't* we open them? What comes out may be ugly, but you have to clean the wounds and clear the infection before real healing can take place.

Ted didn't reopen those wounds. He didn't leak the man's story. Neither did he hide the news of the threatened lawsuit and the subsequent insurance settlement. He had confessed his sin in regard to this man; he had washed the man's feet and thought he had received his forgiveness.

Another indication of wounds that still needed to heal was the number of people who continually reminded Ted of how he had wronged them—even though, from my perspective, his struggle had been a private one and the only person he had really betrayed was me.

"Wait!" I can almost hear you saying. "Didn't he also betray the church? Didn't he betray his friends?"

Did he? How?

Is it that he proved unworthy of their trust in him? or that he failed to perfectly practice what he preached? Okay, I get that. In the weeks following the crisis, I, too, believed that Ted had betrayed everyone. I understood that Ted's closest friends and ministry partners felt betrayed by his lack of confession to them before he was caught in his sin, and I understand that they were hurt and disappointed—and perhaps even afraid that Ted's sin would raise questions about them and affect their reputations and livelihoods.

But the deeper I went into our process of healing, the more I realized that the only thing Ted was "guilty" of regarding the church was falling off the pedestal that some people had placed him on. He never lied to the church. He never preached heresy to the church. He never stole money from the church. He never stopped loving and caring for the people of the church. If people felt betrayed to discover that Ted didn't belong on that pedestal, I have to wonder why they had lifted him to such an exalted position in the first place. We're not supposed to worship our leaders; we're supposed to worship God. Ted would have been the first to tell the people of New Life that he wasn't perfect. His problem was a private sin, one he never embraced, that led to a problem in our marriage.

I drew tremendous comfort from the insight of a dear friend, an elder Russian believer. After Ted had asked for his forgiveness, the man replied in his deep, gruff, Russian accent, "Brother, you have not sinned against me. You have done nothing to harm me. You must make this right with God and with your wife. But as for me, there is nothing to forgive." I read this same message in many letters Ted received from others in the body of Christ. The most meaningful of these letters came from members of New Life.

Ted has never made excuses for his sin or asked to be "given a pass" for what he did. So why do so many people feel that he is beyond restoration or even redemption? Is it the fact that he sinned at all, or just the nature of his sin?

Many Christians seem to recognize an unspoken hierarchy of wrongdoing, in which sexual sins and certain others are judged severely while sins like pride, arrogance, and dishonesty are barely noticed. But all sin displeases God.

Although he initially lied to the media, at no time over the past three years has Ted tried to minimize the severity of what he did. At no time has he tried to cast blame or shift responsibility. Instead, when his sin came to light, he confessed what he had done; he repented of his behavior; he sought help and treatment to gain healing from the underlying causes; and he did everything he could to put his life back together. That should have been enough for those in a position of authority over him to follow the prescription set out by the apostle Paul: "Dear brothers and sisters, if another believer is overcome by some sin, you who are godly should gently and humbly help that person back onto the right path. And be careful not to fall into the same temptation yourself" (Galatians 6:1).

The healthy members of the body of Christ are supposed to help the sick ones, but all too often I've seen our culture make victims out of those who should be healthy and strong. Instead of stepping forward to help their wayward brother back onto the right path, the strong members say, "Let's get him out of here before he hurts anyone else. We're the victims, and we need to heal." But if the healthy ones adopt a victim mentality, then who is left to heal the sick? This is not how God intends for the body of Christ to function.

I remember an episode of *M*A*S*H* in which Hawkeye Pierce stumbles into the operating room too drunk to operate on an emergency patient. Radar O'Reilly, who has always adored Hawkeye, witnesses the incident and is furious with Hawkeye. He pouts and fumes for a couple of days until Hawkeye pulls him aside.

What happens next jolts Radar. Instead of placating Radar with soft words and contrite apologies, Hawkeye glares at him and says something to the effect of, "How dare you put me on a pedestal! I didn't ask to be your hero, and I don't want to be. I'm not a perfect surgeon; I'm not a perfect man."

The fact is, we're all sinners. We all have sinful attitudes and behaviors that we need to confess, repent of, and be healed from. But how can we confess, repent, and be healed if our confession leads to banishment from the fellowship of our local church? And how can our leaders deal with their own human sinfulness if we place them on a pedestal and feel "betrayed" when they turn out to have feet of clay like the rest of us?

I can't help but wonder what would have happened if Ted had confided in his friends before the situation got out of hand. Given how they responded in the aftermath of our crisis, how safe would he have been?

I understand that many of these people have not had the same opportunity I had to express their anger, frustration, disappointment, and pain directly to Ted and to process their anger and their grief. I can understand why those feelings have festered in some people. But even those who *could* have come to confront him chose not to or were discouraged from doing so. That's part of the reason why I believe the entire situation was mishandled. By cutting us off from the fellowship of New Life Church and banishing us to a life outside the state of Colorado, the overseers created a situation that undermined true healing and restoration for *everyone*.

The code of silence that enveloped New Life and prevails at many other churches is neither healthy nor biblical. Jesus commands us to go to a brother who has offended us. We are told to confess our sins to one another and then forgive one another. Communication is crucial. The biblical example is so different from what Ted and I experienced.

When people are allowed to represent themselves, facts can come out. But when they have no voice, they are powerless. One of the most basic tenets of the Western judicial system is the right to defend oneself against an accuser, and this right is firmly rooted in the teachings of the Bible. The lack of proper biblical communication is one of the reasons we finally decided to go public with our story. But our decision to speak out isn't only about us; we want to heal relationships. We want to do what we can to bring healing to those at New Life Church who were hurt. We feel they deserve an explanation and to have their questions answered. We realize the process may be painful, but we're willing to forge ahead to pursue real healing and real reconciliation.

During our first year back in Colorado Springs, countless people stopped by the house to see us. We welcomed them and invited them onto the back deck, where we listened to their stories and filled them in on everything that had happened since we'd left home. Often these conversations lasted for hours as we caught up on everything that had transpired in each other's lives since our crisis.

As the weeks passed and people continued to come to the house, Ted and I talked about the idea of having "healing meetings" at our home. We had heard from so many who wanted to reconnect with us, we thought it might be a good way to organize things.

For the first meeting, we invited twenty couples, all of whom came to the house. Ted opened the meeting by looking around the room and publicly acknowledging that everyone present had, in one way or another, been associated with him in the past. Because they'd been linked with him, his sin had hurt them.

"I have embarrassed you," he told them. "I brought shame into your life, and for that I am so sorry. I apologize and ask your forgiveness."

The first time Ted said that, a current of love seemed to sweep through the room. People began to share, and the ensuing discussion lasted nearly three hours.

Ted and I realized that we'd hit upon a way to help with the healing of those who'd been hurt. We invite people to gather together, Ted apologizes openly and frankly, and we let other people share their feelings, no matter what those feelings may be. The love of God fills the room every time and blesses everyone present, because this kind of communication is what Jesus encouraged.

These "healing meetings" have one primary purpose: to give Ted an opportunity to apologize and to listen to the people he's hurt. We have never wished ill for the people of New Life—we loved the church, and we love it still. We hear rumors that we're out to destroy the church, but that's not true. We would like to challenge the church—*all* churches in the body of Christ—to rise up and do what Jesus taught us.

At the time of this writing, we've had five of these healing meetings. We don't advertise; we simply hear of people who'd be interested. When we have the names of about twenty couples, we e-mail them, indicating a date and time. These meetings are richly satisfying; they are the closest thing to church we've experienced since our return to Colorado Springs. They are the gathering together of believers for mutual edification and fellowship. In these meetings, I can see the literal fulfillment of Matthew 5:23-24: "If you are presenting a sacrifice at the altar in the Temple and you suddenly remember that someone has something against you, leave your sacrifice there at the altar. Go and be reconciled to that person. Then come and offer your sacrifice to God."

To make sure no one is excluded from the healing process, we have invited staff couples from New Life Church to attend our meetings. So far, no one from that group has come, but we'll keep the porch light burning.

When I am afraid,

I will put my trust in you.

I praise God for what he has promised.

I trust in God, so why

    should I be afraid?

What can mere mortals do to me?

PSALM 56:3-4

19

AFTER NEW LIFE'S pastor visited us and released us from the contracts, I became eager to see what God would do next in our lives. Now that Ted and I were free from the separation and restoration agreements, we felt as though we stood on the brink of a new adventure. Ted was more than ready to publicly confess and talk about his repentance process, and I was eager to tell the world what we'd learned through our crisis.

In January 2009, HBO named *The Trials of Ted Haggard* a feature documentary and sent us to the Television Critics Association (TCA) meeting in Los Angeles. They put us up in a beautiful hotel, and several HBO executives met with our family at an afternoon tea. We sat around a long table with everyone who had come to prepare us for the upcoming event. As we shared our story, many people were touched and freely told us so.

The next afternoon, we attended the TCA meeting, where

producers present various programs to critics and reviewers to give context to upcoming shows.

HBO put us on the platform to promote *The Trials of Ted Haggard*, and we spoke publicly about our crisis for the first time. That was a milestone moment, because since November 2006, we hadn't been allowed to speak to the media.

We sat on the stage while Sheila Nevins introduced us. Alexandra Pelosi spoke first, followed by Ted, Christy, Marcus, and me. We had only twenty minutes to present our thoughts and field questions from the audience.

I was a little anxious as I took a seat on the platform—knowing that many in the crowd would regard us with cynicism—but my eagerness to tell our story overcame my fears. I looked past the cameras and digital recorders until I spotted kind faces in the crowd; then I talked to those people.

Most of the reporters' questions were directed at Ted. People wanted to know where he stood in regard to homosexuality. The moderator had to call a halt when our time ran out. As we left the stage, several reporters followed us into the hallway and continued to pepper us with questions. When it was all over, we were relieved and grateful that God had provided at least a brief opportunity to represent ourselves.

During the second week of January, we flew to Chicago to film a one-hour segment with Oprah Winfrey. Sitting together on the set, Ted and I spoke as openly and honestly as we knew how. Ostensibly, we were doing this and other publicity events to promote the documentary, but I saw these interviews as opportunities to represent our faith and bring some degree of accuracy to our story. I wanted to model Christianity's love and forgiveness, in hopes that my attitude would encourage others to respond to

Ted in the same way. We were grateful to Oprah for giving us an opportunity to share the message on our hearts.

Ted's first priority on these occasions was offering a public confession and apology. Only after he had done that would he begin to tell his story or correct the many misconceptions about us. He did *not* want to get into public debates about homosexuality, but the subject always seemed to come up.

The last week of January found us on a fast track. On January 25, we flew to New York, and two days later we taped *The Early Show* with Harry Smith. That was one of my favorite interviews because Harry exhibited a real understanding of and appreciation for our faith. He asked questions that gave us opportunities to say what we really wanted to say.

In every interview, Ted said, "I want to take responsibility. I want to tell the truth. I want to be honest about these things. I want to publicly apologize." Then he gave honest answers to every question, no matter how painful or embarrassing.

On the morning of January 29, we taped an interview with Robin Roberts for *Good Morning America*. Robin was very kind, but she asked some tough questions. Like many of the other interviewers, she quizzed Ted about his sexual orientation—everyone wanted to broach the idea that Ted was actually gay and in denial.

Then Robin asked a question that allowed Ted to fulfill his purpose for the interview: "Why are you coming back into the spotlight?"

"Because I needed to say, 'I'm sorry,'" Ted answered. "We knew people were not healing; that my case was confusing to people. I thought that for them to heal in earnest, they needed to hear my voice, look at my face, and hear me say how deeply sorry I am for the confusion and pain I caused."

Robin pressed on. "And people are trying to understand, and when they hear you say you don't want to be labeled, that you're not gay, you're not straight, you're 'heterosexual with issues,' what *is* that, 'heterosexual with issues'?"

Ted smiled. "I'm not sure; that's the way my counselor describes me right now. I know that I'm in such a better place than I was a year ago, and I was in a better place a year ago than I was two years ago, no question. Because of that, I'm so thankful for this whole process. I'm stronger in my relationship with Gayle; we've been married for thirty years; our relationship is vibrant and dynamic and wonderful; our family is together. So we've gone through a horrible crisis, and we made it."

After we taped *GMA*, we flew from New York to Los Angeles to tape *Larry King Live*. The show would air that night, right after the debut of Alexandra Pelosi's documentary.

I've always thought of Larry King as having an almost fatherly compassion, so I looked forward to that interview. I was anticipating a friendly talk over Larry's desk; but with the revelation of "new" allegations against Ted, the interview had to focus on the "breaking news," even though it was not news to our family. Larry asked the necessary tough questions, especially about the man who'd been paid a settlement by New Life Church. Because that man had just gone public, his story appeared as if it were a new allegation. During the taping, we had to watch a video clip of this man making accusations about Ted, though he stopped short of claiming that there'd been a sexual relationship—because there hadn't been one.

For Ted, those moments were like seeing his sins play out for the entire world to see. Though he dreaded each mention of his painful past, he was willing to face those charges head-on and confess to them over and over again.

The producers of *Larry King Live* connected Marcus via Skype from a studio in Colorado Springs, and for several minutes our son spoke about his father and our family. "We are not going to break up," he said.

Larry treated Marcus with admiration and great respect, calling him the "glue" of our family. I smiled, because that's what Ted has always called me. Ted and I were both so proud of Marcus. How many other twenty-six-year-olds could have handled that kind of pressure with calm and grace?

In looking back over the last three years, I realize that my call to courage came in the first hours of our crisis. Ted's call to courage came in these interviews, when he had to face the cameras and admit the worst, most embarrassing part of himself. He felt as though he had to confess his guilt and apologize in order to move forward, and I admired him for showing such bravery. I knew the interviews were humiliating, but I also knew how important it was for him to face the unblinking eye of the cameras. After each taping, my respect for him deepened. Our crisis required courage from many people, but it demanded the most from Ted.

I also enjoyed watching how interviewers responded to Ted. He's always had a positive relationship with the media, so many of them contacted him during our two years of silence, even though he wasn't able to respond to them. One world-famous interviewer sent him an e-mail to say, "Ted, don't despair; you are not alone."

A firm believer in the First Amendment, Ted never refused a reporter access to our ministry. He always said that if their investigations turned up something negative, we needed to know about it. Those words came back to haunt him, but he'd be the first to admit that his sin needed to be exposed.

❖

Years before our crisis, a nationally known religious broadcaster came to Ted and remarked that Ted functioned as a bridge to many different groups—a bridge between charismatic and more traditional Protestant denominations; a bridge between young and old. "God has given you a voice," the man said, "and I want to give you a voice too. I'm willing to offer my resources to you so you can have a widespread Christian radio ministry."

Ted went up to Praise Mountain to fast and pray about the man's suggestion, but he sensed God telling him not to accept that offer. *I will give you the opportunity to communicate the gospel to more people through secular media than you ever could through Christian radio*, he felt the Lord tell him.

Then our crisis broke—and after Ted and I had begun to think we'd never speak publicly again, we were invited to appear on *The Oprah Winfrey Show*, *Larry King Live*, CNN, ABC, and other leading outlets.

The week after HBO debuted *The Trials of Ted Haggard*, our Web site, www.tedhaggard.com, received 2.85 million hits. Through the Web site, we've received thousands of e-mails, of which only a small percentage have been negative. The letters have come from atheists, Republicans, Democrats, homosexuals, heterosexuals, bisexuals, Christians, Buddhists, liberals, and conservatives. Most of them begin with "I thought I was going to hate you, but now I can say that your life inspires me." Dozens of the letters say, "Your story inspires me and makes me want to read the Bible."

Most of the letters also mention my decision to stand by Ted. People say they marvel at my example and the loyalty of our five children. "The fact that you and your kids love Ted and are firmly planted by his side," several have written, "tells me a lot about the kind of man Ted must be."

Many of those who write say they used to be in the church but they have left because they felt their church no longer represented Jesus' teachings.

I'm hoping this book will serve as a response to some of those messages, because we simply couldn't answer each one personally. But Ted and I read each letter, and we are deeply touched by the struggles so many people are facing. We are grateful for the messages of encouragement and love, and we hope our story will offer hope to those who feel hopeless.

One of our more recent letters stands out in my memory:

Thank you so very much for the interview you did on *The Oprah Winfrey Show*. If it weren't for that, I would never have gone to your site and watched the video from John Bishop's church called "Who's to Judge?" Many things you said on *The Oprah Winfrey Show* and on "Who's to Judge?" directly touched me in so many ways that I can't begin to explain it all.

To make a long story short . . . as of forty-five minutes ago, I was still under the impression that you . . . got what you had coming to you. I am no longer under that impression!

The things you have gone through since 2006, the realizations you have come to, the humble manner in which you present yourself as a renewed man of God, has given me hope in Christianity. I am gay. . . .

There is a good chance I could die from sudden cardiac death due to my heart disease. I need to know that God loves me. I need to know that I will see my mom

again. I need to know that I'm not going to burn for all
eternity. . . .

For the first time in probably twenty-five years, I have
a glimmer of hope I can be "saved." This is due to your
interviews that I saw today, both on TV and on your Web
site. I feel if there was a church in my area with a pastor
like you, I would attend.

If you can do me two small favors (I hate to ask, being
all you have been through), but would you and Gayle
please pray for me? Also, if possible, please let me know
if there is any way that I can still be saved. I thank you in
advance for granting these requests. You and your family
are truly a blessing.[1]

As of this writing, HBO has aired *The Trials of Ted Haggard*
more than forty times. The video is available on DVD, so we have
no idea how many others have watched Alexandra's compilation
of our "home movies." We hope and pray that God will use the
film's message to touch many more lives.

In March 2009, Ted and I were contacted by the people who
produce the television show *Divorce Court*. They wanted us to
come to the studio and tape a show.

At first I was hesitant. *Divorce Court?* Tell our story before a
judge . . . in court?

"This episode won't be about divorce," the producer explained.
"The focus will be on how you stayed together."

Finally, I was convinced. Ted and I flew to Los Angeles to tape
the show, which ended up being a two-part episode. Before Judge
Lynn Toler, Ted explained that he had thought I should divorce
him after our crisis became public news. He repeated what he'd
told me during those dark days—that he'd become so toxic that

divorce *had* to be best for our children and me. He also told the judge my reply: "No way. I'm not going to do that."

The judge looked at me, her sassy demeanor evident in her smile. "So," she said, lifting a brow. "How'd you do it? Why did you stay with him?"

"This is part of Ted's journey," I told the judge. "It's made him a better man. I see what has happened as a divine rescue." I explained that the biblical principles of forgiveness, compassion, and loyalty combined with Ted's genuine repentance to give our family a new start.

The producers connected our daughter, Christy, for a portion of the show. At one point in the interview, Judge Toler asked Christy, "How did it feel when your dad was knocked off that pedestal he had put himself on?"

Christy calmly shook her head. "My dad never put himself on a pedestal; *we* put him up there. And the process for our family has been wonderful because we matter so much to Dad."

I never thought I'd say this, but we enjoyed our appearance on *Divorce Court*. We pray that the show helps other people see that families don't have to dissolve at the first sign of serious trouble.

Though some may insist that God would never use modern media outlets, we've watched him work wonders through the doors he has opened. And he continues to open them. We don't actively seek these opportunities, but they come to us because the Lord is working in our lives. Every morning I wake up and wonder what new surprise the day will bring.

Not everyone loves us. Not everyone understands what we're doing. But in the light of such unexpected evidence of the Lord's leading in our lives, the criticism is easier to bear. While some are still saying, "Be silent and go away," Ted and I remain willing to talk to a world that is eager to hear how sin can be forgiven, marriages healed, and families strengthened.

When others criticize Ted in person, he listens respectfully to their comments. "Scorn and derision would be total justice for me; I deserve that for what I have done," he says. "That's why I'm so grateful for people who show me grace."

The Spirit of the LORD is upon me,

for he has anointed me to bring

   Good News to the poor.

He has sent me to proclaim that

   captives will be released,

that the blind will see,

that the oppressed will be set free,

and that the time of the LORD's

   favor has come.

LUKE 4:18-19

20

WHY DID I stay married to Ted Haggard?

I think the more pertinent question—the one I had to settle in my heart—was, *Why should I go?* My reasons for staying with Ted were far more compelling than any that would have propelled me toward divorce.

I stayed with Ted because to me he's worth the struggle. As you might imagine, I was devastated in the beginning. After the crisis broke, I felt totally let down and betrayed. My heart was thoroughly broken. But even in the midst of my pain, I believed Ted loved me, I loved him, and our relationship was real. I had settled in my mind the fact that he was and is so much more than the battle that raged within him. I decided that he was worth fighting for, our marriage was worth fighting for, and our family was worth fighting for.

If I had walked away, it would have meant that everything I had devoted my life to no longer held value. But I believed it all had tremendous value. This was the hill I was willing to die on.

I stayed with Ted because *commitment* means something to me. I've committed my life to God, which means that I've chosen his ways and I follow his example of love and forgiveness. I'm committed to our marriage, to stay in this journey till death do us part. I am committed to our children, and I want to restore honor and dignity to their lives.

My decision to stick by Ted boils down to this: Jesus said, "There is no greater love than to lay down one's life for one's friends" (John 15:13).

Jesus is my example. If he could lay down his life for me, surely I could lay mine down for my husband. When I saw that others weren't going to do that for Ted, I realized that not only did I want to honor our marriage commitment because I loved him, but I also wanted to be his friend and represent the body of Christ for him.

Doing so meant walking through the darkest hours of my life, as I had to face not only the pain of my husband's betrayal but also the pain of his punishment. Ted warned me that I should divorce him, that staying with him would only lead to greater ruin for me. But I couldn't. Walking away would have been a denial of everything I believe about the worth of a human being, about friendship, and about love.

"We know," Paul writes, "that God causes everything to work together for the good of those who love God and are called according to his purpose for them" (Romans 8:28).

Throughout the Bible, we find examples of God's faithfulness to people during their darkest hours. Take Joseph, for example. Though his brothers sold him into slavery, Potiphar's wife falsely accused him of rape, and Potiphar unjustly imprisoned him for years, Joseph remained true to God, and God kept his hand on Joseph. And when Joseph stood before his brothers as second-in-command over all Egypt, he was able to say, "You intended to harm me, but God intended it all for good. He brought me to this position so I could save the lives of many people" (Genesis 50:20).

I am grateful to have been a part of Ted's journey. Ted never rejected God, never turned away from the Lord. God has responded to the prayers that Ted has prayed over the years, and he has rescued Ted from the terrible trap that had ensnared him. Ted's process shouldn't shock anyone, because we are all on a journey with God.

Ted once told me, "In the beginning of my crisis, people talked about 'Ted's sin,' but did you notice that it didn't take long before they were talking about 'Ted and Gayle's sin'? That's because even though you didn't do anything wrong, you were willing to be counted with me. So many of my friends and the other guys at the church were not willing to be counted—or even *associated*—with me; but Jesus is, and you are."

I studied Ted's face and nodded. Where was he going with this?

"I think," he said, a sheen of purpose in his eyes, "God has a unique plan for us. When he's ready, he's going to lead us to a different kind of ministry. No one on earth will ever place me on a pedestal, but I can live among sinners and serve them as God leads me. After all, that's what Jesus did."

Grateful that he had begun to look to the future, I rested in the knowledge that we both understood our new calling. I was grateful that we had suffered together, learned together, and grown together. And this new calling was *ours*, Ted's *and* mine. No one else had earned that place by his side.

As I consider what we've lived through in the last three years, one story keeps coming back to me: Victor Hugo's classic *Les Misérables*. You are probably familiar with the tale—the convict Jean Valjean is released from a French prison where he served nineteen years for stealing a loaf of bread. No one in the town of Digne is willing to give him shelter because he is an ex-convict, still a criminal in name, if not in deed. A kindly bishop shelters Valjean and feeds him, but Valjean repays this kindness by stealing the bishop's silver candlesticks. He is apprehended and claims that the candlesticks were a gift . . . a story the grace-filled bishop confirms with a benevolent lie when the police summon him. When Valjean tries to express his gratitude for this kindness, the bishop asks him to go his way and be an honest man. Valjean does just that, but he is haunted and hunted by Javert, the police chief, who will not let Valjean forget his criminal past.

Ted and I have Javerts in our lives, those who will not accept the fact that God the Father has welcomed his prodigal son home. Those who by their own words and actions have become opponents of forgiveness and mercy in Ted's life.

Grace versus punishment. Forgiveness versus persecution. I would much rather err on the side of grace and forgiveness.

I think you can see why *Les Misérables* resonates with me.

I'm sharing my story with the world because I want to inspire others to choose the risk of love, even in the midst of the worst devastation. This is what Jesus taught us to do. It is a way of healing for all of us. At the end of the day, we'll be stronger people in our churches, our families, and our friendships if we choose to love and to do the hard work of forgiveness. If we set our trajectory on forgiving each other's wrongs and loving each other, we'll find that love covers a multitude of sins and gives us hope that our lives can be better.

Probably the most difficult part of this journey for us has been the separation from New Life Church, the work into which we poured twenty-two years of our lives. I viewed the church as my family and felt deeply devoted to my brothers and sisters in Christ. I never dreamed I would be separated from them in my darkest hour. Ted and I would have preferred to have our crisis handled within our church family. To my way of thinking, families pull together when facing trials, and that's how they contribute to the healing of their weak or wounded members. I believe a commitment to this process leads to a strong, healthy family and a strong, healthy church. Even now, I want to honor the people of New Life with the choices I am making. I believe that, given the opportunity, many of them would have made the same choices. I hope one day they'll be able to say I represented them well.

I forgive those who have followed a different path in response to Ted's sin and who have caused me and my family such pain as a result. That's different from what I would have chosen, but I still choose to love them because God's grace extends to them as well.

The paradox in our situation is that God has used our trials to bring us to a better place. I believe we have attained greater spiritual maturity as this journey has taken us to new depths and new heights of understanding God's passion and love for us. I believe he is using our experience to shape us and position us where he wants us in the future. I am thankful to be where we are today and to have learned what we've learned. Our marriage and family are stronger, our close friendships are better grounded and healthier, and we have a greater understanding and appreciation for the gospel as it relates to the human condition. I thought we were happy and free before our crisis, but now we are much more so.

To other women who are facing trials regarding their husbands—I don't know who you are married to, so I can't presume to know the best course for you. Ted gave me the gift of repentance, and he chose, as I did, to heal our marriage. But I know that not all men choose to do that. Even so, I encourage you, as much as you are able, to do what Jesus instructed us to do: forgive and love. Only you can determine what that will look like in your life.

You will still have to process your pain, your anger, and your sense of betrayal. This will be difficult, but set your trajectory toward forgiveness and love. Remember all the things you appreciate and respect about your husband, and know that these things are still true about him. You have no control over his choices or behaviors or the pain he has caused, but you do have the power to choose how you will respond. You have to determine what is truly valuable and worth fighting for. Decide who you are going to be in the midst of your pain. I have confidence you will choose well, because you know you are not alone.

And always remember—love covers a multitude of sins (see 1 Peter 4:8). When I pressed toward forgiving and loving Ted, I healed. When I judged and scrutinized him for all the pain he had caused, I only spiraled further into despair.

Love never fails (see 1 Corinthians 13:7). If we choose love and let it do its work, we are all better for it. Not only does Jesus instruct us in the way of forgiveness and love, but his Spirit empowers us to act accordingly. What we have afterward is a relationship that has been strengthened through fire. For Ted and me, this means we have each other and we have our family.

The apostle Paul's exhortation to the Romans is simple and straightforward: "Don't just pretend to love others. Really love them" (Romans 12:9). To the Colossians he writes, "Make allowance for each other's faults, and forgive anyone who offends you. Remember, the Lord forgave you, so you must forgive others. Above all, clothe yourselves with love, which binds us all together in perfect harmony" (Colossians 3:13-14).

No one benefits from the scrutiny of others. We all need love to cover our wrongs, and we'll be so much happier if we offer and receive love from one another. But if we persist in judging and pointing out one another's faults and sins, we will lose hope and tumble down into darkness and fragment our relationships. On the other hand, if you choose a path of forgiveness and love, you and your family can overcome tremendous difficulties together.

Before Jesus ascended to heaven, he breathed on his disciples and said, "Receive the Holy Spirit. If you forgive anyone's sins, they are forgiven" (John 20:22-23). In doing this, he gave them the power to forgive each other's sins. That's the power the church can offer the world—the forgiveness of sins. I don't think we should ever give up on a human being, but we should take the time to listen to and see that person. We all have a deep need to be truly *seen*, to be truly valued, to be known as our best selves, not our worst selves. God is the one who really sees us (see Genesis 16:13-14). If we can offer that gift to one another, we'll all be much better off.

When Ted and I were enduring the first few painful weeks after our crisis broke, we received a letter from Bob Stamps, the campus chaplain who introduced Ted and me at Oral Roberts University. He enclosed a copy of *Life Together: The Classic Exploration of Faith in Community* by Dietrich Bonhoeffer.

"God has a plan for you," Bob wrote. "Do not allow anyone to help you who will not first confess his sins to you."

As Ted has often said, "Our response to someone else's sin reveals whether or not we understand the central message of the New Testament." Do we respond with scorn and ostracism or with love and forgiveness? Do we reflect the message of the New Testament and the primary reason that Jesus came?

I am not writing this book to disparage anyone. I am confident all the people in my story did the best they knew to do, given the very difficult circumstances and the church cultures we have created. However, we heard repeatedly that they did not have a guidebook to show them how to navigate our crisis, and they knew they made wrong decisions along the way.

Having experienced the repercussions of those decisions, I am writing to challenge the ideas that evolved in our church culture and guided the choices that were made. I hope to provide information that will produce a better template for the future. Too many Christians have been left wounded and have fallen through the cracks of our established systems. I believe it is time we return to a biblical model that is in keeping with the teachings of Jesus and the instructions of the New Testament writers.

Even though the particulars of our situation were unique, as every situation is, I think the Bible offers a better way to navigate situations like ours. I hope the information I have shared will inspire a more gracious, more healing, more biblical way to handle those situations, which are all too common. I hope this book provides information that will help create a better path for the church's future.

I know I've written some hard truths in these pages, but I'm not trying to point fingers or criticize. Over the past few years, I've witnessed how many churches deal with sin, and I've seen how certain methods fall short of the biblical model. As the body of Christ, we can and should do better. If anything I've said in this book feels like an indictment against the church, then perhaps we who belong to the body of Christ—and I include myself in that number—should see if there are attitudes we need to reconsider in order to fulfill the teachings of Jesus.

Churches should provide a safe place for mutual confession and support. I really believe in the liberating power of confession. Once we expose our sins to the light of day, the enemy can no longer keep us in bondage to shame and secrecy. I can't imagine anything that shouldn't be confessed . . . as long as you direct your confession to the people who have been affected by your sin and to someone who can wisely help you overcome it. Some people may find healing by confessing to a good friend, someone who will listen.

I know some women don't want to hear everything from a spouse who has betrayed them; perhaps they don't want to have to face the details. In our situation, I wanted to know everything, but people are different. If you ever find yourself in this situation— and I pray you don't—you'll probably sense what's best for you.

We have to realize that it's okay not to be okay. Through my process, I have begun to see how many people view the church as a community of the righteous (and consequently the self-righteous) instead of as a community of sinners who are grateful they've met the Savior. I used to stand before the women of New Life and teach that they could win the battle over sin. I'd emphasize that sin could be conquered, and victory achieved, and that they could move beyond it.

I still believe that, but now I am not so adamant that this is a simple process. Now I understand that sin dwells within us; it's part of our fallen human nature. We'll battle sin as long as we live in these corruptible human bodies. I know this because even those who have been on their journey in God for a lifetime still sin. That's why I'm grateful for the gospel of Jesus Christ. In this gospel, a righteousness from God is revealed, a righteousness that comes by faith (see Romans 3:21-22). That is our hope. None of us is righteous in ourselves: "When we display our righteous deeds, they are nothing but filthy rags" (Isaiah 64:6). But God can forgive us and cleanse us.

Though I didn't break my marriage vows, dealing with our crisis brought out the sin in my own heart—I found myself dealing with bitterness, anger, and pride. Those sins may not make the television news, but they're as real—and perhaps even more destructive—than sexual immorality.

Job discovered this principle. The Bible tells us that Job was a wealthy, blameless, and godly man who became a test subject in an experiment conducted by God and Satan. Satan asked for permission to test the depth of Job's faithfulness to God, and God granted it. Then, in the space of one day, Job lost his ten children and all his cattle and sheep. He went from being the most prosperous man in the region to being the poorest. But he remained faithful to God.

So Satan arranged for round two: "Skin for skin!" he challenged God. "A man will give up everything he has to save his life. But reach out and take away [Job's] health, and he will surely curse you to your face!" (Job 2:4-5).

So God granted permission for another round of calamities. Satan attacked Job with boils that appeared all over his body, so many that Job couldn't sit or stand or lie down without excruciating pain. Still, he did not curse God. He did not abandon his faith. But he did do something else; he revealed his spiritual pride.

As Job's friends gathered around to demand that he confess whatever terrible sin he'd committed to deserve such divine punishment, Job kept insisting he had done no wrong. He proclaimed that not only had he not committed injustices; he had spent his life doing good deeds. Then he cried out, "If only someone would listen to me! Look, I will sign my name to my defense. Let the Almighty answer me. Let my accuser write out the charges against me. I would face the accusation proudly. I would wear it like a crown. For I would tell him exactly what I have done. I would come before him like a prince" (Job 31:35-37).

Then, in a whirlwind of glory that must have rendered Job speechless, God answered: "Who is this that questions my wisdom with such ignorant words? Brace yourself like a man, because I have some questions for you, and you must answer them. Where were you when I laid the foundations of the earth?" (Job 38:2-4).

As Ted and I worked through our crisis, I found myself relating to Job. We were being chastised for something Ted—not I—had done, and as I chafed under the restrictions forced on us, I found myself counting off the good things *I* had done for the church. And then, like Job, I realized I was far from blameless. In feeling proud of my goodness, I was guilty of spiritual pride.

Sin in another person can bring out the arrogance in ourselves. I've seen the evidence in my own life. I inwardly bristle when people look on me with pity. I can scrutinize in an instant; I can judge in a heartbeat. And when my judgment against someone else comes out, it's dark. Standing by Ted, suffering with him, brought out the sin in my own heart.

My son Marcus described me as a "saint" on *Larry King Live*, but I smile at this because I know I'm still a sinner, and I will be until I reach heaven. I've watched so many people in this process. I've seen the "righteous" not recognize their own sins, even to the point of denial. I don't want to be like that anymore. Those who don't recognize their own sins hurt others.

I know that many in the church think Ted has been disqualified from pastoral leadership. I grew up with that kind of thinking. People read 1 Timothy 3:2—"an elder must be a man whose life is above reproach"—and assume that Ted no longer fits that description. But while a leader who *embraces* sin certainly isn't living above reproach, one who fights to resist sin and embraces repentance certainly is.

I know Ted saw himself as permanently disqualified for leadership, and initially I agreed with him. But as time passed, I began to question that line of thinking. I saw that Ted and I had received the answer to our prayers, and that the process of repentance had taught us so much about God's mercy and grace that we were more equipped to minister than ever.

The Bible taught me that many effective leaders in history had fallen into sin, recovered, and went on to fulfill their gifts and callings in God—Moses (who committed murder), David (who committed adultery and murder), and Peter (who denied Christ publicly), to name a few. I realized Ted was on a journey like everyone else, but he never stopped praying, and God never stopped speaking to him.

I began to realize that God might be using our painful process to give hope to the hopeless. That morning in my closet, God had assured me that he had great purpose for us; and as time passed, I began to believe that the full meaning of restoration—*to bring something back to its original state*—might apply to Ted.

I have written this book because I'm committed to the purpose God has given me—to bring grace and the gospel to the people who need it most: people like you and me.

I believe God has moved Ted and me to a ministry outside the parameters within which we once operated. He has broadened our boundaries. After spending time in exile and mourning the death of our former dreams, we have been resurrected to new opportunities, and we've decided to finish our race well. What more can anyone do to us now? Our reputations have been destroyed. Our occupations have vanished. Our once-dependable source of income is gone. We've been told we're no longer welcome where we once thrived.

Now we live to tell the world about Jesus and demonstrate God's mercy and grace to undeserving sinners like us. I resonate with what Paul says in Acts 20:24: "My life is worth nothing to me unless I use it for finishing the work assigned me by the Lord

Jesus—the work of telling others the Good News about the won-derful grace of God."

More and more often, I find myself saying that this is the best season of my life.

I love the Bible stories that involve women. I feel I can identify on some level with each of them. CeCe Winans sings a song called "Alabaster Box," with lyrics based on the story found in Luke 7:36-50. Jesus entered the house of a Pharisee called Simon, a devout and religious man. While the men were dining, a sinful woman entered the room and knelt at Jesus' feet. When Simon saw her, he said to himself, "If this man were a prophet, he would know what kind of woman is touching him. She's a sinner!" (Luke 7:39).

But Jesus, who knows people's thoughts and hearts, said, "Simon, I have something to say to you" (Luke 7:40).

Simon smiled, ready to receive . . . what? A compliment for the dinner? A compliment for his outstanding adherence to religious laws and traditions? Praise for his obvious holiness?

Jesus then told the story of two debtors—one who owed his master five hundred pieces of silver and one who owed fifty. When neither of them could repay what they owed, he forgave both debts.

Jesus looked at Simon. "Who," he asked, "do you suppose loved him more after that?" (Luke 7:42).

Simon tugged on his beard, probably wondering if this was a trick question. "I suppose the one for whom he canceled the larger debt" (Luke 7:43).

Jesus then looked at the woman who was still huddled on the floor. She had poured a bottle of costly perfume on his feet, and now she wept quietly, wiping his feet with her hair. She didn't look up but rather knelt before him, bent in submission, kissing his feet in gratitude.

Jesus said to Simon, "I tell you, her sins—and they are many—have been forgiven, so she has shown me much love. But a person who is forgiven little shows only little love" (Luke 7:47).

I imagine that Jesus then bent, lifted her chin, and looked her in the eye when he said, his voice gentle, "Your faith has saved you; go in peace" (Luke 7:50).

At the beginning of our crisis, I felt a bit like Simon. I was secure in my church world, I took pleasure in doing good things for God, and I delighted in our ministry. When our crisis came, ushered in by God's sovereign will, I found myself torn from all the things that had formed my identity—everything except my husband, my family, and my personal relationship with God.

Over time, as Ted submitted to God's discipline and divine restoration, I learned that I had as much in common with the kneeling woman as I'd had with Simon the Pharisee. I was a sinner. I needed forgiveness. I needed to see the world and my role in it with new eyes. And once I learned to see, I knelt at Jesus' feet and thanked him through grateful tears.

At one point in "Alabaster Box," CeCe sings, "You don't know the cost of the oil in my alabaster box."

I know what Ted and I have walked through. His sin cost us almost everything, yet it was worth all the struggle to receive the grace of God and the understanding that his grace exists for everyone.

I don't know the sins in your life, and you don't know all the sins in mine. But I do know that together we can find forgiveness from God, who so willingly gives it.

When my family arrived in Florida right after Ted's story broke, I went for a solitary walk on the beach. I walked far away from the house where we were staying until I found a stretch of deserted shoreline. There in the sand, I sat and lowered my head to my bent knees, weeping as I prayed.

My anguished soul didn't know what to do with all the hurt I felt. I wasn't sure what to do with the things Ted had confessed on the plane the day before.

As I prayed amid the rumble of the waves, I sensed the Lord speak to me: *You are the Shunamite.*

My mind ran through the story, and I remembered that early in my marriage, I had felt a disconnect between Ted and me. He was so busy, and I excused him, thinking that he had to pour more of himself into his ministry than into his marriage. Our physical relationship was satisfying, but for years I struggled with feeling that I occupied a lower place in my husband's priorities. I finally came to the same decision point the Shunamite reached: a resolution to accept what could not be changed and move on.

But the man of God asked her, "What can I do for you?"

The Shunamite woman's closed-off heart had harbored a yearning for a child.

My heart harbored a desire for a more intimate relationship with my husband.

"Don't go there," the Shunamite had said, and I was saying the same thing. I didn't want to revisit that point of pain. God was moving toward an area I'd already sealed off. In the process, he would change my life, destroy my old fortresses of refuge, and bring me to the intimate place I'd always wanted to share with my husband.

I would never recommend the path we took to get us where we've ended up, but now the connection between Ted and me is everything I've ever longed for. I think back to the day I sensed the Lord telling me, *Trust me; it had to happen this way.* I *had* to be ripped out of the church I loved. I never would have volunteered to make such drastic changes in our lives. Not until I was forced from the life I cherished did I see its limitations. Now I see so much more; I wouldn't *want* to return to what I had before.

God answered both our prayers. Mine for intimacy; Ted's for freedom from his compulsive thoughts that led to his sin.

After the Shunamite's son was raised from the dead, the man of God sent them to a far-off land because their homeland was entering a time of famine. Later, when she and her son returned, they visited the king, who restored everything they'd lost.

That part of our story is beginning now, after three years of pain.

I don't know what you have sealed away in your heart—what kinds of struggles, fears, or unfulfilled longings you have locked up. Perhaps you are trapped in sin and don't know where to turn for help. Perhaps your heart aches because all you want is to be seen and loved. Maybe you are struggling with your sexuality, addiction, arrogance, or pride.

No matter what your situation, I want to give you hope. I want you to know that God sees you and he cares enough to rescue you and heal you. In him, you will find forgiveness and love. Jesus will show you the way.

You can trust him. He will not abandon you in the midst of pain. With him, you will never be alone. And his forgiving love covers a multitude of sins.

Epilogue

A few days ago, I was relishing a particularly beautiful Colorado September day. Summer was giving way to fall, and the afternoon was warm and sunny, even though the leaves on the deciduous trees were brilliant hues of yellow, orange, and red. When the doorbell rang, I came down the stairs to find my granddaughter Hadessah and her protective Brittany spaniel playing peekaboo with a woman who was standing outside our screen door. I recognized her and the other two women who soon joined her and welcomed them into our home. These longtime friends had been with us for most of the twenty-two years we were at the church. They appeared to have a purpose in coming to see Ted and me. Once we were all seated in our living room, they proceeded to tell us how very much they loved us and missed us. When we responded in like manner, they interrupted, "So what is next? We believe God has more for you to do, and we want to hear what it is."

Almost three years have passed since our crisis, and my darkest days have begun to give way to increasing light. Since our return to Colorado Springs, our family has been on a steady path to healing and regaining trust among ourselves and with others in our community. Our marriage continues to feel stronger and more intimate than ever. Our children are once again pursuing their individual goals and establishing their own lives. Almost daily we encounter people from the church we once pastored and others from the community who demonstrate their love for us and allow us to demonstrate our love for them. We hug, we talk, and we laugh together again.

So what *is* next?

Only God knows for certain.

In the meantime, my prayer is that because we have experienced God's grace so deeply in the last three years, we can more authentically represent it to those, like us, who need it.

Notes

CHAPTER 2

1. Jeff Sharlet, "Soldiers of Christ: Inside America's Most Powerful Megachurch with Pastor Ted Haggard," *Harper's Magazine* (May 2005): 42.

CHAPTER 4

1. Bylaws of New Life Church, article 13, paragraph 2.

CHAPTER 6

1. Naomi Zeveloff, "You've Been Punk'd," *Colorado Springs Independent*, November 9, 2006.

CHAPTER 10

1. Paul Asay, "Second New Life Pastor Steps Down," *The Gazette*, December 19, 2006.

CHAPTER 11

1. Mark Galli, "We've Won the Lottery—Now What?" *Christianity Today* online, July 30, 2009, http://www.christianitytoday.com/ct/2009/julyweb-only/130-41.0.html?start=2 (accessed August 27, 2009).
2. Paul Asay, "There Are No Secrets," *The Gazette*, January 7, 2007.
3. Barry Corbin, *Unleashing the Potential of the Teenage Brain* (Thousand Oaks, CA: Corwin Press, 2007), 18.

CHAPTER 12

1. John DeCecco, "Confusing the Actor with the Act: Muddled Notions about Homosexuality," *Archives of Sexual Behavior* 20 (1990): 421–423.
2. Jeffrey Watson, *Biblical Counseling for Today: A Handbook for Those Who Counsel from Scripture* (Nashville: Word, 2000), 190.
3. Ibid., 189.

CHAPTER 13

1. New Life Overseers and Restoration Committee, letter to Ted and Gayle Haggard, undated.
2. New Life Overseers and Restoration Committee, letter to Ted Haggard, January 11, 2007.
3. The agreement simply cited the verses, but I've added the text so that readers will know what the verses actually say. The quote from 1 Peter 5 is verses 5 and 10.
4. C. S. Lewis, *Reflections on the Psalms* (London: Geoffrey Bles, 1958), 27.
5. New Life Church and Ted Haggard, separation agreement, signed January 24, 2007.
6. New Life Overseers and Restoration Committee, letter to Ted and Gayle Haggard, undated.
7. Cary Leider Vogrin, "Board to Lead Congregation in 'Day of Hope' at New Life," *The Gazette*, February 9, 2007.
8. Associated Press, "Haggard's Former Church Holds 'Day of Hope,'" *The Christian Post*, February 19, 2007, http://www.christianpost.com/article/20070219/haggard-s-former-church-holds-day-of-hope/index.html.

CHAPTER 14

1. John Piper, "Measures of Faith, Gifts of Grace, Ministry in Small Groups," www.desiringgod.org/ResourceLibrary/Sermons/ByDate/1998/1050_Measures_of_Faith_Gifts_of_Grace_Ministry_in_Small_Groups (accessed September 1, 2009).
2. "Reopening Old Wounds for New Life," *Ministry Today*, January 27, 2009, www.ministrytodaymag.com/index.php/ministry-news/65-news-main/18250-reopening-old-wounds-for-new-life (accessed August 28, 2009).
3. Radio interview with Michelangelo Signorile, February 4, 2009, www.youtube.com/watch?v=H7QnUCEDOfU.

CHAPTER 15

1. Howard J. Markman, Scott M. Stanley, and Susan L. Blumberg, *Fighting for Your Marriage: Positive Steps for Preventing Divorce and Preserving a Lasting Love* (San Francisco: Jossey-Bass, 2001), 312–313.

CHAPTER 16

1. Thomas Hendrick, "Security Guard: 'God Guided Me And Protected Me,'" *Denver News*, December 10, 2007, www.thedenverchannel.com/news/14817480/detail.html (accessed August 29, 2009).

2. New Life Overseers and Restoration Committee, letter to Ted Haggard, January 31, 2008.
3. Press release from New Life Church, Colorado Springs, undated, unsigned.

CHAPTER 17

1. Christopher Lisotta, "When Ms. Pelosi Talked to Mr. Haggard," *The Advocate*, January 24, 2007, www.advocate.com/exclusive_detail_ektid41342.asp.
2. Ibid.
3. Ibid. Bracketed words are in the original article.
4. Alexandra Pelosi, interview by David Neff, "Haggard 'Deserves What He Got,'" *Christianity Today* (January 28, 2009), www.ctlibrary.com/ct/2009/januaryweb-only/104-31.0.html. Bracketed words are in the original article.
5. Ibid.
6. Ibid.
7. Ibid.
8. Howard J. Markman, Scott M. Stanley, and Susan L. Blumberg, *Fighting for Your Marriage: Positive Steps for Preventing Divorce and Preserving a Lasting Love* (San Francisco: Jossey-Bass, 2001), 302.
9. Mark Barna, "Haggard Living in Springs Again," *The Gazette*, June 25, 2009, http://findarticles.com/p/articles/mi_qn4191/is_20080625/ai_n27957643/?tag=content;col1.

CHAPTER 18

1. Unsigned letter to Ted Haggard, October 29, 2006.
2. Shelly Holloway, "He Fell into the Hands of God," letter to Ted Haggard, November 7, 2006.
3. Karen Gallagher, letter to Ted Haggard, March 19, 1998.

CHAPTER 19

1. Name withheld, e-mail correspondence to Ted Haggard, June 30, 2009.

About the Authors

GAYLE HAGGARD IS a speaker, a teacher, and the wife of Ted Haggard, former senior pastor of New Life Church in Colorado Springs and past president of the National Association of Evangelicals. Ted and Gayle founded New Life Church in the basement of their home in 1985. By 2006, it had grown to a congregation of 14,000 people, and Gayle was directing women's ministries, in which she oversaw 150 small groups and taught classes to women of all ages. She also launched a ministry called Women Belong, which was based on the principle that no woman should ever feel alone, because we all belong to God and to each other. Soon, however, everything Gayle believed and taught was put to the test. On November 1, 2006, Ted Haggard was accused of having a secret life that involved infidelity and illicit drug use, and Gayle's world came crashing in on her. "In a few short days," she says, "my life as I had known it, that I had so lovingly embraced, was demolished." Over the past few years, Gayle and her husband of thirty-one years have emerged from their crisis and now feel that their faith, their marriage, and their family are stronger than ever because of what they have learned and experienced. In addition to *Why I Stayed*, Gayle is the author of *A Life Embraced: A Hopeful Guide for the Pastor's Wife*. She and Ted reside in Colorado Springs with their five children and one grandchild.

ANGELA HUNT writes for readers who have learned to expect the unexpected in novels from this versatile author. With over three million copies of her books sold worldwide, she is the best-selling author of more than one hundred works ranging from picture books (*The Tale of Three Trees*) to nonfiction books to novels. Angie and her husband live in Florida with their two mastiffs— one of their dogs was featured on *Live with Regis and Kelly* as the second-largest canine in America. Angela admits to being fascinated by animals, medicine, psychology, unexplained phenomena, and "just about everything" except sports. Books, she says, have always shaped her life—in the fifth grade she learned how to flirt from reading *Gone with the Wind*. Her books have won the coveted Christy Award, several Angel Awards from Excellence in Media, and the Gold and Silver Medallions from *ForeWord* magazine's Book of the Year Award. In 2007, her novel *The Note* was featured as a Christmas movie on the Hallmark Channel. Angie has recently released the sequel to *The Note*—*The Note II: Taking a Chance on Love*. Romantic Times Book Club presented her with a Lifetime Achievement Award in 2006. In 2008, Angela completed her doctorate in biblical studies. When she's not home reading or writing, Angie often travels to teach writing workshops at schools and writers' conferences. Visit Angela's Web site at www.angelahuntbooks.com.